NEW STUDIES IN ARCHA

Symbols in action

Ethnoarchaeological studies of material culture

NEW STUDIES IN ARCHAEOLOGY

Advisory editors

Richard I. Ford, *University of Michigan*
Glynn Isaac, *University of California, Berkeley*
Colin Renfrew, *University of Cambridge*
David Thomas, *American Museum of Natural History, New York*

Symbols in action

Ethnoarchaeological studies of material culture

IAN HODDER

Lecturer in Archaeology, University of Cambridge

CAMBRIDGE UNIVERSITY PRESS

CAMBRIDGE

LONDON   NEW YORK   NEW ROCHELLE

MELBOURNE   SYDNEY

CAMBRIDGE UNIVERSITY PRESS
Cambridge, New York, Melbourne, Madrid, Cape Town, Singapore, São Paulo, Delhi

Cambridge University Press
The Edinburgh Building, Cambridge CB2 8RU, UK

Published in the United States of America by Cambridge University Press, New York

www.cambridge.org
Information on this title: www.cambridge.org/9780521105088

First published 1982
This digitally printed version 2009

A catalogue record for this publication is available from the British Library

Library of Congress Catalogue Card Number: 81–10207

ISBN 978-0-521-24176-2 hardback
ISBN 978-0-521-10508-8 paperback

TO MY FATHER

CONTENTS

Acknowledgements   *page* ix

1 Introduction: the nature of material cultures   1
1.1 Cultures   2
1.2 Cultural similarities as reflecting degrees of interaction   8
1.3 Culture as reflecting behaviour   9
1.4 Conclusion   11

2 Ethnicity and symbolism in Baringo   13
2.1 The Baringo district (with F. Hivernel)   13
2.2 Field method   17
2.3 Material culture patterning   18
2.4 Conclusion   35

3 Maintaining the boundaries   37
3.1 Pottery production and distribution   37
3.2 Njemps stools   48
3.3 Hearth position   54
3.4 Conclusion   56

4 Disrupting the boundaries   58
4.1 Metal production and spears   59
4.2 Calabash decoration   68
4.3 Conclusion   73

5 Within the boundaries: age, sex and self-decoration   75
5.1 The dominance of older men   75
5.2 Age symbolism   77
5.3 Sex symbolism   83
5.4 Boundary maintenance and disruption   84

6 Hunter-gatherers and pastoralists on the Leroghi plateau   87
6.1 The Lonkewan Dorobo and Samburu   90
6.2 Artifact types   92
6.3 History and explanation   97
6.4 The maintenance of overt identities within tribes   102
6.5 Conclusion   103

7 A state of symbiosis and conflict: the Lozi   105
7.1 Introduction   105
7.2 Present-day cultural patterning   111
7.3 Production and distribution   118
7.4 Status symbolism   119
7.5 Within-site patterning   122

8 Dirt, women and men: a study in the Nuba Mountains,
Sudan   125
8.1 The Nuba   127
8.2 Regional patterning in material culture   134
8.3 Explanation of regional patterning   151
8.4 Within-site patterning: bone refuse   155
8.5 Other aspects of refuse   161
8.6 Burial   163
8.7 Aspects of design   170
8.8 Conclusion   181

9 Implications for archaeology   185
9.1 Cultures   186
9.2 Within-site artifact distribution   190
9.3 Settlement patterns   193
9.4 Burial   195
9.5 Exchange   202
9.6 Style   204
9.7 Social stratification   207
9.8 Conclusion   210

10 Conclusions and prospects   212
10.1 'Wholeness'   212
10.2 The particular historical context   215
10.3 Applying the contextual approach in archaeology   218
10.4 Summary and some further prospects   228

Bibliography   230

Index   239

ACKNOWLEDGEMENTS

The fieldwork in Kenya (chapters 2 to 6) was funded by the British Academy, the Sir Ernest Cassel Educational Trust, and Leeds University. A research permit (Ref: OP.13/001/C 1977/16) granted by the Office of the President, Nairobi, made the work possible. Help in Kenya was provided by Richard Leakey, the National Museum, Nairobi, and the British Institute in Eastern Africa. My special thanks to Mary, Matthew, Dave, Lucia and Sami for supporting me in the field.

The Zambian work (chapter 7) was funded by the British Academy and the University of Leeds, and was made possible by the cordial aid of the Permanent Secretary, Western Province, Zambia. Gwyn and Miriam Prins, Lindsay and Austin Sedgley provided essential help in Zambia.

The research in Sudan (chapter 8) was funded by the Social Science Research Council. Official permission and assistance in Khartoum were provided by the National Council for Research, the Board of Anthropology, N. M. Sherif, the Director General of Antiquities, and A. Mohd Ali Hakem, Department of Archaeology, University of Khartoum. Guiding me through the formalities, Khidr Ahmed provided invaluable help, as did Else and Arvid Kleppe and Paul Callow. Thanks most sincerely to Mary, Jane, Andy and Sami for putting up with me in the field and for so willingly collecting so much of the nonsense I wanted.

Richard Bradley, Linda Donley, James Faris, Danny Miller, Henrietta Moore, Paul Spencer, Chris Tilley and Owen Wheatley read all or various parts of the typescript and the final draft has taken account of their criticisms. An article similar to chapter 2 has been published in D. Green, C. Haselgrove and M. Spriggs (eds.) *Social organisation and settlement*, British Archaeological Report, 1978, and the pottery section of chapter 3 is published in M. Millett (ed.) *Pottery and the archaeologist*, Institute of Archaeology, London, 1979. Chapter 7 is an expansion of parts of a paper published in I. Hodder, G. Isaac and N. Hammond (eds.) *Pattern of the past*, Cambridge University Press, 1981. The section on burial in chapter 9 is developed from an article published in P. Rahtz, T. Dickinson and L. Watts (eds.) *Anglo-Saxon cemeteries 1979*, British Archaeological Report, 1980.

Most of the photographs were taken by Sami Karkabi, Ministry of Tourism, Beirut, who accompanied me in all the fieldwork except that in Zambia. I am extremely grateful to him for his patience and care and am only sorry that more of his excellent photographs could not be included in this book.

I must also thank my Cambridge students from whom I have learnt so much. Many of the ideas in chapters 9 and 10 grew out of frequent and intense seminars in the academic year 1979–80, and it is no longer possible to know from whom the ideas originated. My debt to the members of the group, whose own work will be published, is immense.

It is difficult for me fully to appreciate how much this book owes to Françoise. It was she who took me to Baringo in the first place and started the whole thing off. Her practical sense in the field (Baringo and Zambia), and her patience and criticism at home provide the bases and framework on which the research is built.

I

Introduction: the nature of material cultures

This book presents a series of ethnoarchaeological studies of material culture patterning and the background to the enquiry and the reasons for undertaking the fieldwork will be described in this introduction. The initial aim of the research was to see what material 'cultures' (geographical areas with recurring associations of artifacts) represented and were related to in a living context. The concern was to shed some light on the analysis and interpretation of cultures in prehistoric archaeology. In this the aim was similar to my interests in *The spatial organisation of culture* (1978), but in that book, a combing of the ethnographic and anthropological literature failed to produce detailed evidence of material culture patterning and its relationships. While many ethnographic cultural studies in North America (in particular the work of Kroeber and the Californian studies of cultures) and Africa were referred to in that book, few had examined cultures in the detail and manner suitable for answering the questions of the prehistoric archaeologist. When do ethnic units identify themselves in material culture? What is the spatial patterning that results? What happens at material culture boundaries? After compiling *The spatial organisation of culture*, it seemed that it might be valuable to carry out the series of ethnoarchaeological studies presented here.

My interest in finding out more about the nature of 'cultures' can be related to a widespread disillusionment within European prehistoric archaeology about the value of the term. In the 1960s and 1970s many archaeologists expressed embarrassment about the use of the word, and some reacted by finding alternatives (e.g. Cunliffe's (1974) use of 'style zones'). Since the ethnoarchaeological studies were a product of these doubts and disillusion, this chapter will begin by examining how the concept of cultures developed and came to be questioned in prehistoric archaeology. The major interpretive model currently available for cultural similarity, that is, flows of information and degrees of interaction, will then be discussed. In the final part of this chapter I will show how the aims of the ethnoarchaeological work came to be expanded by the realisation that the interpretation of cultures was just one example of a more widespread problem in archaeology.

1.1 Cultures

In continental Europe, the Austro-German school of anthropological geographers (1880–1900) was concerned with the mapping of cultural attributes and correlation of the distributions with environmental variables (Frobenius 1898; Ratzel 1896), and the geographical tradition has had a long and major influence in European prehistoric studies. For example, between 1950 and 1963 a journal entitled *Archaeologica Geographika*, started by H. J. Eggers in Hamburg Museum and University, was devoted to the collection of large numbers of distribution maps of different types of prehistoric artifact. The main contributors, such as Kossack, Hachmann and Jankuhn, in line with other workers in Europe at the same time, were content to catalogue and to build up a more complete set of distribution maps. Gross correlations were made with environmental features, and changes through time were noted. But there was little attempt at explanation. The emphasis on description has been argued through the seventies (e.g. Lüning 1972), with, for example, Knöll's (1959) exhaustive account of the northwestern European Trichterbecher culture distributions being refined and filled in by Bakker (1979).

The explanatory models which have been used in western continental Europe have largely concerned the relationship between cultural distributions and peoples. Yet the main aim of the *Archaeologica Geographika* was to develop and refine cartographic methods and there has on the whole been little emphasis on making ethnic correlations. This hesitancy is partly the result of the nationalism and racism associated with Gustaf Kossinna's (1911; 1926) interpretation of cultural distributions. In Germany the efforts made to demonstrate by maps and collections of distributions that the different components of culture did not always coincide helped in the rejection of Kossinna's ethnic correlations. Interpretation in terms of peoples came to be little discussed (see however an article by Sturms in *Archaeologica Geographika* for 1950, and Bergmann 1968). In Russia and eastern Europe, on the other hand, the sixties and seventies witnessed a large number of articles (listed by Klejn 1977) debating the explanation of cultures in terms of ethnic groups. Here the emphasis was on the importance of understanding the archaeological culture theoretically rather than on the summing of traits to produce archaeological entities.

The interpretation of archaeological cultures in continental Europe developed with little integration of the anthropological functionalism and cultural ecology of England and America. There was an archaeological, geographical and historical interest in the definition of cultures and cultural distributions, and few attempts were made at interpretation in any other way than in terms of ethnic groups. In England and America, on the other hand, the closeness of the links with functionalist anthropological traditions led to a different line of development, with a gradually decreasing interest in cultures and with an emphasis being placed on ecological relationships.

Early in the twentieth century, archaeologists in Britain often assumed an immediate relationship between peoples and things in that cultural material indicated races of people. Macalister's (1921) *Textbook of European archaeology* used phrases such as 'the Mousterian type of humanity' and the 'race called Mousterian' (*ibid.*, 575, 581). Burkitt, while realising some of the difficulties involved, also used the terms 'Neolithic races', 'Upper Aurignacian race', 'Solutrean race' (1921, 44, 135, 189; 1923, 116–117). Crawford had used the word 'cultures' as early as 1912 (p. 192), and in 1921 (p. 79) he defined culture as 'the sum of all the ideals and activities and material which characterise a group of human beings'. Thus, distinct human groups could be identified by their particular material culture.

These early ideas of the relationship between material culture and people were taken and greatly developed by Childe. While he rejected, in line with contemporary work in Europe, any general racial, linguistic, political or 'tribal' interpretation of cultures, he still retained the notion that cultures in some sense represented peoples (Childe 1951). The artifact types which make up cultures were seen as being inventions that had been socially successful. The invention became a 'type' by being accepted as a norm of behaviour for the members of a group. Types make up models which present accepted and successful ways of doing things and which can be passed from generation to generation. Types thus represent a collective and tested wisdom and groups of types distinguish peoples. But in asserting that the peoples so represented were rarely linguistic, political or tribal, Childe expressed the beginnings of a doubt that increased in later workers in Britain, such as Daniel (1962, 114–115) and Higgs (1968). Childe had to conclude that the 'people' forming a 'culture' had no other reality. A social unit of people was represented, but 'what sort of unit that society was – a tribe, a nation, a caste, a profession – can hardly be decided from purely archaeological data' (Childe 1956, 19). In the end, the 'people' producing a 'culture' was only definable by the material 'culture' itself. The 'culture' was a purely archaeological entity.

An abstraction of material cultures so that they had no relationship to other realities was taken further by David Clarke (1968). Archaeological entities such as cultures were not necessarily of any relevance to entities defined in other sciences such as social anthropology. Although Clarke examined the relationship between material culture and linguistic and tribal similarity, his main theoretical stance in 1968 was that archaeological entities could be studied as entities in their own right. Like Childe, he saw material culture as representing coded survival information passed from generation to generation. While information theory could be used to examine the transfer of cultural data, the characteristics of the information flow could be studied in abstract, with less attention paid to the relationship between material culture and the people who produced it.

At the same time as the expression of doubts concerning the relationship between cultures and ethnic units increased, prehistorians in Britain began to emphasise the importance of an alternative ecological viewpoint less concerned with cultural norms and more attracted to studies of environmental relationships. Despite his frequently diffusionist interpretations, much of Childe's work was concerned with local processes and development in an ecological setting. He declared (1951, 16) that 'a culture is the durable material expression of an adaptation to an environment, human as well as physiographical, that enabled the society to survive and develop. From this point of view the buildings, tools, weapons, ornaments and other surviving constituents are interrelated as elements in a functioning whole.' Renfrew (1974, 36) is quite justified in viewing Childe as a precursor of a systems approach to cultural change. Childe saw cultures as organic wholes 'whose constituent elements are integrally related' (Childe 1950, 177) so that a change in one facet affected all others. For example, a change in economy inevitably affected most other aspects of social behaviour (Childe 1958, 294). 'Material culture is...largely a response to an environment: it consists of the devices evolved to meet needs evoked by particular climatic conditions, to take advantage of local sources of food and to secure protection against wild beasts, floods or other nuisances in a given region' (Childe 1948, 20–2). Childe saw cultural variability as 'divergent adaptation to local conditions' (1962, 55). Childe clearly had the utilitarian view of culture so clearly examined and criticised by Sahlins (1976), but this is not to say that he was an environmental determinist. Geographical factors are just the background, the constraints within which change occurs.

Grahame Clark presented similar views. Much of his explanation of culture change used ecological and economic factors. Culture was seen as 'essentially no more than a traditional medium for harmonising social needs and aspirations with the realities of the physical world, that is with the soil and climate of the habitat and with all the forms of life, including man himself, that together constitute the biome' (Clark 1968, 175). However, Clark accepted that environmental factors only set certain limits within which there is room for behavioural variety. The importance of ecological adaptation was continued in Britain in the work of Higgs (1972; 1975) and in Clarke's (1968) view of material culture as holding survival information.

In North America a similar line of development led to a decreasing interest in cultures and to an emphasis on ecological relationships. By 1914 Holmes had already divided North America into 'cultural characterisation areas' based on archaeological data. Students such as Holmes defined geographical areas based on pottery and other artifact types, but their concern was descriptive rather than explanatory. During the twenties and thirties work by, for example, Kidder (1924) and the Gladwins (1934) established cultures which could be fitted into spatial and chronological 'slots'. The main purpose of such studies, as for early cultural research in Britain, was to provide analytical units for the establishment of a chronological scheme. Description and spatial-temporal location were also the reasons for the definition of 'cultural tradition' by Willey in 1946. But during the thirties and forties there was also an emphasis on explaining what cultures represented, and there was from the beginning a divergence between 'normative' and 'behavioural' explanations. As examples of the 'normative' approach, Martin felt that culture concerned a body of meanings held by a society and transmitted by tradition (Martin, Lloyd and Spoehr 1938), and Rouse (1939) entertained similar views. The emphasis was on cultures and types as mental templates in the minds of the original makers and users of the artifacts, but there was also disillusion with attempts made to correlate cultures with other entities. Childe's doubts noted above may have been influential, and by 1958 Willey and Phillips (p. 49) could suggest that cultures had little social reality. As Willey and Sabloff (1974) have demonstrated, the normative view has always had to contend with an alternative behavioural or functional approach in American archaeology. Artifacts were early listed according to functional category, and by the fifties, in parallel with the ecological emphasis of Grahame Clark's European prehistory, a concern with functional links with the environment was widespread in North America, from the specific studies of Wedel (1941; 1953) to the more general influences of Julian H. Steward's *Theory of culture change*.

White's (1949) emphasis on culture as man's extrasomatic means of adaptation was developed in archaeology by Binford who, in his 1965 article, suggested processual definitions of cultural variation. He indicated that culture should be viewed as a system composed of subsystems, and that different parts of the cultural system function in different ways. He separated adaptive techniques from interaction spheres, large areas with stylistic similarity and within which social interaction occurs. Yet to identify cultures as adaptive systems or interaction spheres is not to interpret them in social terms. If discrete cultural units in a range of technical and non-technical traits do exist in geographical space, what social units do they represent and what precise adaptive value do they have (Renfrew 1977b)? The functional approach does not really answer the normative question, 'What do cultures relate to?' The functional argument has taken away the emphasis from such questions, concentrating instead on the adaptive role of the components of cultural systems.

In both England and America there has been a move away from a concern with cultural entities and an increasing awareness that cultures do not always equal ethnic groups. The trend has been towards an examination of the ecological and adaptive significance of cultural items. But the culture concept has also decreased in use for another reason: the empirical realisation that distinct cultures may not exist in the archaeological data anyway.

All definitions of cultures from Crawford to Childe and Clarke have been very similar. They concern geographical areas in which traits are repeatedly associated. Yet monothetic blocks of culture seemed hard to find. Childe (1951) noted that the various fields of material culture did not necessarily coincide. Clarke (1968) formalised the idea that cultures were made up of overlapping distributions by giving them a polythetic definition. He emphasised that lists of traits at neighbouring sites might not be identical but that quantitative analysis would still recognise general cultural affinities between sites within a region. The different and overlapping artifact distributions could be related to different subsystems in much the same way as Binford had suggested.

Doubt about the the existence of cultures was further developed by making a distinction between random and non-random association groups (Hodder and Orton 1976). Hodder and Orton suggested that a continuous trait distribution could be likened to a circular disc. The discs, of varying diameters, could be thrown at random over a region, to produce a complex series of overlaps. Imagine a series of sites within the region, each site with the array of artifacts represented by the discs which happened to overlap at that point. Because the distributions (discs) are continuous, any two nearby sites in the region would have similar assemblages. At least, the nearby assemblages would usually be more similar than distant assemblages. Such 'random' association of overlapping cultural distributions produces a continuum of cultural similarity across the region. As we move from site to site over the area, cultural assemblages gradually change. Starting from any one point within the area we can produce a 'culture' by moving outwards to arbitrary boundaries. Within the 'culture' so defined sites *are* more similar to each other than they are to sites outside the 'culture'. But the culture is an arbitrary construct (random association group) within a continuum of variation over space. This theoretical expectation has been identified in practice in Shennan's (1978) elegant study of European Beakers.

Doubts about the empirical existence of distinct cultures encouraged Renfrew (1977b, 94) to suggest the total abandonment of the notion of culture as a recognisable archaeological unit. Yet there is another type of culture little discussed in Renfrew's abandonment. His concern was mainly with random association groups. But there are also non-random association groups. Spatial analysis can distinguish whether artifact distributions are randomly overlapping or whether they overlap in a non-random way to form distinct groupings. Analysis can distinguish whether cultural similarity between sites is spatially continuous or

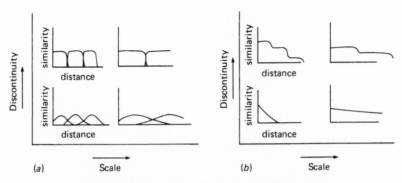

1. Patterns of regional similarity at different degrees of
discontinuity and scale: (*a*) site-to-site similarities and (*b*)
decreasing similarity with reference to a single site.

discontinuous with marked boundaries. It can also identify the spatial
scale of cultural variation. Two aspects of material culture distributions
(scale and discontinuity) are shown in figure 1. Analysis of late Iron Age
distributions in southern England (Hodder 1977b) has indicated non-
random overlap and discontinuities in material culture similarity around
such small-scale groups as the Durotriges. If Renfrew is right in
abandoning random association groups as cultures is he also right in
abandoning these more distinctive non-random groupings?

It has been shown that two general approaches to the interpretation
of cultural distributions can be identified in both England and America.
The first concerns the question, 'What do cultures indicate in terms of
people and norms?' Such considerations, often labelled 'normative',
have recently been thought to be lacking in explanatory value. The
second approach has emphasised the importance of answering questions
concerning the adaptive role of cultural items in different environmental
contexts. Within such a processual approach the value of defining
cultures as norms has decreased. But whether a normative or a processual
stance is taken, it is necessary to differentiate between the two types of
cultural distribution shown in the lower and upper parts of the graphs
in figure 1. What factors cause some societies to be associated with
random association groups and others with non-random association
groups?

One aim of the ethnoarchaeological studies in this book was to examine
whether the disillusion and doubts concerning the use of the culture
concept should really lead to a rejection of interest in the normative
explanation of cultural entities. Could anything be salvaged from
'cultures'? At least the question could be asked: under what conditions
do marked cultural discontinuities relate to the boundaries of ethnic
groups? But as well as examining the normative approach, it was also
necessary to consider the value of particular processual interpretations

of spatial cultural variation. Beyond the general statements about the adaptive role of cultural distributions, some specific hypotheses had been suggested which needed to be tested in the ethnoarchaeological work.

1.2 *Cultural similarities as reflecting degrees of interaction*

In rejecting the normative view of culture and in substituting a functional or ecological emphasis many archaeologists have recently aimed to relate cultural and behavioural variability. One example of this trend which is directly relevant to the interpretation of cultures is that the spatial patterning of material culture is seen as reflecting degrees of interaction. At the within-settlement scale, the interaction hypothesis was used in the Longacre–Deetz–Hill matrilocal residence theory (to be discussed in chapters 7 and 9). Daughters learn potting from their mothers and because of this close contact and interaction, similar pots are made. At the regional scale the hypothesis again suggests that cultural and stylistic variation reflect variation in degrees of interaction (see Plog 1976 for a range of examples), and that social boundaries hinder the movement of objects (Ericson 1977, 118; Sidrys 1977). Alternatively, artifact similarity is functionally related to the information and communication network (e.g. Wobst 1977). The nature of the interaction and information flow is often related in turn to the pattern of available resources.

The direct relationship assumed between resources, interaction and cultural similarity is evident in many studies. Yellen and Harpending (1972, 251), for example, state that poor and highly variable resources lead to cultural homogeneity among hunter-gatherers because of the greater need for contact between specialised groups, while rich or uniform resources favour differentiation. Similarly, Sherratt (1981) relates the greater variability in the resource base in the later Neolithic in Europe to the widespread pottery styles found at that time. In these and other studies (Struever and Houart 1972; Sherratt 1972, 525; Hodder 1978) a straightforward relationship is assumed between interaction and cultural similarity. Clarke (1968, 414) notes that one of the main factors affecting artifact similarity is the 'efficiency of the person to person contact' and 'the extent and continuity of contact'. Cohen (1977, 82) suggests that widespread homogeneity of ceramic styles should occur in hunter-gatherer societies when there is considerable movement of individuals from camp to camp. 'Conversely, local specialisation in artifact styles should be indicative of relative isolation among populations' (*ibid.*).

Stephen Plog (1976) has attempted to provide an independent archaeological test for the hypothesis that cultural similarity reflects degrees of interaction, by taking distance and geographical models as measures of interaction. This would seem to be a difficult line of argument since there is little evidence that social interaction and distance are directly correlated in traditional societies. If it is impossible to examine the relationship between interaction and cultural similarity in an archaeological context, it is necessary to turn to ethnoarchaeology, and the studies in chapters 2 to 7 specifically examine the assumptions involved in the interaction hypothesis. The aim of the ethnoarchaeological work was not only to examine the relationship between peoples and cultures, but also to find out if cultural similarity reflected interaction and, if it did not, what other factors intervened.

But before moving on to the ethnoarchaeological studies some indication will be given of the way in which the aims of the fieldwork studies came to be expanded. A widening of focus resulted from the fact that the interaction hypothesis is just one of many similar hypotheses that are applied in all fields of archaeological work.

1.3 *Culture as reflecting behaviour*

According to the interaction hypothesis, cultural similarity 'reflects' degrees of interaction. By 'reflects' is meant that direct predictive links are assumed between culture and human behaviour. Given a higher degree of interaction one could ideally predict a higher degree of cultural similarity. Such direct links between culture and behaviour are assumed in many spheres of prehistoric archaeology.

For example, direct links are assumed in much of the work on the relationship between artifact styles and the nature of the production of the artifacts. In chapters 4 and 7 it will be shown that the scale of production of pottery and metal items is often assumed to have a direct relationship with the scale of stylistic similarities. The scale of the former can be deduced from the scale of the latter.

In recent studies of burial traces in archaeology it has frequently been asserted (Binford 1971; Tainter 1978) that variability in mortuary practices is related to variability in the form and organisation of social systems. For example, a direct link is assumed between the complexity of the status structure in a society and the complexity of differential treatment of people in burial ceremonies. As with the study of interaction, the study of burial now seems to be suggesting relatively straightforward links between behaviour and artifacts.

The same point is relevant to recent work on refuse and discard. This may seem a surprising claim since much of, for example, Schiffer's (1976) important contribution is concerned precisely with showing how behaviour in respect to discard can distort the relationship between, on the one hand, activities and social organisation and, on the other, distributions of artifacts on archaeological sites. But, in a sense, the link between behaviour and artifacts is still seen as direct in Schiffer's work. Discard behaviour is related directly to variables such as size of site, length of occupation, and life-span of artifacts, while Binford (1978) has emphasised the role of curation. The artifact distributions are interpreted directly, using laws, in terms of the functioning and organisation of the site system.

In settlement studies, the size of sites is often assumed to have some statistical relationship to population size (Wiessner 1974) and there have been many attempts to relate the organisation of house and other structures within settlements to social organisation (e.g. Clarke 1972). At the regional scale, it is now commonly accepted that settlement patterns reflect social organisation (Renfrew 1972; Hodder 1978).

In studies of regional exchange systems, it has been suggested that there must be some direct relationship between the spatial patterning of the artifacts exchanged and the process of exchange (Earle and Ericson 1977). For example, fall-off curves have been studied in attempts to suggest relationships between the shapes of the curves and reciprocal, redistributive, down-the-line and prestige exchange (Hodder 1974; Renfrew 1972; 1977a).

All these examples, which will be examined more fully in chapter 9, demonstrate the attempts made by archaeologists to set up predictive links between culture and social behaviour. This emphasis on the reflective nature of material culture patterning has been associated with a functional and behavioural trend in prehistoric archaeology. Artifacts are seen as assisting people in their articulation with the world around them (both physical and social; Flannery 1972). Material culture is made up of tools functioning between man and his environment. Such an emphasis has a long history in America, as has already been shown, and in prehistoric studies in Britain as the works of Childe, Clark and Clarke attest. But the idea of culture as man's extrasomatic means of adaptation is better known today through the work of Binford (1972). Since artifacts and cultural features are seen as being involved in the adaptive strategies of the prehistoric people who made them (Cordell and Plog 1979, 409), 'laws' can be used to set up links between material culture and society. For example, Schiffer (1976, 13) describes 'correlates' which relate behavioural variables to variables of material objects. The link between people and things concerns utility and function. The link is predictable, lawlike and fairly direct.

But the functional link is now seen as only 'fairly' direct because of the recognition of the importance of depositional and post-depositional effects. Schiffer's (1976) cultural transformation processes demonstrate that archaeological remains are a distorted reflection of past behavioural systems. But the degree and nature of this distortion can be ascertained by the application of cultural and non-cultural laws. As with the 'correlates', these laws of artifact deposition are related to adaptive strategies. There are, for example, predictable behavioural relationships between artifact patterning and site size and intensity of use. Binford (1973, 242) suggests: 'it is clear that the character of the archaeological record and the degree that it is a reflection of the activities performed at any given location will vary inversely with the degree that there is an efficient economising techno-logistics systems in operation'. Once the distortions of the depositional processes have been predicted on the basis of adaptive strategies or techno-logistics systems, material culture still 'reflects' or 'correlates' with social behaviour.

In this section I have tried to emphasise certain aspects of what I take to be the dominant attitude to material culture amongst prehistoric archaeologists today. Material culture patterning is a distorted but predictable reflection of human behaviour. Material items of all forms function to enhance adaptation to the physical and human environment. These various aspects and points will be returned to later in this book, and in chapters 9 and 10 an alternative view will be presented. The points have been made here briefly because they provide the background to the examination of the interaction hypothesis in the ethnoarchaeological studies.

1.4 *Conclusion*

The concern with 'cultures' which stimulated the ethnoarchaeological work grew out of a widespread disillusion in prehistoric archaeology with the value of describing and defining cultural entities and with the possibilities of interpreting them. It had become clear that cultures did not always equal ethnic units. The main alternative to this idea had come from processual and behavioural archaeology with the notion that areas of cultural similarity reflected areas of high social interaction. These hypotheses had to be tested in ethnographic contexts.

But if, in the course of the ethnoarchaeological work, it could be shown that cultural similarity did or did not reflect degrees of interaction, a contribution would also be made to the general behavioural and ecological emphasis in archaeology. Does material culture 'reflect' human behaviour in adapting to environments? Can we find material 'correlates' for social variability? Is the functional, adaptive viewpoint sufficient or are norms and beliefs perhaps also relevant? Such questions became dominant as the fieldwork progressed and they are the main concern of the concluding chapters in this volume.

Finally, what is meant by the phrase 'symbols in action'? In following through the ethnoarchaeological research and its implications, emphasis came to be placed on material items as symbols. The word 'symbol' refers to an object or situation in which a direct, primary or literal meaning also designates another indirect, secondary and figurative meaning. The term 'symbolic meaning' is used in this book to indicate the secondary references evoked by the primary meanings.

'In action' has a double significance in this volume. The first concerns the use of 'action archaeology' as a term for ethnoarchaeology (Kleindienst and Watson 1956), since the major part of this book consists of ethnographic studies undertaken for archaeological purposes. The second reason for the use of the word 'action' concerns the particular view of symbols that will be put forward. This is that symbols do not 'reflect' but that they play an active part in forming and giving meaning to social behaviour. To explain more fully this view would be to anticipate the discussion in the chapters which follow. It will be possible to understand the title 'symbols in action' more adequately by the end of chapter 5.

2
Ethnicity and symbolism in Baringo

The first man who fenced in an area and said 'this is mine', and found people simple enough to believe him, was the real founder of civil society.
(Rousseau, *Discours sur l'origine de l'inégalité parmi les hommes*, 1754)

As described in chapter 1, the initial aim of the ethnoarchaeological work was to examine what cultures represented in terms of ethnic units, interaction and information flow. In a living context, what do material cultures look like, and what do they reflect? As archaeologists, how can we infer behaviour from the cultural distributions? In answering such questions it seemed necessary to conduct field research in a range of societies with different resource bases associated with different patterns of exchange and interaction, and with different patterns of social organisation and with varying emphases on the importance of adherence to ethnic status. The first study examined egalitarian groups within a relatively uniform but poor environment in the Baringo district, Kenya. The groups are mobile pastoralists but have a long tradition of overtly expressing distinct ethnic allegiances. The research considered the way in which artifacts reflected areas of social interaction within this physical and human environment.

2.1 *The Baringo district* (with F. Hivernel)

The Baringo area situated in north central Kenya was one of the few unexplored places left in East Africa at the beginning of the nineteenth century, probably a result of its remoteness and difficulty of access. From the coast, one has to cross large expanses of desert lying to the north and east of Baringo, while the southern approaches pass through the land of the Maasai, whose 'ferocious' reputation used to be widespread.

During the nineteenth century the area was on an Arab trading route which used the Njemps settlement to the south of Lake Baringo as a trading post. But with the completion of the Ugandan railway in 1901, the importance of Baringo as a stopping place on caravan routes diminished. The area became part of British possessions in 1890, and by

2. View of the Tugen Hills to the west of Lake Baringo, showing Tugen compound.

1904 a British station had been built near the shores of Lake Baringo at Arabal (southeast of the lake), and then at Mukutan (east of the lake) in 1914. These headquarters were finally transferred outside of the area covered by this study to Kabarnet in the Tugen Hills in 1924. A taxation system was set up by the British administration in 1908.

Lake Baringo lies in the Rift Valley between, on the west, the Elgeyo escarpment, and on the east, the Laikipia escarpment. Altitude ranges from 975 m on the Baringo floor to about 2134 m on the plateaux (Elgeyo and Laikipia). The Tugen Hills to the west of the lake (figure 2) rise up towards the Elgeyo escarpment. Rainfall averages 50 to 75 cm a year around Lake Baringo, but the amount is highly variable and there are frequent droughts. The main rainy season generally occurs between April and August. There are no permanent rivers, although the Perkerra and Molo rivers to the south of the lake generally have some water until quite late during the dry season.

The soils of the area are poor and the land of the Tugen, Njemps and East Pokot is amongst the most eroded in Kenya. This is partly due to the accumulation of large herds of cattle, sheep and goats, and over-grazing. Quarantine restrictions were imposed in the past which attempted to control the movement of stock in the hope of controlling disease. The decreased mobility of animals resulted in more intense grazing, with disastrous effects.

The area of ethnographic study (figure 3) includes the Tugen and Pokot tribes (both in the Kalenjin cluster), and the Njemps (in the

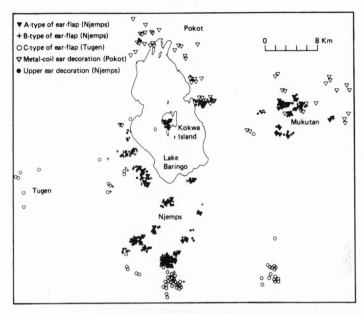

3. The distribution of types of female ear decoration. The difference in the distributions of the A-type of ear-flap and the upper ear decoration on the one hand and the C-type on the other allows a line to be drawn between the Tugen and Njemps to the south and west of the lake (see figures 8 to 13 and 15).

Table 1. *Tribal estimates provided by the District Commissioner for the Baringo district in 1936*

	People	Cattle	Sheep/goats	Land (sq. km)
Tugen	22,280	29,456	188,327	4,022
Njemps	1,610	5,498	27,800	647
Pastoral Pokot	5,299	38,075	135,869	4,248

Maasai group). A census of the general stock of these tribes in the Baringo district was made in 1936 by the Veterinary Department. For the same year, figures for the human population have been supplied by Major Bonds, District Commissioner of Baringo (Maher 1937) (table 1).

These figures must not be taken too seriously as people tend to hide the real numbers of their cattle in order to avoid paying taxes, and the figures for the human population are estimates and not real counts. Discrepancies occur between the figures in table 1 and those published by the Kenya Land Commission (1933) for 1931 (table 2). By 1948, the Tugen had increased to 61,500 and the Njemps to 3423.

Inaccurate as these figures may be, they do indicate the relatively large

Table 2. *Tribal estimates provided by the Kenya Land Commission for the Baringo district in 1931*

	People	Cattle	Sheep/goats
Tugen	33,255	51,297	322,240
Njemps	2,262	12,215	29,858
Pastoral Pokot	7,350	100,000	275,000

areas covered by the Tugen and Pokot when compared with the small enclave of Njemps, living nowadays on an even smaller parcel of the floodplain immediately to the south of Lake Baringo. The figures also demonstrate that the pastoral Pokot have the largest numbers of cattle per head of population while the Tugen, with their more mixed agricultural/pastoral economy, have least. Although in the past they practised irrigation agriculture, the Njemps are now trying to become full pastoralists and today they live at a higher population density than the other tribes around Lake Baringo.

The Kalenjin tribes (including the Tugen and Pokot) all speak related languages. The Njemps speak a Maasai language, and they mainly derive from the Samburu (chapter 6). The Kalenjin tribes have oral traditions of a common origin although the Pokot may have been an early offshoot. Recent research (see Hivernel 1978) indicates that all these tribes are probably agglomerations of numerous individual peoples, and that they have absorbed large numbers of 'foreigners'. The heterogeneity of origin makes the cultural uniformity within the tribes, to be described below, all the more remarkable.

The three tribes (Tugen, Njemps, Pokot) have similar patterns of social organisation, characterised by a lack of centralised authority. There are a number of local councils or groups of elders who have some localised authority, and men of local standing are accepted as 'chiefs' by the colonial and present Kenyan government. These chiefs are not traditional. There are no meetings at which the whole tribe gathers at one time. Marriage is virilocal and polygamous, and ties of kinship spread over fairly wide areas – a 15 or 25 km radius or more is common. There are exogamous dispersed clans, and a system of age-sets means that members of the same age-set over wide areas can treat each other as social equals.

The settlement pattern consists of huts and granaries in dispersed compounds. Nowadays there are no villages apart from the small shopping centres which have supplemented the local markets, and where one can buy outside items such as soap, blankets, aspirin, flour and matches. But at the beginning of this century the Njemps were clustered into a few large and tightly packed villages (Dundas 1910; Johnston 1902, 812) which no longer exist. The Tugen and Njemps compounds are fairly permanent. 'Western' influence varies very much within the region studied, but it has affected the whole region to some extent. There are mass-produced imported goods, but on a small scale and only items of minor importance. More remote areas with less 'European' goods and where the nearest tarmac road is about 95 km away were chosen for study. Here there were few or no European items to be found in the huts. Although there have been many recent changes, dress remains mostly non-European. The Baringo area remained relatively untouched by early colonial settlement and influence because of its arid environment and rather less fertile soils (Middleton 1965, 344), and because the area was not on the main railway route (Mungeam 1966, 94).

Although, in the context of Kenya as a whole, the Baringo district is relatively traditional in many aspects of life, the effects of colonial and more recent governmental control have undoubtedly been felt in the area. The establishment of non-traditional chiefs, the spread of local schools, and the policing of the area to prevent warfare and raiding are some important recent changes which have had considerable effects on the structure of society. The factor which has perhaps caused the greatest change in the traditional way of life is the bringing of relative peace and stability to the area. Policing of the district has largely stopped the cattle raiding and fighting in most of the localities studied (although not completely – see below). It is possible that the bringing of security from outside the traditional system has greatly affected the nature of the tribal groupings, and this possibility will be discussed later in this chapter. These factors do not make ethnographic study in the Baringo area invalid. In fact, the impact of central government control can be identified in the material culture patterning, and this will be discussed. What is important for this study is that traditional methods of manufacture and exchange of many items still exist in the area, although in the author's opinion such methods are on the verge of disappearing. Every attempt was made to avoid localities with a non-traditional aspect such as the irrigation scheme near Marigat, and the small factory concerned with fish processing near Kampi-ya-Samaki. Compounds containing young men and women who had been to school and were wearing European dress were not studied. Precautions of this nature, although the influence of the central Kenyan government should not be ignored, allow patterning in the traditional material culture to be compared with the patterning of a particular mode of human organisation and behaviour.

2.2 *Field method*

During the fieldwork, over 400 hut compounds were visited in the Njemps area and on the fringes of the Tugen and Pokot tribes. Without reliable maps of the total present-day settlement pattern it is difficult to determine accurately what percentage of compounds was visited. In the areas near the Tugen–Njemps border it is estimated that about 50 % of compounds were studied. Figure 3 does, however, give some indication of the relative densities of settlement in the different parts of the area examined.

Personal life histories were collected for over 500 adults. This information included age, place of birth, where they had lived, date of marriage and languages spoken. These data were collected through interpreters. It should be stressed that some of this information may be imprecise, especially that regarding age. Although it was possible to obtain the age of individuals within a 20 to 30 year bracket, an attempt was also made to determine when the items of material culture studied had been made or bought. Dates were given, through the interpreter, by reference to age-sets, famines or other major events, but many may have been exaggerated. However, it is hoped that, as long as one is only interested in approximate dating, this information may be of some general value. Indeed, the clear internal consistency in the patterning which results (Hodder 1977a) goes quite a long way to corroborate the value of the dates. Other information was also collected on the material culture in the compounds. Details of self-adornment were recorded. Sketch plans were made of the compounds and insides of the huts. Measurements and details were recorded of pots, basketwork, wooden containers, stools, spears and shields etc. For each item, information was also obtained on who made it or from where it was acquired.

It was necessary to make some choice of items to be studied. To avoid too arbitrary a choice, an attempt was made to study all artifact types within the main categories of objects – utility, personal dress and decoration, weapons. The only widely found objects not studied, as far as the author is aware, are the metal cooking pots which are now coming into use. Rarer items such as circumcision dresses were also not studied in detail.

2.3 *Material culture patterning*

In this section, some general comments will first be made about the tribal borders in the Baringo area, and then the difference between the nature of the borders will be examined in some detail.

An important point to make about the borders is that there is usually very little ambiguity or blurring about the tribal group to which a person belongs. Each tribe is characterised by distinctive styles of dress. The people themselves know very clearly whether at any one moment they are identifying with the Pokot, Njemps or Tugen, and this identification is shown overtly in items of dress, particularly ear decoration (figure 3). Types of dress and ear decoration worn by Tugen, Njemps and Pokot women and Pokot men are shown in figures 4 to 7.

Individuals can move across the borders and change their homes.

4. A Tugen woman wearing fawn-coloured cloth and the C-type of ear-flap.

5. An Njemps woman wearing red-coloured cloth, the A-type of ear-flap and upper ear decoration.

6. A Pokot woman with skin dress, metal-coil ear decoration and 'plates' of necklaces.

7. A Pokot man with typical head and ear decoration and holding a common Pokot type of stool.

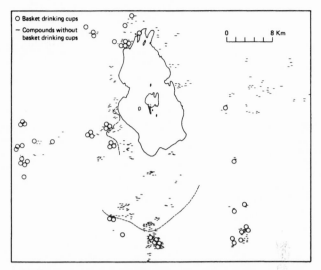

8. The distribution of basket drinking cups (*tokei*; see figure 14: 4). Broken lines indicate the more distinct borders between the Tugen and Njemps (see figure 3).

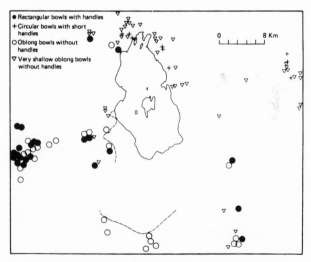

9. The distribution of types of wooden eating bowl (*tubē*; see figures 14: 6 and 7). For broken lines see figure 3.

When they do this they will usually change their dress to conform to the tribe in which they live. But if they make a return visit to their original tribe for a short period, they might well change their dress again. So, whatever a woman may feel she really is, she can outwardly express different identities, and there is rarely any ambiguity about which identity she is overtly expressing at any one time. The individual herself

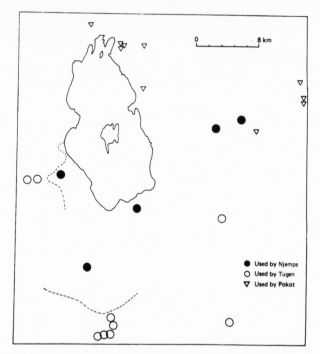

10. The distribution of shield types used by the Njemps, Tugen and Pokot. For broken lines see figure 3.

and an outside observer would always come to the same conclusion about the tribe with which a particular person was identifying.

Having made this general statement it will be shown below that certain of the border areas do show some between-tribe blurring. But even these borders must be considered abrupt relative to the great stretches of cultural homogeneity within the tribal areas behind the borders. Various aspects of dress, then, as well as other items of material culture show fairly clear breaks at the tribal boundaries (figures 3 and 8 to 10). Distributions such as the ear decoration (figure 3) allow lines to be drawn between the Tugen and Njemps to the south and west of the lake. The same boundary is seen in the smaller samples of basket drinking cups (*tokei* – figure 8), wooden eating bowls (*tubē* – figure 9), and shield types (figure 10). But what happens to the relationships between people at these boundaries? Why do the boundaries exist and what does it mean to be a Tugen as opposed to a Njemps? And why have the differences in material culture been maintained over at least the last eighty years?

The inadequacy of many of the answers favoured by archaeologists for these types of question has been discussed elsewhere (Hodder 1977a), but what is particularly clear is that the cultural differences are not the result of a lack of between-group contact. In fact there has been a long history

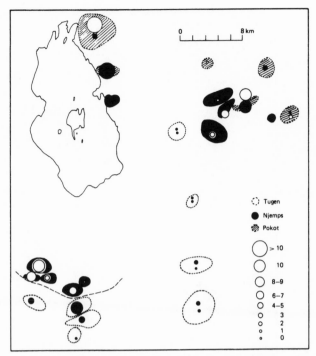

11. The average numbers of in-laws from other tribes in tribes of informants in various settlement clusters (surrounded by dashed lines). The size of circle in each cluster indicates the average number of Tugen, Njemps and Pokot in-laws of informants.

of interaction and movement between the tribal groups. For example, although those living near the tribal borders show a preference for marriage within their own tribe (Hodder 1977a, figure 7), cross-border marriages *are* fairly common, so that most people near the borders have some in-laws in the neighbouring tribes. The average numbers of immediate in-laws (brother-, sister-, parents-, and children-in-law – the Tugen word is *kabikoi*, the Njemps word *lautan*) per informant are shown in figure 11.

Also, most people have 'cattle friends' and partners in other tribes. It is common practice for a tribesman to leave some of his cattle and goats with partners dotted around the countryside at considerable distances from his dwelling-place. These partners look after the animals and use the milk from them (in Tugen such partners are *ingor*, in Njemps *ngitaat* and in Pokot *sirah*). In this way a man's stock is safeguarded against localised disease and raiding. Such animals can always be recalled. A rather different practice occurs when one man *gives* cattle and goats to another man. In these cases a man relinquishes his rights to the animals, but he expects a similar gift in return at some unspecified time (the Tugen

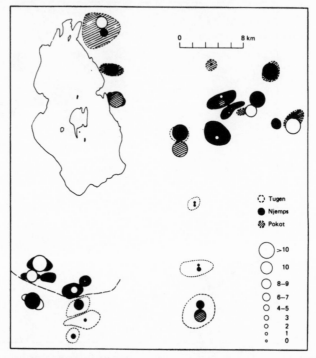

12. The average numbers of cattle exchange friends in other tribes for informants in various settlement clusters. The size of circle in each cluster indicates the average number of Tugen, Njemps and Pokot cattle friends of informants.

words for such 'exchange friends' are *tinyei besentenya*, in Njemps they are *silē* and in Pokot *ghosia*). Any one man may have from five to fifty of these cattle partners and exchange friends. Figure 12 shows that informants near the borders generally had such partners in neighbouring tribes. So the pattern of the individual's fields of contacts and relations cannot be used to explain the material culture differences. Even if a man has many friends and relations in other tribes, it does not follow that he therefore dresses like the other tribe.

In the same way that the borders have not been eroded by cross-border marriage and interaction, neither have they been eroded by migration and the movement of whole families from one tribe to another. When a family wishes to move into another tribe the husband must begin discussions with its elders, and he will usually have to give a bull to be eaten by the young men or warriors of the area. When the members of a family move, they will often change their dress and material culture completely so that they become almost indistinguishable from the local community. In the past it seems that there has been much movement and absorption of this sort throughout the Baringo and Turkana areas, without any watering down or erosion of the cultural differences.

Factors of the type already discussed do not explain why it is that to be a Tugen, Njemps or Pokot involves demarcating clear and distinct identities in terms of dress and material culture. Why is it that the 'us' and the 'not-us' categories are so clearly displayed?

One further suggestion that might be made is that the differences are in some way related to different economies and ways of life. It is true that there are slight differences in economic emphasis between the three groups (Tugen, Njemps, Pokot) as already mentioned. But this argument seems only relevant to part of the cultural assemblage. Certain traits such as milk jugs, hut construction and compound plan do seem to be related to economic variation. For example, there are some purely pastoral Njemps in the Mukutan area who have temporary houses built like those of the pastoral Pokot. But this type of argument cannot be used for the whole cultural inventory. There is clear homogeneity in material culture within tribes and fairly clear breaks at the borders. The economic variation is much more gradual, localised and complex so that it is difficult to see it as the cause of all the material culture variation.

So far in this section no adequate explanation for the clear differences in the identities expressed by the different groups in the Baringo area has been offered. Perhaps it should be added that to be a Tugen rather than a Njemps means that one has slightly different social customs – for example, a different bride price and different penalties for wrong-doing. But these differences are very slight and those individuals crossing the borders easily adopt and fit into the new institutions. It is difficult to see these minor features as causing the material culture differences.

The initial explanation to be offered here concerns the relationships between groups. There is, and has been for some considerable time as far as one can see, a great deal of economic competition between the Baringo tribes. This competition mainly takes the form of cattle and goat raiding (although it will be suggested that the real economic advantage of such raids is often slight) and major disputes over grazing lands. Even today the Pokot and Turkana are fighting over cattle and land.

The young circumcised but unmarried men (the *moran*) have a special role to play in the competition between groups. The *moran* are the warriors who carry out the raiding to obtain cattle from other tribes. But, perhaps more importantly, they are the people who are involved in the expansion of the tribal area and who will retrieve the cattle belonging to members of the tribe if they are stolen by another tribe. So, by being a member of a tribe one qualifies for the protection of the *moran* of that tribe.

While working amongst the Pokot in 1977, the cattle of one family north of Mukutan were stolen at night by the Turkana. The next day 150 Pokot *moran* set off to retrieve them. Although this particular expedition was unsuccessful, the example illustrates the very real extent to which membership of a tribe bestows a considerable degree of support and aid.

In more general terms, Sahlins (1968) has suggested that certain types of reciprocal exchanges occur within tribal areas. Such exchange involves balanced and generalised reciprocity. But the 'them' category may be treated differently from the 'us' category. Across the tribal border there may be negative reciprocity involving barter and haggling and theft – the desire to get something for nothing. Between-group contact may involve a distinctive type of relationship between people because it is based on the differences between them. For example, it may be the very differences between groups which allow each group to gain resources (in the Baringo case, land, cattle and goats) from the other tribe without giving anything in return. I would suggest generally that, as competition over resources and conflict between groups increase in the Baringo area, there are greater advantages in groups overtly stressing their differences. It is the differences which allow one to take and not to give in return, which allow 'them' to be treated differently from 'us', and which allow the resources of groups to be increased. At the same time, identities may be stressed in a warring, competitive situation for another reason. If a person is dependent for his security on the voluntary and spontaneous support of his own community, self-identification as a member of this community may need to be explicitly expressed and confirmed. So, in periods of instability and insecurity, one might expect greater material culture conformity within regional communities, and greater cultural differences between communities.

Perhaps it would be useful to explain here in more detail the importance to an individual of belonging to one Baringo tribe as opposed to another. As has been suggested, the factor which most closely correlates with being a Tugen, Njemps or Pokot is that one's security and livelihood are guaranteed by the existence of the wider group to which one belongs. Having been born or become a member of a tribe, informants were always clear that reparation for the theft of one's belongings (mainly cattle) was the responsibility of the group as a whole. So the logical relationship between the economic base of society and material culture is apparent. Ultimately, the very livelihood and security of a family depend on support from the wider group to which it belongs. Because in the Baringo context, one's reliance on the wider group is so fundamental, it is expressed immediately and overtly in the outward signs with which one is associated – i.e. in material culture.

The way in which material culture is used to communicate information about group membership is brought out by the responses obtained when women were asked why they did not wear different decoration, say that of other tribes. The most common type of answer was that women did not wear uncharacteristic dress because 'they did not want to be a stranger' in their own tribe. One woman said that it might be thought that she would be attacked as a foreigner in Njemps land if she dressed like a Pokot, although in practice there is a lot of travelling in different tribes. A Tugen woman said that the women in her area had been told by their local 'chief' to wear their distinctive dress 'so that they could be recognised as friends, and not enemies in times of fighting'.

These comments support the idea that items such as ear decoration express identity with a group and conformity with its rules. The same is evident amongst those women changing tribe on marriage. A Pokot woman married to an Njemps man said she wore full Njemps dress because when her parents gave her to another tribe, she had promised to agree to follow the Njemps customs. The material culture associated with her expressed her conformity and identity. Extended or even short visits back to the original tribe often result in changes back to the first tribe's style of dress. In fact, an individual's guise may be transient and temporary, depending on context. Another Pokot woman married to an Njemps man said that when she wanted to be like the Njemps she wore Njemps articles. This attitude stresses the importance of material culture as a medium for communication.

But it should be emphasised that the material culture differences do not only communicate or signal which group one belongs to in order to achieve security and group support. As already indicated, the cultural differences form the basis for negative reciprocity between groups. They 'justify' the theft. The 'them' category can be treated differently from the 'us' category because 'they' *are* different. The material differentiation provides the framework within which between-group relations can be unstable, competitive and unbalanced. It is insufficient to talk about material culture 'expressing' group identity because it does much more than that. The material culture constitutes the group differences and is actively articulated in relations of negative reciprocity.

The suggestion made above, that several aspects of the material culture patterning in the Baringo district are related to competition and conflict over resources, may still seem rather weak, especially since the colonial and present Kenyan government brought a certain amount of peace and stability to the area. So it is necessary to examine how useful the explanation is in accounting for variation in the sharpness of the borders, and changes in the nature of the borders through time.

Variation in the sharpness of the borders

First, then, variation in the sharpness of the different borders will be examined. At the northwestern edge of the lake, the Pokot adjoin the Tugen. But this border is by no means clear-cut. Tugen and Pokot houses are found intermingled, and one woman may wear both Pokot and Tugen items of decoration. When a woman marries a man from another tribe living in this border area she does not necessarily change her style of dress. Certain other material culture traits, such as wooden milk jugs, spread from the Pokot well into the Tugen area.

An initial interpretation of the relative blurring of this border was that

Pokot and Tugen are both Kalenjin. That is, they are both members
of the same wider language and historical grouping. But more recent
work on the northeastern side of the lake has identified the same blurring
between the Pokot and a non-Kalenjin group, the Njemps. Once again
the Pokot and Njemps compounds are intermingled, and large numbers
of women wear both Njemps and Pokot traits.

What is the social situation responsible for the material culture
blurring at these borders? In the first place there is no more, nor less
cross-border marriage and exchange of cattle (as far as a border can be
identified) than across other borders (figures 11 and 12). In these areas
the Pokot are moving southwards towards the Tugen and Njemps
because of pressure from the Turkana to their north. But many of the
Pokot in the two border areas had been there for some time, often living
in fairly permanent compounds. Any tendency towards economic stress
and competition in these areas is, to a certain extent, relieved by two
factors: (i) those living in the two border areas make up quite a large
part of their diet by fishing in the lake; (ii) the Njemps and Tugen
cultivate maize and other crops while the Pokot do not do this. These
factors relieve any stress which might otherwise have occurred through
direct conflict between identical needs. There is, in any case, fairly rich
grazing land around the edge of the lake while the density of occupation
in these areas remains relatively low. So the material culture mixing, and
the relative lack of clear stressed identities in the areas to the north of
the lake, relate to a low level of economic competition and strain.

However, moving eastwards and upwards away from the lake to the
Mukutan area, the Pokot are again found bordering the Njemps. Yet
here the situation is slightly different. The Pokot have moved into this
area fairly recently (in the last five years) because of Turkana raiding,
and to a lesser extent because of cattle disease and drought in Pokot areas.
The Pokot compounds in this Mukutan area are more temporary than
those near the lake. The population density is again low. These factors
mean that the Pokot do not represent a huge threat to the Njemps and
their grazing lands. In addition, the Njemps in the area tend to grow
more maize than the Pokot. Other differences in the economies of the
two groups are that the Njemps have no camels and fewer goats and
sheep. Perhaps as a result of all this, there has been no recent fighting
between the two tribes in this area. Indeed, the Pokot obtain all their
drinking water in the dry season from a river running through Njemps
territory. Nevertheless, there is greater economic stress in this area than
at the north of the lake. At Mukutan both the Njemps and the Pokot
have a heavy reliance on cattle, and this far from the lake there is no
possibility of fishing relieving the economic competition. There is a
scarcity of grazing land, and this is seen quite clearly in the fact that some
of the Njemps in this area have adopted a more mobile and pastoral way
of life. They have changed to this because the lack of grass in the

Mukutan area makes permanent habitation and grazing there difficult. The Njemps were certainly aware of the threat posed by the arrival of the Pokot in the area, and, at the time of the study, had begun moving into and consolidating their border with the Pokot.

Related to both the fact that the Pokot are recent arrivals in the area and to the increasing economic strain and competition, there is less blurring of identities and material culture in this area. The identities expressed in terms of dress and material culture were kept rigidly distinct so that no people were found wearing items of both Njemps and Pokot dress. However, there was a certain amount of blurring in some other aspects of material culture, Njemps and Pokot compounds were intermingled, and in one case Njemps and Pokot families inhabited two halves of the same compound.

Up to this point the relationship between the Pokot and other tribes has been considered. In general, it might be expected that any border with the Pokot would tend not to be strongly marked since the Pokot have a more nomadic way of life than the Tugen and Njemps. The presence of the Pokot is temporary and may, therefore, pose less of a threat.

To the south and west of the lake, the border between the Tugen and Njemps presents a different situation. The flat plain in this area was first inhabited by the Njemps, but over the last thirty to fifty years the Tugen have been moving onto the plain from the hills to the west, in search of better grazing land. There is now an extremely high density of occupation on the plain, and both Tugen and Njemps are moving into and consolidating their border areas. The Tugen also moved round to the east of the Njemps and took over the upland Arabal area which was traditionally a seasonal grazing zone of the Njemps.

The Njemps are therefore surrounded by, and being encroached upon by, the Tugen. Also, unlike the areas discussed above, the economies of these two groups are very similar. There is little or no fishing here because of the distance of the border itself from the lake. Both groups collect honey, grow maize, and place a strong emphasis on cattle, especially the Njemps. As a result of this, and unlike the other areas, there has recently been raiding and small-scale fighting in this locality. Most people in the Njemps–Tugen border areas south and west of the lake do not take their cattle to graze in each other's lands (figure 13) and said that they would be scared to do this without permission and without relatives in the other tribe. Some Njemps said that they would never be able to take cattle into the Tugen area, even in a very bad year.

So there is clear evidence here of conflict over grazing lands. Yet the amount of intermarriage between tribes is about the same as in other border areas (figure 11). Many people living up to 5 km from the border have some in-laws in the other tribe; as they do cattle partners (figure 12). Also the different tribes cooperate in the growing of maize. There

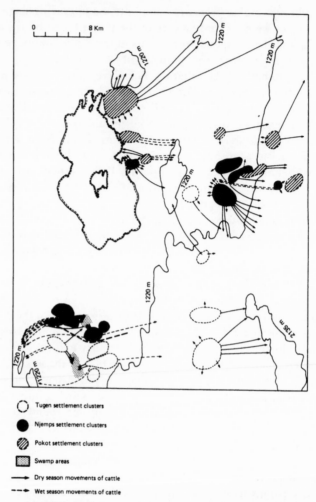

13. Cattle grazing movements in the Baringo area. The clusters
of settlement shown in this figure are as in figure 11. Land over
1220 m and 2135 m is shown. The boundary between the Tugen
and Njemps to the south of the lake is shown (heavy broken
line).

is a large communal maize field just inside the Tugen area south of the
lake. Individual Tugen allow Njemps people to plant maize in their part
of the field in return for some of the maize, or for beer. Alternatively there
is an obligation to return help later if needed.

In spite of this between-tribe contact, there is no doubt that there is
a higher population density and greater economic stress and competition
in this area than elsewhere. Corresponding to this there is a marked
boundary between the two groups in several aspects of material culture,

especially in the ear decoration worn by women (figure 3). But the boundary is also seen very clearly in the distribution of *tokei* (figure 8), *tubē* (figure 9), shield types (figure 10) and ceremonial dresses. No women were found wearing a mixture of Tugen and Njemps ear decoration. In fact, on the border itself there are only two compounds in which there is any indication of a mixture of characteristically Njemps and Tugen traits. No case was found of a Tugen or Njemps living in the other tribe and retaining differences of material culture, so that a line can easily be drawn between the Tugen and Njemps areas (figures 8 to 10). Marriage moves across the border result in quick and complete assimilation in terms of material culture and dress (at least this is true for marriages which have taken place in the last twenty years. The earlier situation is discussed below).

Apart from marriage moves, two families were found who had moved as units from the Tugen area into the Njemps area thirty to forty years ago. They had achieved this by talking to the elder Njemps men, paying a bull, and by becoming involved in the Njemps way of life. For example their children were circumcised with Njemps children in the same ceremonies. Also, they changed their dress and material culture completely. However, in both families the children had later married Tugen in preference to Njemps and had retained a large number of Tugen cattle partners. This suggests that, although families might become fully incorporated into another culture and way of life and express their incorporation overtly, they might still think of themselves as different and prefer to marry back into their own tribe.

Some of the evidence from Baringo has been mentioned which shows that distinct identities are overtly stressed most clearly at those boundaries where there is greater economic competition between groups. It is suggested here that this is because one's rights to land, and protection from raiding, depend on one's being a member of a particular group. Where there is greater competition over land, and more fighting and raiding for resources, identities are most clearly displayed. The cultural differences are maintained because it *is* the differences that ensure one's security and justify the competitive access to resources.

Changes in the nature of borders through time

So far the situation in the Baringo area at the present day has been considered. But, as already suggested, the present situation differs markedly from that in the past, in that policing of the area has had some degree of success in maintaining peaceful conditions and preventing cattle raiding. Is it possible to discover what border relations were like before this relative peace? Probably border conditions varied considerably through time and from place to place. But some fairly clear pictures emerged for a few areas by talking to older men about the situation just before the colonial impact. In several areas it is quite apparent that there

Table 3. *The number of Njemps and Tugen women of different ages wearing ear-flaps of types A, B and C*

Ear-flap type	Age					
	16–25	26–35	36–45	46–55	56–65	66–75
Njemps women						
A	14	12	5	1	2	0
B	6	7	9	8	5	8
Tugen women						
C	10	14	15	5	1	0
B	1	0	2	3	6	0

was a considerable amount of raiding and warring across the borders before the colonial peace. Related to this there was no grazing of cattle in different tribal areas and cultural boundaries were fairly distinct.

For example, older men in the Mukutan area talked of a long period of conflict with the Tugen over the Arabal area to the south of Mukutan. However, there is plenty of oral evidence that at the same time fairly large numbers of Tugen opted to 'become' Njemps. They settled in the Njemps area, completely changed their dress and material culture, and became incorporated in Njemps society. These adopted Tugen were and are indistinguishable from the Njemps. So, as has already been shown, distinct borders and economic competition do not relate to a lack of interaction and migration. But, about twenty years ago, central government control extended up into this area and the tribal fighting ceased. As a result, the Tugen who had moved into the Njemps part of the area near Mukutan in the last twenty years have *not* become fully incorporated into Njemps culture. Because of the relative lack of conflict there is nowadays less need to display clear identities with the tribal group within which one lives.

However, in some areas, such as to the south and west of the lake, the material culture shows a clearer boundary now than it did in the recent past, and there was some suggestion from informants that at the time there was fairly fluid nomadic movement. The A-type of ear-flap decoration (figures 3 and 5) is a relatively new fashion, having been introduced in the last ten years. Table 3 shows that it is preferred by the younger women. Older women still prefer to wear the older B-type (table 3 and figures 3 and 39). The two types have different distributions (figure 3) to the south and west of the lake in that the B-type is worn by Tugen women living near the Njemps. It is also of interest to examine the distribution of the *kerebē*, a simple basketwork bowl (figure 14). These are seldom made now, but in the past they were frequently used to contain millet. In fact the Tugen used to take their millet in them when

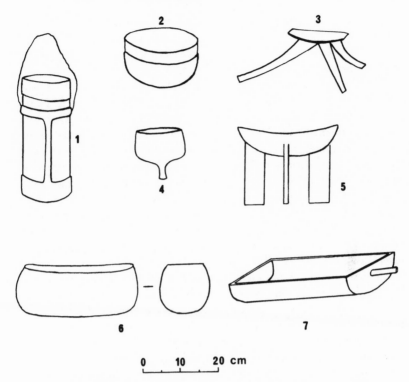

14. Types of artifact found in the Baringo area. 1 = wooden honey pot. 2 = basket eating bowl (*kerebē*). 3 = three-legged stool. 4 = basket *tokei*. 5 = four-legged stool. 6 and 7 = wooden eating bowls (*tubē*).

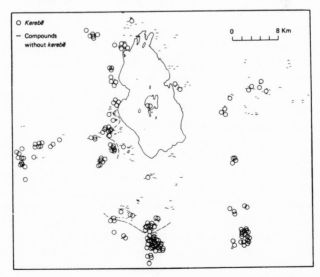

15. The distribution of the basketwork bowl called the *kerebē*.

exchanging for Njemps goats at the great *manyattas*. These were the villages in which the Njemps lived before their dispersal and adoption of cattle. The *kerebē* (figure 15) show a considerable degree of overlap into the Njemps area.

What factors can be put forward to explain the fact that these, and various other traits (Hodder 1977a), indicate a sharper Njemps–Tugen border south and west of the lake now than in the recent past? One suggestion might be that early colonial officers tended to classify people into groups such as the Tugen or Njemps for administrative convenience. The sense of separate identities may have resulted from categorisation from outside (cf. Fried 1968). This type of explanation seems inadequate for the full complexity and variability of border situations in the Baringo area. In any case, there is a chronological problem as the change in ear-flap styles and distributions occurred in the last ten years. Colonial administration and taxation to the south and west of the lake began several decades earlier (Hennings 1951).

An alternative explanation again concerns competition over resources. Up until the 1920s, the Njemps lived in villages and had practised irrigation agriculture. After about 1926 they gradually dispersed and began to change their emphasis to cattle. Only very recently, however, has a heavy reliance on cattle been taken up. There is plenty of oral evidence that while the Njemps maintained irrigated fields, they exchanged goats for Tugen millet and conducted other transactions with the Tugen. At that time there were clear differences in the economies of the two tribes, and a less competitive, symbiotic relationship existed. There was no need, then, for traits of material culture to be retained within distinct identity categories, and traits were copied across the borders. But as the economies of the two groups have become more and more similar, and as the tribes have come nearer to each other and population densities have increased, competition over grazing land has become a significant aspect of life. It has, therefore, recently become necessary to display clear and distinct identities in terms of material culture. In fact, this type of explanation may show why there was a change of ear-flap fashion. Since the B-type ear-flap had already diffused across the border, the only way in which the Njemps could adequately assert their distinctiveness was to adopt a new style of what is perhaps the most characteristic and easily distinguishable cultural item. But the ear-flaps are also used to assert age differences and we need to examine this aspect of the patterning (chapter 5) before we can achieve a fuller understanding.

A comparable sequence of events is found for the development of relations between the Pokot and Turkana. In 1977 these two groups were fighting over land and cattle (although there were Pokot with cattle partners and marriage relations amongst the Turkana), and the Pokot interviewed were very much aware of the cultural and dress differences between them. However, the Pokot and Turkana do have many traits of material culture in common. When asked about this, Pokot men said that it was the result of earlier friendly relations between them and the Turkana. Certainly there is some oral evidence that until fairly recently the Pokot and Turkana had reasonably peaceful relations. Thus it seems that much of the temporal variation in material culture patterning, as well as the spatial variation, can be related to conflict and competition over resources and the resulting need, in the Baringo context, to stress overtly clear, unambiguous identities.

2.4 *Conclusion*

It has been shown that cultural similarity in the Baringo area plays a part in the adaptive strategies of competing ethnic groups. But problems are beginning to emerge with the hypothesis that cultural patterning reflects patterns of interaction since the distinct material culture boundaries in the area studied are foci of interaction, not barriers. There are always many types of social and economic interaction to be found within a living society, and the forms of contact which have been demonstrated at the Baringo borders are 'reflected' by dissimilarity in the particular material items which have been discussed, while other types of within-group information flow are reflected by cultural similarity.

Only some aspects of the Baringo borders have begun to be uncovered in this chapter. But it is already clear that we cannot, as prehistoric archaeologists, assume that material culture 'reflects' (in the sense defined in chapter 1) degrees of interaction because the *nature* of the interaction and the degree of competition between groups also play a part. Certain artifact types are held back from expressing between-group contact because they are used to support within-group interaction and to justify between-group negative reciprocity and competition where there is a scarcity of resources. Partly because there are none of Rousseau's fences in the Baringo area, material culture of the baskets and trinkets kind is used most effectively to constitute and reproduce ethnic group distinctions despite the long history and high degree of inter-ethnic flows.

The enquiry has not led so far to a reconsideration of the more general hypothesis described in chapter 1 that material culture patterning 'reflects' human behaviour. The hypothesis concerned with degrees of interaction has simply been replaced by a hypothesis which suggests straightforward predictable links between material culture boundaries and competition over resources. Within this ecological framework, an initial answer to the question posed in chapter 1, 'Under what conditions do marked cultural discontinuities relate to the boundaries of ethnic groups?' would be 'In conditions of marked competition over resources'. It will become apparent later on that this answer is only one small part of a complex picture, but it will have to suffice for the moment.

The only addition that can so far be made to the notion that material culture reflects behaviour concerns the active part played by the artifacts studied in the relations between groups. An emphasis on material culture reflecting, mirroring or expressing behaviour tends to suggest that artifacts have a passive role. While it has been shown that in the Baringo area material culture does reflect and express groups and their competition, it is also clear that material symbols can actively justify the actions and intentions of human groups. The non-passive role of material symbols will be examined more closely in the studies which follow.

3
Maintaining the boundaries

In this chapter the distributions of pottery, stools and hearths are examined in order to show how they reinforce ethnic distinctions and act to make the ethnic competition and negative reciprocity acceptable within the Baringo context. In addition, it is important from the archaeological point of view to demonstrate what material culture boundaries look like and how they might be recognised in archaeological data.

3.1 *Pottery production and distribution*

Njemps pottery

Most of the pottery used by the Njemps is made on the largest island in Lake Baringo (Kokwa Island), although other potters (all of whom are women) work in the Mukutan area to the east of Baringo, and have worked in the past on other islands in the lake. It is generally agreed by all the Njemps potters that the clay on Kokwa Island is the most suitable for potting. When interviewed, the Kokwa potter (figure 16) said that she had tried making pottery on the mainland near her main market at Kampi-ya-Samaki, but had been unsuccessful. Therefore, one constraint on the distribution of Njemps pottery is the localisation of good potting clays and this is a factor which has been discussed more generally by Arnold (1978).

The Kokwa potter makes two forms of vessel, one for cooking with a wide open mouth (figure 17), and one for water storage with a long narrow neck and a small mouth. In making the pots, the clay is first collected from ant hills at preferred spots on the island, and the dry clay is pounded down to a fine dust. Water is then added and worked into the clay. No tempering material is added. The pot itself is then gradually built up by the addition of coils, and smoothed out by hand and with the aid of pieces of calabash (figure 16). No base or support is used to hold the pot during its formation, the whole process being carried out with the potter resting the pot on her lap. After drying in the shade, the pots are fired in small bonfires.

37

16. The Kokwa potter in the process of making a cooking pot, smoothing the sides with a piece of calabash.

17. Artifacts from Baringo. Left: honey pot, and cooking pot from Kokwa. Centre (top and bottom): *tubē*. Right: calabash and *kerebē*.

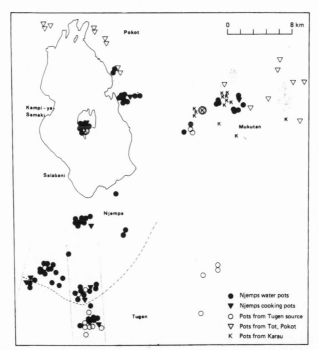

18. The distribution of pottery types. Double circles enclose the potters at Karau (K) and on Kokwa (X). The dotted lines to the south of the lake represent transects used for quantifying fall-offs of pottery (see figure 19).

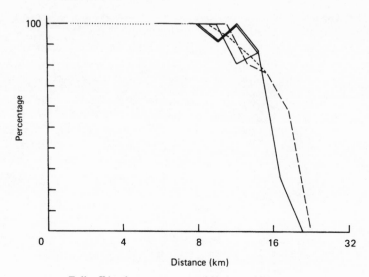

19. Fall-off in the percentage of Kokwa (Njemps) pottery to the south of the lake. The different lines are for different transects (for the transects to the south of the lake see figure 18).

The amount of pottery made by the Kokwa potter varies seasonally, since the clay is too wet in the rainy season for potting. On average she makes only ten pots a month in the dry season, so that she is able to carry out agricultural tasks as well.

There are two main ways in which the Kokwa potter's products are dispersed. Batches of pots are sometimes taken by the potter to the main markets in the mainland, and in particular to Kampi-ya-Samaki, on the western edge of the lake. Consumers buy the pots at this market and there is no secondary dispersal via traders. Only on rare occasions does the potter take her wares to smaller markets such as Salabani. But many of the pots are obtained directly by the consumers travelling in small reed fishing boats to the island. This method of obtaining pots is not confined to those Njemps living nearest the lake. All the Kokwa pots found to the east of the lake had been obtained by this direct method. To the south of the lake, of the eighteen informants who were asked this question, nine had obtained their pots by going to the island, eight had obtained them from Kampi-ya-Samaki, and one from Salabani.

The Kokwa potter said that she sold her wares to any tribe. But the data themselves show that her wares are largely confined to the Njemps. This is shown in figure 18, where the majority of Kokwa pots are in compounds which would be designated Njemps on other grounds (see also Hodder 1977a).

It is clear that the Njemps pot distribution correlates with the distributions of a series of other Njemps traits such as ear decoration, shield type and house plan. This non-random association suggests the play of boundary constraints in the distributions.

The second non-random aspect of the Njemps pottery distribution concerns the fall-off curves. If the relative amount of Kokwa and Chebloch (the Tugen source; see below) pottery in bands southwards away from the Kokwa source is considered (figure 19), plateaux and sudden fall-offs occur at what is, on other evidence, the Njemps boundary. (It will be shown below that this fall-off is, in reality, even more marked than appears in the figure.) The different fall-off lines in figure 19 indicate data from different positions and angles of transect in order to examine the variation which results from the methods used. The problem of how deviation from expected 'random walk' fall-off curves is to be measured is considerable, but the analysis of fall-off curves resulting from different random walk procedures (Hodder and Orton 1976) makes it clear that the type of fall-off obtained in figure 19 (i.e. with plateaux and very steep gradients; see figure 1) could not be simulated by an unconstrained random walk process, and the play of some particular constraints is again suggested.

To understand these constraints, it is helpful to know more about the Kokwa potter herself. Born on the island, she started making pottery in 1961, when she was 16 years old. She learnt the methods from her mother who in turn had learnt from her mother. Both the present potter and her mother were the only potters on the island. The methods have been guarded in the family and it is possible that other Njemps potters working elsewhere (for example, at Karau) are from the same family (see below). The Kokwa potter said that she usually works in isolation because if other people on the island learnt her techniques she would be losing money. This desire for secrecy is heightened because the potter can earn more than her neighbours who fish and farm. She is, therefore, fairly prosperous. With the limited demand it would be disadvantageous if others started making pottery in the central Njemps area.

It is of further interest that no evidence could be found for any innovations in pottery making and decoration over recent decades. The Kokwa potter acknowledged that she produces exactly the same forms and decoration as her mother and grandmother. Yet the potter does come into contact with, and see, other people's pots. Marigat pots, for example, are ubiquitous (see below), and frequent contact with other tribes would have introduced her to their wares. So, why does she not absorb these new or outside influences? One reason might be that all women in Baringo societies are especially conservative and conforming (p. 84).

It is suggested here that the conformity of the potter herself, as well as the conformity of pot choice by the Njemps people as a whole, can only be explained by social and economic forces acting within societies, and by the effect of competition between groups. Ownership of a distinctly Kokwa pot, different from the pots used by other tribes, is part

20. Artifacts from a Tugen compound. Front row, from right to left: *tokei*, *kerebē*, two *tubē*, stool, honey pot. The pots in the middle and back rows are from Chebloch with the exception of the pot at the centre back from Marigat (see chapter 3).

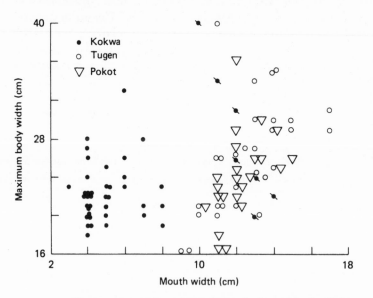

21. The mouth widths and maximum body widths for Kokwa, Tugen and Pokot pots used for water. Crossed circles are pots claimed to be of Kokwa origin in Tugen compounds.

and parcel of the formation of group identities. Although the non-random patterning is less marked than for the ear decoration, it is still there in the Kokwa pot distributions and it attests to the same underlying desires and needs.

If pots are used to form group membership, it is clear that the pots must be visibly different from group to group. Of the two types of pottery made by the Kokwa potter, the cooking pot is not made by any of the neighbouring tribes. However, water jars are made and used in adjacent groups. Yet the necks and mouths of the Kokwa products are narrower than those used by the Tugen (figure 20) and Pokot. This is shown by figure 21 where mouth width has been plotted against maximum body width for all the measured pots. The only overlap into the sizes of pots used by the Njemps on the one hand and by the Tugen and Pokot on the other concerns pots found in Tugen compounds outside the Njemps area but where the informant claimed a Kokwa origin. In view of the exact relationship between the wider neck and the non-Njemps compounds it is reasonable to suppose that the information supplied about these pots is incorrect. This highlights the problem of using interview data rather than, for example, petrological analysis, and suggests that the fall-off curve in figure 19 should in fact be rather more marked than appears.

In figure 18 is indicated the compound of a woman potter at Karau in the higher lands to the east of the lake. Several of the pots attributed to the Kokwa potter in this area may have been made by the Karau potter, since her existence was not realised until a relatively late stage in the fieldwork. The distribution of Karau products is further complicated by the existence of another potter in the Mukutan area (see below).

The Karau potter herself was over 50 years old in 1977. On marriage she had moved to Kokwa, or more probably to another island in the lake, where she was taught by two Njemps wives who were the potters there. When her husband died in about 1940 she moved to the area where she now lives. The soil is less good for potting than on the Baringo islands, but she used to make ten to fifteen pots a month. She stopped making pots four years ago.

Although, therefore, she could not be observed making pots, her description of her methods corresponded exactly with the Kokwa potter's techniques. The forms she produced appeared identical to those of the Kokwa potter, and although only two cooking pots were measured these had a width and height well within the range of Kokwa pot dimensions (figure 22). From an economic standpoint, the making of Kokwa-type pots would appear not to be the best path for the Karau potter to follow. In order to sell her wares it might be thought desirable to distinguish them in some ways so that she could build up a reputation for herself and become widely known through her distinctive products. But in terms of Njemps society this would not be the best thing to do.

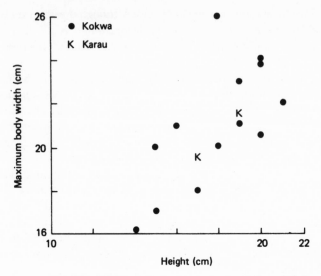

22. The heights and maximum body widths of Kokwa and Karau cooking pots.

Owning a Njemps-type pot is part and parcel of being Njemps. The Karau potter can best sell her wares by satisfying the need to conform, not by differentiation.

The same arguments apply for another woman working in the Mukutan area about 9·5 km to the northeast of the Karau potter. She again makes the same two pot forms by the same methods. In 1977 she was 35 years old, and she had started making pottery after her marriage at the age of about 15. Born locally of a locally born father, her mother came from Kokwa and taught her the potting techniques.

Tugen and Pokot pottery

The Tugen and Pokot prefer to obtain their pottery from sources other than Kokwa, even though many of them live as near or nearer the island than many Njemps. The majority of the pots used by the Tugen are made by related Kalenjin tribes to the west in Elkeyo-Marakwet. These are brought to the market of Chebloch just within the western Tugen border. Most of the Tugen compounds visited contained pots which had been obtained by travelling directly to Chebloch. This is even true of compounds found to the east of the Njemps, south of Mukutan (figure 18).

The Pokot go to great lengths to obtain pottery from a market in a different area; in this case from the market at Tot, well to the northwest of Lake Baringo.

The relative costs of the pottery. Up to this point, various aspects of the pottery distributions in the Baringo district have been discussed in terms of the social and economic pressures which cause individuals to express overtly their membership of identity groups. Further light is thrown on this situation by examining the relative costs of the pots from different sources. Many pots are now paid for in cash rather than by the exchange of maize, millet or goats as in the recent past. Two tins of maize flour used to be paid for a Kokwa pot, while one informant said she had paid a goat for a pair of Kokwa cooking and water storage pots, although this is likely to be an exaggeration. In considering the following cost data, it should be remembered that informants may well have exaggerated the prices in the hope that we might want to buy their pots. The Kokwa potter herself said that a cooking pot cost 8 Kenyan shillings, and a water jar 10 Kenyan shillings (in 1977 there were about 14 Kenyan shillings to the English pound), but other informants said they had paid from 5 Kenyan shillings to 10 Kenyan shillings. The prices of the Kokwa pots show no indication of decreasing or increasing with distance from the source. This is to be expected in view of the nature of the trading system.

The prices paid for the Karau potter's products are in the same range as those for the Kokwa pots (4 Kenyan shillings to 10 Kenyan shillings). The small amount of data obtained for the Chebloch pots suggests similar figures. However, the prices paid for Tot pots amongst the Pokot are considerably higher in the northwestern area near the lake (10 Kenyan shillings to 25 Kenyan shillings). The higher price paid for Tot pots may be the result of the Pokot's greater propensity to exaggeration. But, on the other hand, the distance to Tot from the northwest of the lake is 72 km, the distance from the western margin of the lake to Chebloch is 47 km, and the maximum distance reached by Kokwa pottery is 26 km. Thus, the greatest distance to source occurs with the most expensive pottery. This may only be an apparent relationship between cost and distance, not a true one, since there are no data available on the cost of Tot pots near Tot itself. Yet this consideration of costs highlights a further characteristic of the distributions. Those Pokot living to the east of the lake in the Mukutan area have obtained pots from about 97 km away (even taking their seasonal pastoral movements into account), and paid a high price for them. Yet cheaper Njemps pottery is available either from Karau (only 8 to 16 km away) or from Kokwa (24 km away). There is, therefore, a clear preference for the pot types associated with one's own tribe even though more effort and cost might be needed to obtain them. A similar situation is found to the south and southeast of the lake (figure 18), where the Tugen have obtained pots from Chebloch, even though Kokwa is nearer. This pattern is again perhaps best explained in terms of the desire to express conformity with particular identity groups.

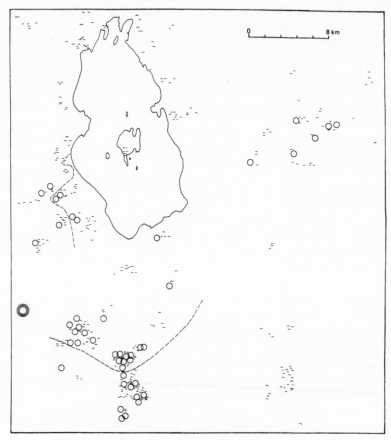

23. The distribution of pottery obtained from Marigat.
Horizontal dashes = sites without pottery from Marigat.
Concentric circles enclose Marigat.

Pots from Marigat

The Tugen, Njemps and Pokot pots mentioned above are predominantly
water jars and cooking pots, and each tribe obtains its own products from
a preferred market. In the compounds these pots were often found broken
and out of use. In place of them, in the last four to five years, the
inhabitants of the Baringo region have begun using, in addition to some
metal containers, a different kind of pottery. Wide-mouthed bowls with
out-turned necks (figure 20) are made in the Kisumu area near Lake
Victoria and these are now found widely in Kenya. In the Baringo area
the main local market for the sale of these products is Marigat. The pots
are manufactured by people who are not related to the Kalenjin (such
as the Tugen) nor to the Njemps, and they are widespread mass-produced
items. Perhaps because of this, these pots are not used as tribal identity

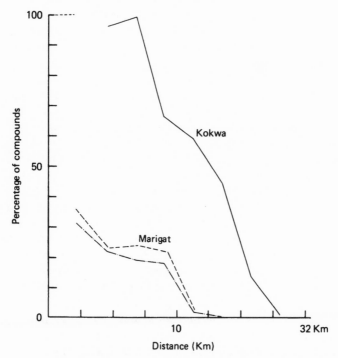

24. Fall-off in the percentage of compounds with Kisumu/Marigat pottery with distance from Marigat, and the fall-off of compounds with Kokwa pottery away from source.

markers and their distribution is not restricted to any tribal groups in the Baringo area (figure 23).

Figure 24 shows the fall-off in the percentage of compounds with Kisumu/Marigat pottery in bands away from their local source at Marigat. A fairly gentle fall-off with a low overall gradient occurs. The fall-off in Kokwa pottery, using that data in the same form (figure 24), shows a much sharper fall-off from higher values. The Marigat fall-off is similar to what can be simulated by a random walk process with general distance constraints (Hodder and Orton 1976). It would not be easy to simulate the sharp gradient of the Kokwa fall-off without introducing specific additional constraints. It is suggested here that the difference between the two fall-off curves occurs because social constraints of the type mentioned above are being placed on the dispersal of Kokwa pottery.

A further lesson can be learnt from the Marigat pottery fall-off curve. It has been demonstrated elsewhere that fall-off curves of this general form (slightly convex with a low gradient) occur when highly valued objects are passed on via several steps from source to final destination (Hodder 1974; Renfrew 1977a). Yet the Marigat pots are cheap utilitarian objects (see below) which are obtained by direct travel to the market. There is no secondary exchange within the Baringo area itself. The reason that this process of dispersal produces a fall-off curve of the observed, unexpected, form is that women visit Marigat rarely and for special purposes. Women travel long distances to this centre to obtain less common goods and for particular social events. Thus, although the women may buy pots of low value in Marigat, the trip has a special social purpose and women travel in from long distances. The resulting pot fall-off curve, therefore, has a form which is usually associated with higher valued goods moving longer distances. It is clearly dangerous to make broad generalisations about the processes causing different types of fall-off curves. This example shows that, while the earlier work (Hodder 1974) may have been justified in noting the importance of 'value' for determining the type of fall-off curve, the nature and value of the trip to source may in certain cases be more significant than the value of the artifact itself.

Marigat pottery is generally cheaper (3 Kenyan shillings to 4 Kenyan shillings) than the more locally produced wares, and this presumably provides one reason for its recent flooding of the Baringo market. Production on a large scale at Kisumu has allowed cheap pots to enter the area, thus hastening the decline of the local traditional industry.

The importance of the Baringo pottery example for the archaeologist is that variation in form of the distributions can be seen to relate to social and symbolic factors. The shape of fall-off curves can be examined in order to identify the presence and nature of constraints in the pottery distributions. Those types of pottery which are used as symbolic markers of group identity form distinct spatial patterns which can be recognised and compared with other evidence. The constraints are imposed by the individual, but they leave a distinctive and recognisable trace in the archaeological record.

3.2 *Njemps stools*

The stool is another exchanged artifact type which has distinctive distribution patterns as a result of being used to support and reinforce identity groups. The wooden stool type to be discussed here is four-legged (figure 14) and the distribution (figure 25) shows that many of the stools were obtained from carpenters. Several of these stoolmakers were visited.

Lerupē was visited in 1976 when he was about 75 years old. He had lived in the locality shown in figure 25 since he was 20. Lerupē said that he had learnt stoolmaking by copying local stools and stools made by Kikuyu. He made the roughouts for the stools in the bush near the trees from where he obtained the wood, and finished them in his compound. He said that he used to make one stool every two days, and exchanged each one for a sheep. Customers could obtain stools only by coming to his compound. Lerupē could point to no difference between his and Letrugga's stools.

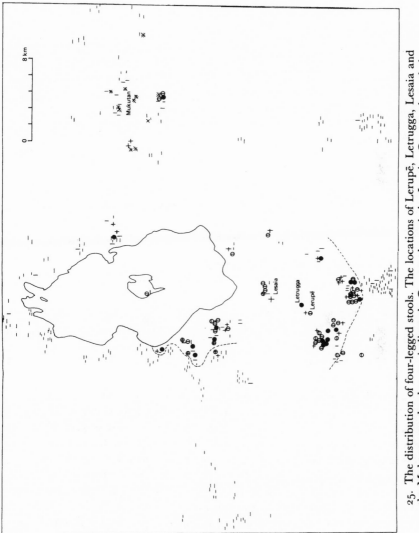

25. The distribution of four-legged stools. The locations of Lerupē, Letrugga, Lesaia and the Mukutan stoolmaker are indicated: ⊕ = stools made by Lesaia. ⊖ = stools made by Lokridi. Ⓟ = stools made by Lerupē. ● = stools made by Letrugga. ✳ = stools made by Mukutan stoolmaker. | = four-legged stools made in the owner's compound.
+ = four-legged stools present but no information could be obtained as to source.
– = four-legged stools absent.

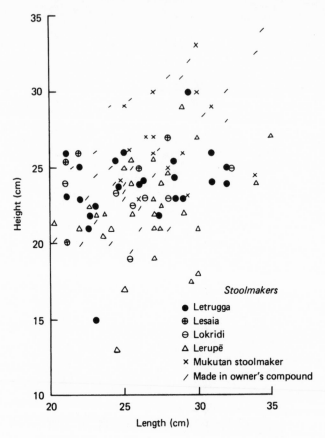

26. The heights and lengths of Njemps stools.

When *Letrugga* was visited in 1976, he was about 85 years old. He worked in a way similar to Lerupē, each stool taking up to eight hours to finish. He had learnt from an old Njemps stoolmaker (not a relative) when he was 15 to 20 years old, and had made stools ever since, while still retaining cattle and fields like other Njemps. Although the stools are mainly used by men, women tended to be the customers who came to ask him to produce a stool in return for a goat or sheep. He was aware that his customers were mainly Njemps.

Lesaia, who worked in the same area as Lerupē and Letrugga, had died before 1976. The main stoolmaker in Mukutan was visited. As well as making stools he made honey pots and swords. The stools were made from three trees (*nchanoti, ilngaboli, sumaati*) and he made up to six stools a month, being able to make two a day. He began in 1969 and had not learnt from his father but simply copied other stools. He said he sold many to Njemps, rarely to Tugen, and that Pokot disliked this kind of stool and did not buy any (this information was contradicted by the

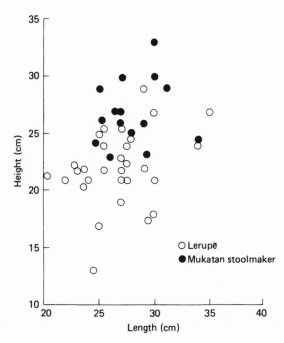

27. The dimensions of stools made by Lerupē and by the Mukutan stoolmaker.

compound survey; see below). This stoolmaker was quite emphatic that he could make any type of stool the customer wanted. This tendency to make what the customer wants explains some aspects of the distributions which will be discussed below.

Many of the stools are thus made on demand by part-time carpenters. But many are made by Njemps men for their own use, or by people who make a few for their friends. Even 'foreigners' are quickly able to adopt and reproduce the same style. For example, a Turkana man (Lokridi) who 'became' Njemps in Mukutan before moving to the area south of the lake made Njemps stools in both areas. Turkana do not have this type of stool, but figure 26 shows that Lokridi's stools are indistinguishable from those of the other 'indigenous' stoolmakers.

No differences could be identified in the styles and shapes of the stools made by the different craftsmen. This is reinforced by figure 26 which shows the heights and seat diameters of the measured examples. Each craftsman copied each other's products and was aware of the similarities. However, if we compare the stools of Lerupē with those of the Mukutan stoolmaker (figure 27) there is some evidence of a slight difference. The Mukutan carpenter knew of the work of Letrugga and Lerupē and was aware of no differences between his and their work. This example simply shows the slight stylistic variation that may occur within tribes due to

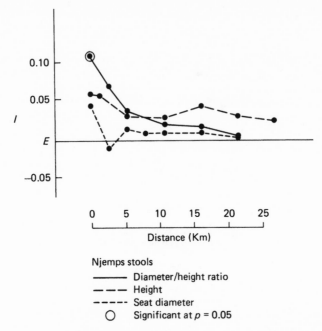

28. Spatial autocorrelation values (I) at different distances for Njemps stool measurements.

'incorrect' copying. It is here that the 'interaction' hypothesis (p. 8) is of some value, and the idea of 'random drift' in styles has been suggested by Binford (1972). As distance increases copying is less likely to be perfect. But the 'incorrectness' that is permissible will vary according to cultural context.

In view of the slight stylistic variation, it is of interest to determine the nature of the spatial patterning in similarities between stools. Spatial autocorrelation tests were applied to the 183 stools for which there was sufficient information. The aim was to see if there was any spatial dependency in the height, seat diameter, and height/seat diameter ratio, for the stools. The results for the I coefficient (Hodder and Orton 1976) in figure 28 show little evidence of significant spatial autocorrelation. However, the height/seat diameter ratio does show evidence of spatial dependency at a very localised level (significant at $P = 0.05$ under the null hypothesis of randomisation). Thereafter the spatial dependency decreases rapidly with increasing distance. By 3 to 5 km between stools there is no evidence of any correlation between stool dimensions. This extremely localised scale of similarities parallels that found for the spears, which are also largely produced by specialists, while the patterning is similar to that found for the locally produced calabashes (p. 68) but contrasts with items such as baskets and wooden containers (figure 29) which are the results of dispersed production and which show no evidence

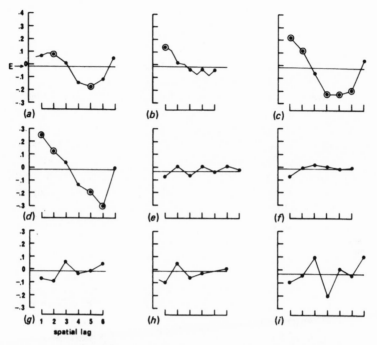

29. Spatial autocorrelation values (I) for spear and other measurements. The diagrams show the changes in spatial autocorrelation at different spatial lags (distance bands). E = expected value of I coefficient under hypothesis of no spatial autocorrelation. Encircled points = evidence of significant departure from null hypothesis. (*a*) to (*d*) = measurements and ratios taken from the spears. (*e*) = handle length/length ratio of *tubē*. (*f*) = width/height ratio of *kerebē*. (*g*) = length of three-legged stools. (*h*) = width/height ratio of honey pots. (*i*) = width/height ratio of *tokei*.

of localised style clusters. In the case of the stools, the pattern seems to derive from the common practice by which a customer orders several stools at a time, which often turn out to be identical or very similar. Also, local copies of stools may be made and, as we have seen, the carpenters produce stools according to local preferences. Localised style clusters rather than large-scale regional stylistic trends can thus result from specialist production. But the spatial autocorrelation tests have detected very minor variation. The general similarity in the products of the different carpenters (figure 26) results from the consumer demand for tribal-wide conformity. No informant was aware of the slight differences between the dimensions of the stools of Lerupē and the Mukutan stoolmaker. This variation and the localised style clusters are within the unconscious limits set by the more or less conscious desire for conformity in Njemps society.

The dispersal pattern (figure 25) of the stools is informative. All stools which are obtained from the specialists are obtained by direct contact, but there is a limit to which people will travel in order to obtain a stool. Thus, it is on the fringes of the areas served by Lerupē, Letrugga, Lesaia and Lokridi that other stoolmakers can obtain a 'market' – near Kampi-ya-Samaki to the west of the lake, and at Mukutan to the east. Within the central area, the stools of Lerupē and the other carpenters cover very similar areas (although the stools of Lesaia are perhaps more common to the southwest than to the south and east of the lake).

The overall distribution of the Njemps stool type is remarkably skewed. The stools of the Lerupē group move up to 23 km north and northeast, but only 7 km south. This very sharp fall-off southwards and the overall highly skewed distribution would be easily noticed by archaeologists as comprising an 'odd' or highly constrained pattern. In this case the pattern is related to the tribal boundary to the south of the lake. Tugen rarely obtained this style of stool 'because they are Njemps stools'. The stools symbolise the quality of being a Njemps and they are part of a world view which is 'other' to the Tugen. They are used in Njemps ceremonies, and for the Njemps they are associated with men, especially with the deliberations and status of older men. The stools are thus both part of the internal structure of the Njemps world view and a symbol of the Njemps/Tugen dichotomy.

3.3 *Hearth position*

Variation in hearth position inside the huts is of interest since, in contrast to many items of dress and portable objects such as pots and stools, it is less clearly part of the overt expression of identities. Individuals from different tribes do sometimes enter each other's huts, but most discussions and meetings take place in the compound outside the huts. The inside of the Njemps hut (figure 30) is more part of the individual personal world, the interior cool and darkness contrasting suddenly and blindingly with the brightness and heat outside the door. How, then, is this internal world ordered in the different societies?

Figure 31 shows the distribution of the different hearth positions in the Njemps, Tugen and Pokot huts. While the Tugen may place their hearth, which is lined with large stones, either in the right or left sections of the hut as seen from the entrance, the Njemps keep to a fairly rigid rule of having it in the right section. To the south of the lake, no Njemps have their hearths in the left section. But to the north and east of the lake, including the Mukutan area, the Njemps sometimes do place the hearth on the left, while there is considerable copying of hearth positions between Pokot, Njemps and Tugen. Thus all the cases in which the left hearth position is not used by Njemps and where the borders are more distinct occur in the areas where there is less socio-economic tension (to the south of the lake as was shown in chapter 2).

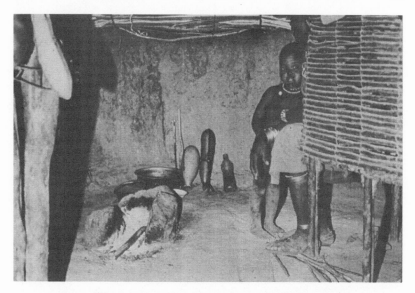

30. The hearth and bed (to right) within a Njemps hut.

We thus see that the internal world, as well as the exterior world, is more ordered and clearly categorised in areas of socio-economic stress. There is an internal desire for 'everything to be in its place' which is stronger when the overall organisation of society is under strain. This helps to explain the different border patterns, but why do the Tugen permit more variability in hearth position than the Njemps? The very marked internal order amongst the Njemps is also visible in the positions of beds and lofts in the huts (Hodder 1977a). There is a remarkable conformity in the arrangement of many aspects of the Njemps hut interiors. In general, the Njemps are contained at a high density within a restricted environment. They inhabit a much smaller area than the Tugen (p. 16) and there are less possibilities for flexibility and movement in hardship. Each man has more wives than amongst the Tugen and this adds competition amongst the men to the other tensions. Njemps society is under greater tension and demands greater conformity. This is both overt (chapter 2) and internal, as is seen in the spatial patterning of hearth positions.

This evidence that the internal, private world may be ordered in the same way, and to the same extent, as the exterior, overt world is in direct contrast to Wobst's (1977) hypothesis that identity differences are expressed most in clearly visible items – especially those visible at long distances. There is a continual interplay between the different spheres and types of material culture. The ethnic differences are constituted in the mundane as well as in the decorative. The tribal distinctions and negative reciprocity become acceptable and are 'naturalised' by their

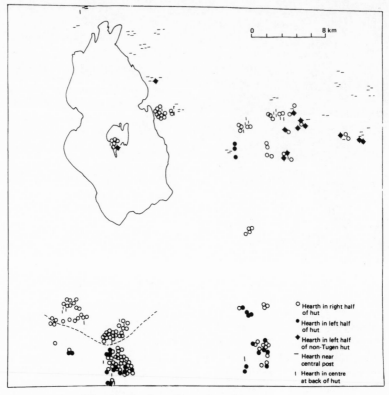

31. The distribution of hearth positions.

continual repetition in both public and private. The Baringo research
did not examine why the left or right parts of the huts were used for
hearths, nor how these hearth positions fitted into the overall symbolism
of spatial relationships within the huts. But it is at least clear that
hypotheses such as that suggested by Wobst, which are only concerned
with the 'expression' of identities and the 'reflection' of interaction, are
of limited value since material culture also actively forms ethnic differences
and makes them acceptable.

3.4 *Conclusion*

In their various ways, the pots, stools and hearth positions all exemplify
the remarkable extent to which the inhabitants of Baringo continually
reinforce and repeat the same regional patterning of material symbols (see
Hodder 1977a for further similar distributions). Especially in the border
areas where there is greatest tension and competition, material culture
of many forms is used to justify between-group negative reciprocity and
to support the social and economic dependencies within groups. The

non-passive role of material symbols has been intimated in the study of the Baringo hearths.

Yet the picture that has been given so far of distinct material culture entities is inaccurate. In fact many artifact types do cross the tribal borders. While many forces within the Baringo societies and many material symbols are concerned to maintain overt ethnic distinctions, many other forces are concerned to deny or disrupt the clear material culture distinctions.

4
Disrupting the boundaries

Chapters 2 and 3 have shown the inadequacy of the view that similarity in material culture merely reflects degrees of social interaction. Despite frequent interaction across the Baringo tribal borders, clear material culture distinctions are maintained in a wide range of artifact categories. Rather, the cultural distinctions play an active role in between-group competition. The material culture patterning of pots, stools and hearths reflects tribal groupings and within-tribe information flow because it also supports the tribes in competitive between-group interaction. Many material items are selected to symbolise within-group relations, with the result that the majority of the artifact distributions actually contrast with the intense, frequent and long-existing between-group interaction.

However, some artifact types in the Baringo district do cross ethnic boundaries. The spear and calabash types examined in this chapter have distributions which cut across the tribal groupings. The complex way in which these items are manipulated as part of conflicts and tensions within Baringo societies will be discussed. Rather than referring to the interaction hypothesis, it will be necessary both to understand what symbolic meaning is given to the artifact types within the particular Baringo context, and to understand how that symbolism is manipulated as part of the social strategies of individuals and groups within the different tribes.

As well as examining further the interaction hypothesis, another aspect of the view that 'material culture reflects behaviour' can be assessed in this chapter. As noted in chapter 1, it has frequently been assumed by prehistoric archaeologists that the scale of production of craft items has a direct relationship with the scale of stylistic patterning. In the discussion of Baringo stool types in the preceding chapter, some questioning of this hypothesis was occasioned by the localised variation of centrally produced items. The relationship between the scale of production and the distribution of styles will be examined more closely in the discussion of Baringo spears.

4.1 *Metal production and spears*

In the discussion of regionalisation in metalworking styles, archaeologists are nowadays wary of the mention of 'cultures' and regional 'traditions', and often use the terms 'industrial organisation' (Rowlands 1976), 'industry', or 'industrial tradition'. For Childe (1956, 33) an 'industry' was an assemblage of typologically related objects distinguished by the material they are made of and/or the technical method used to produce them. An 'industrial tradition' has been described, like a 'culture', as a broad group of similar material, temporally or spatially defined, which may be placed in some sort of relationship or sequence with one another (Coles 1963–4, 126–31).

But what do these groupings of metal types mean – even if they can be correlated with metal composition groups? It has long been recognised that straightforward tribal interpretations are incorrect. Two major sorts of alternative explanations seem to be preferred. The first relates to the word 'industry', and supposes that regional differences in metallurgy are the work of different smiths, or schools or workshops of smiths. For example, an 'industry' has been defined (Rowlands 1976, 115) as relating to a specialist activity whose products have 'an area of influence' which can, at least partly, be reconstructed from typology and distributional studies.

Thus the nature of 'industrial organisation' is seen as being fundamental to the formation of spatial patterning in metal styles. For example, in Rowlands' (1971) important and interesting work on the ethnography of metalworking, he states that 'regional and chronological differences in the context of metalwork should therefore be related primarily to the industrial organisation that produced them'. And later, in a study of the regional distribution of Middle Bronze Age palstave types, it is stated that the types show 'localised differences indicating that palstave production was carried out at a local level and distributed over a relatively small region. Contact between these local smiths must have been frequent enough however to maintain a general uniformity' (Rowlands 1976, 121).

In this last sentence we meet the second type of explanation that has recently been preferred for interpreting stylistic similarities and differences in metal items. It is assumed that, as interaction or contact increases, there is greater similarity and *vice versa*.

It seems natural to assume that different patterns of industrial organisation and production on the one hand, and interaction on the other, will produce different stylistic groupings. As we have seen, this general assumption has an underlying theme that human behaviour is reflected or mirrored in material culture. I hope to show in this section that it is incorrect to assume that metal style patterning simply reflects human behaviour. In particular, there is no simple relationship between industrial organisation, interaction patterns and cultural patterning, and we certainly cannot infer the nature of industries and interaction from stylistic patterning alone. I will examine the Baringo evidence of metalworking, and consider first the supposed reflection of industrial organisation in cultural patterning, and then the supposed reflection of interaction in styles of metal items.

The main evidence from Baringo concerns iron spears which are the major items of metal produced locally and traditionally. Spears found in hut compounds were measured (width and length of blade, length of upper section, length of middle wooden handle, length of lower section). Information was also obtained on where and when each spear was made, by whom, and how it was obtained.

The spears mainly come from three different sources: one is the Marakwet smiths well to the northwest around Tot, another is the Samburu smiths to the east, and the third is the Tugen smith living just to the southeast of Lake Baringo at Arabal. The latter smith, who seems to be representative of the rest, was visited (figure 32). In 1977 he was 55 to 60 years old. He obtained his iron from the Kenyan Farmers' Association. But when young he, and his father before him, obtained metal ore in Arabal and smelted it down themselves. Nowadays the smith works in a small workshop near the family compound. The workshop contains wood and skin bellows, a charcoal furnace, which is a fire surrounded by large stones and a clay channel for an opening, an anvil set in the ground, other tools and a hole filled with water for quenching. The smith now sometimes makes two spears a day, but he boasted that when he was young he could make ten. However, it took him a whole morning to make the two metal parts of one spear – the lower and upper portions – starting at 9.30 a.m. and finishing at 1.30 p.m.

The smith does not fix the wooden handle. This is done by the customer to his own liking in order to achieve the right balance. But it took the smith four hours to make the metal parts. In the past, including the smelting, the smith's work could obviously be fairly time-consuming. This is especially so since he also made small hoes, cowbells and swords. In fact, the smith worked all the year round, more or less full-time. Although he must be described as a full specialist, the rest of his family, his wives and children, participated in normal subsistence activities with cattle, goats, honey collecting and arable fields.

Thus, although a specialist, the smith does not depend totally on the society outside the family for support. But what is the attitude of the Tugen to their smiths? Generally the blacksmith (*kitongindet*), even today, is feared as someone having some of the potential powers of a witch (Ott, pers. comm.). He has an anomalous character, similar in some respects to strangers, who are suspicious, and potentially dangerous. It is possible that Tugen smiths are put in this category by the society as a whole, because there is a danger that they may become too rich and use this

32. The Arabal smith in the process of beating out the blade on the upper metal section of a spear.

wealth to wield political power. Certainly by making spears, each of which is worth a goat, a man could amass large herds, as in the case of the Arabal smith visited. If smiths have a 'different', 'stranger' status, they can be prevented from using their wealth to become powerful. The special character of the smith may allow sanctions to be brought in which prevent him gaining prestige. Equally, however, the smith may use his 'witch' aspect to discourage others copying his skills and so decreasing his potential wealth. The skills are handed down from father to son and others are discouraged from acquiring them.

Although the smith does not work seasonally, he prefers to make large lots of spears and to sell them off as people want them. Thus, if these periodic bursts of activity were to result in hoards, we could not assume that this indicated seasonal activities.

The dispersal of the spears occurs in two ways. Usually people come to the smith himself to get a spear. But when there is a low demand, the smith takes the spears round to try and sell them. Most of the work in the Baringo area was located fairly near the Arabal smith and the vast majority (89%) of the spears which were found in compounds, and which had been obtained from the Arabal smith, had been acquired by going directly to him. In the same area, the Njemps use spears from the Samburu. The great majority of these spears (85%) from the more distant source had been obtained from travelling salesmen and smiths and through secondary exchange. Work on the Leroghi plateau (chapter 6) near the source of these Samburu spears showed that in this area most were obtained by going directly to the smith. The evidence thus suggests that, in Baringo, the customer tends to travel up to 32 to 48 km to the smith. But beyond this, and up to 80 km, most spears are obtained by secondary exchange and from salesmen, hawkers and the smiths travelling themselves.

The Baringo pattern of spear production, then, involves a few specialist smiths scattered widely over a large area. The archaeologist would therefore often assume widespread similarities in the spears at least in the 80 to 160 km wide area of influence of each smith. In general, the spears are all very similar. The trouble is that when we look at the details of the measurements, we no longer find marked uniformity. On the contrary we find marked localisations of styles.

Figure 29 (*a* to *d*) shows the results of spatial autocorrelation analyses for different dimensions and ratios on the spears. A high degree of spatial autocorrelation means that the measurements of nearby spears are strongly and positively correlated with each other. Very low degrees of spatial autocorrelation mean that the spears a given distance apart are strongly dissimilar to each other. This analysis shows that there are clear localised areas of similarities in spears. Each of the spatial lags in figure 29 is 3·2 km wide. Thus the spatial and stylistic localisations are a maximum of 9·6 km wide, nothing like the 80 to 100 km wide areas of influence of some of the smiths.

This spear evidence is in marked contrast to the evidence from some other artifact types. Figure 29 (*e* to *i*) indicates results on measurements of other objects. There is no evidence of any spatial and stylistic localisation, and yet these items are made by men and women in their own homes – that is by dispersed non-specialist production. Thus we find a complete reversal of what the archaeologist might expect on the basis of his simplistic assumptions about the way in which material culture 'reflects' human behaviour. The specialised production and wide dispersal of spears leads to localised traits, and the localised non-specialist and dispersed production of other items leads to widespread uniformity of traits.

This pattern supports the evidence from Zambia (chapter 7) that we cannot infer the scale of production and industrial organisation from stylistic patterning. Where specialists provide wide areas with their products, the local desires of the consumers and preferential movements of traders can lead to localisations of traits. This is because it is the social context of the customer, his wants, demands and desires, that must be taken into account. 'At Kerma, Nubia, the customer has considerable influence over the form and decoration of the implement that a smith makes for him' (Rowlands 1971, 221).

Conversely, the dispersed production of non-specialist items can lead to widespread uniformity in styles if the social context demands such expressions of conformity in certain items. We cannot infer industrial organisation from typological studies of metal items. It is essential to compare typological patterning with independent evidence of industrial organisation – hoards, workshops, metal analyses – and to attempt to understand the stylistic variability in the context of what is known about a particular society from other evidence.

The second type of explanation that archaeologists favour for inter-preting stylistic similarities and differences of metal items is the intensity of interaction and contact. As far as the spears are concerned, the first thing that one would expect as a result of this hypothesis is that the number of spears should fall off with distance away from the smiths, and that as they do they increase in price.

Certainly there are fewer spears as one moves away from the smiths. The farthest reached by the spears of the Tugen Arabal smith is 39 km, by those of the Samburu smith at Sukuta lol Marmar about 64 km, and by those of the Tot area smiths about 80 km. At first sight it appears as if the spears are always the same price wherever exchanged. They cost one goat or about 40 Kenyan shillings. But, of course, a lot depends on the age and quality of the goat and the exact amount paid. The Arabal smith said he asks more if he takes the spear to the customer, less if the customer comes to him, and less still if the customer brings his own metal. This pattern was to some extent supported by interviews with spear owners, although the information is very unreliable. As soon as one asks a person how much a spear cost, he thinks one wants to buy it and so doubles or trebles the price. In general, Arabal spears from near the source were usually said to be bought for 30 Kenyan shillings, while those coming from the farther Tot and Samburu sources cost 40 Kenyan shillings. Near the Samburu source the spears cost 30 Kenyan shillings.

So far so good. The interaction fall-off hypothesis works. But there is

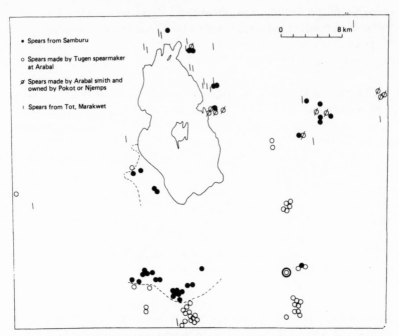

- Spears from Samburu

o Spears made by Tugen spearmaker at Arabal

ø Spears made by Arabal smith and owned by Pokot or Njemps

ı Spears from Tot, Marakwet

0   8 km

33. The distribution of spears from different sources. Concentric circles indicate the Arabal smith.

some very 'odd' patterning in the spear distributions. Of the spears made by the Arabal (Tugen) smith, 71 % end up in Tugen hands, 21 % in Njemps hands, and 7 % in Pokot hands. This is the reverse of the pattern claimed by the smith himself. He said that he sold fewest to the Tugen and most to the Pokot!

Thus the Tugen prefer spears made by the Tugen smith. This is seen most clearly to the south and west of the lake (figure 33). Here there is a very clear border between Tugen and Njemps in other material culture, as we saw in chapters 2 and 3. The neighbouring Njemps obtain *all* their spears from the Samburu smith. The Njemps are related to the Samburu and they prefer this source even though the Tugen source is much nearer and the Tugen spears cost less.

But to the east and north of the lake, where there are borders between Tugen, Njemps and Pokot, the pattern is less clear-cut. Spears from the Tugen Arabal source are owned by Njemps, and spears from the Samburu source are owned by Tugen.

Why do we find marked distorted patterns with unequal distributions around the source, and the clear tribal preferences for particular smiths especially in some areas? The answer has certainly nothing to do with intensities of interaction. I have already described (chapter 2) the large amount of contact and interaction across the marked border south of the

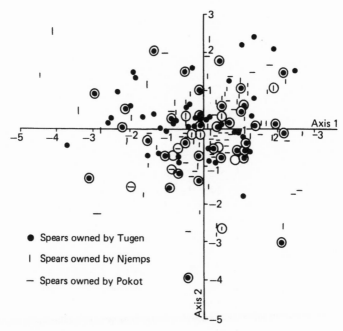

34. Spears plotted in the first two principal components.
Encircled symbols indicate spears made by Arabal smith.

lake. People from different tribes are always meeting each other to exchange items and foods, helping each other in communal fields and travelling with cattle. There is some evidence of greater intensities of certain types of interaction at the borders, not less. What the distinctions do relate to is within-tribe tension and inter-tribal competition over cattle and grazing land. To the south and west of the lake, where there is greater socio-economic stress (chapter 2), the distributions of spear origins are most distinct. To the north and east, there is less composition and the tribal differences in the origins of the spears are less clearly marked.

So the cultural patterning is part of the mechanism by which people demonstrate that they belong to one group in opposition to others. In this case, cultural patterning relates not to the intensity of interaction but to its nature. If intensity is involved at all, cultural differences become more marked in a competitive situation as the intensity of interaction increases. The more interaction there is, the greater the premium which may be placed on clarifying differences symbolically. In the high competition areas to the south and west of the lake, it is obviously considered important that one gets one's spears, if one is a Tugen, from the Tugen smith, and if one is Njemps from the Samburu source, even though there is no stylistic or functional difference between the spears. It is clearly unacceptable to break this convention in high conflict areas but less unacceptable in low conflict areas.

Table 4. *Mean values (cm) of spear measurements owned by the different tribal groups*

	Tugen	Njemps	Pokot
Blade length	20·5	21·4	20·1
Metal upper section	68·0	67·2	71·0
Wooden handle length	49·4	51·4	57·3
Metal lower section	87·8	87·3	89·9

This is despite the fact that the spears made by the different smiths are virtually identical. There are small localisations of stylistic detail (as shown by the spatial autocorrelation results) but an archaeologist would certainly put all the spears into one 'type'. A Principal Components Analysis was unable to distinguish between the spears owned by different tribes (figure 34). Table 4 shows a possible tribal distinction in the length of the wooden handles fitted by the owners. There is some evidence that Pokot-owned spears tend to have longer handles. This is only a slight tendency, there is no sharp distinction as the Principal Components Analysis has identified.

Thus, even across very clear borders such as that between the Tugen and Njemps to the south of the lake, the general *styles* of the spears are the same (even though the origin is different). In the past there is some evidence that Tugen and Kalenjin (the wider group to which Tugen belong) borrowed spear styles from the Maasai even though they were fighting against them.

To understand why there is such widespread copying of generalised spear styles, we need to understand more about the uses of spears, their social context, and their symbolism. The spear was not the primary weapon in warfare. The most effective weapon was the bow and poisoned arrow, made by each man for his own use. During battles the Tugen employed the bow and arrow in much the same way as English archers at Agincourt. Only half the warriors (or less) carried shields. These protected the archers who would carry bows and up to seventy or eighty poisoned arrows which they loosed in flights at the enemy. The warriors did carry two spears, but from Tugen and European accounts the poisoned arrow and their skirmishing guerilla tactics were more effective against an enemy (Ott, pers. comm.).

Equally, a man rarely uses his pair of spears for hunting. The bow and arrow, on the other hand, are frequently used for fishing and killing small wild animals. Despite the fact that his spears are not used very much, a young Tugen, Njemps or Pokot man is rarely seen without one. He leaves his spear outside a compound when he enters, but otherwise he nearly always carries one, when herding, dancing or participating in

Table 5. *Mean values (cm) of measurements of spears made by smiths in the different tribal groups*

	Arabal (Tugen)	Samburu	Tot (Marakwet)
Handle length	52·04	50·96	56·18
Metal lower section	87·84	89·34	91·50

Table 6. *Comparison of the mean values (cm) of measurements of spears made by the Tugen Arabal smith and owned by the Tugen and Njemps*

	Owned by Tugen ($N = 38$)	Owned by Njemps ($N = 11$)
Handle length	51·5	48·2
Metal lower section	87·2	91·5

other activities. Why is this? Amongst the Nuer, Evans-Pritchard described the spear as a projection of the self, so when a man hurls his spear he cries out 'my hand'. Ott (pers. comm.) has suggested a similar though less clear-cut significance for the spear in Tugen society. The Tugen do implicitly associate the spear with socialisation and conformity to young male society. The spear is also associated with sexual prowess.

The spear is the most important symbol of a young man's social position and virility. It is thus directed symbolically towards both women and older men. In the Baringo area, young men are prevented from marrying until their age-set matures, when some may be over 30 years old. Once a man marries he carries a spear less often, if at all, and instead he carries a wooden staff with a carved wooden knob at the end. Older men carry such staffs casually but they are most frequently seen when the elders meet to discuss issues at the traditional meetings of the locality or at other public meetings. At these gatherings, to speak without a stick is to talk like a woman.

The spears of young men are symbols of an age difference (see further chapter 5). The major source of conflict of interests for young men are the older men who maintain a monopoly over wives and cattle resources. Spears are part of the mechanism by which young men demonstrate their unity and strength. Their bravery in raids and their prowess demonstrate their worthiness for being accepted into full male society. The spear symbolism, then, is partly directed against the older men, and the young men from different tribes ape each other across tribal boundaries in their attempts to demonstrate strength and warrior ability. Thus, in the past, the young men would copy the spear types and other decoration of the Maasai, whose young men were widely renowned and feared as raiders and warriors. This happened even though they were fighting against the Maasai.

The spear types are similar over wide areas when other things are very different between tribes because the young men of all tribes wish to demonstrate their prowess and readiness for elderhood and their opposition to the older men. The various tensions between the age and sex groups in Baringo societies will be discussed more fully in chapter 5. But any understanding of why spear styles disrupt the tribal borders by crossing them must be based on the internal symbolism of the spears within Baringo societies and their association with the young warrior *moran*. So it is of little value to say that the spears reflect between-group interaction. Rather these artifacts are used as part of the strategies of particular age and sex groups. The spear symbolism is manipulated by the young men in their relations with the old.

We can begin to answer questions such as 'Which artifact types are used in such a way that they "reflect" a particular information flow?', by examining the symbolism of the artifacts in local strategies. This point can be clarified by considering decoration on a very different type of artifact, the calabash or gourd.

4.2 *Calabash decoration*

Calabashes are of especial interest because, in contrast to most of the other artifact types from Baringo, they are often decorated. Containers made from calabashes (figures 35 and 36) are used mainly for storing milk, and each woman incises her own decoration on her calabashes which only last for a few years. Many of the motifs she puts on are common and widespread in distribution. But others show marked localisations (figure 37). The spatial patterning is not clearly related to social boundaries on the tribal scale. There is greater localisation in these calabash distributions than in many other artifact categories, and there is variation within tribes. These calabash distributions relate to the local community contacts and relationships of women. Designs are copied between women within small neighbourhoods and settlement clusters which sometimes cut across tribal boundaries. Designs are copied between families as much as within families. Thus, decorative style distributions of calabashes play a part in local dependencies and relationships rather than tribal-wide identities.

But again, it is not simply a question of material culture reflecting a particular scale of interaction. Rather, the calabash decoration can be seen as being involved in the strategies of women in relation to older men. In chapter 5 the highly limited and controlled role of women in Baringo

35. A collection of Njemps calabashes.

society will be documented. Their overt symbols of dress and pottery demonstrate conformity and acceptance of the strict control held over them by older men. But calabash decoration does not have to conform in this way. The men pay little attention to the decoration, which is often badly executed, and they consider it of peripheral importance. The men certainly do not make the demands of conformity in relation to the calabashes that they do to items of female attire. The calabashes, then, are appropriate for use as a medium for silent discourse between women. In contrast to the overt, controlled symbols of dress by which women demonstrate their conformity and the tribal dichotomies, women use calabashes to disrupt the boundaries in opposition to the older men and to form their local independence. Across the Njemps–Tugen borders, the calabash decoration supports family ties of marriage and birth. As with the spears of the young men, the motifs of calabash decoration are manipulated by a section of society in terms of its relations with older men.

But as well as examining the distributions of particular calabash decorative motifs, the distributions of different design organisations of the motifs can be studied. The Njemps frequently decorate calabashes and they use exclusively zoned designs. By 'zoned' is meant bordered lines of horizontal decoration (cross-hatching, zig-zags etc.) alternating with blank areas (figures 35 and 36). The Tugen and the Pokot, on the other hand, rarely decorate calabashes (nor other containers), and when they do, the designs are often 'floating' – that is, they are placed 'haphazardly' over the calabash. Why should there be these differences in the nature

36. An Njemps calabash.

of calabash decoration? The greater use of decoration amongst the Njemps can first be considered. In the Nuba study to be reported in chapter 8, decoration, including calabash decoration, plays a part in the 'purification' of eating, drinking and other activities. Decoration protects by surrounding what is seen as impure. The Nuba groups have a strong

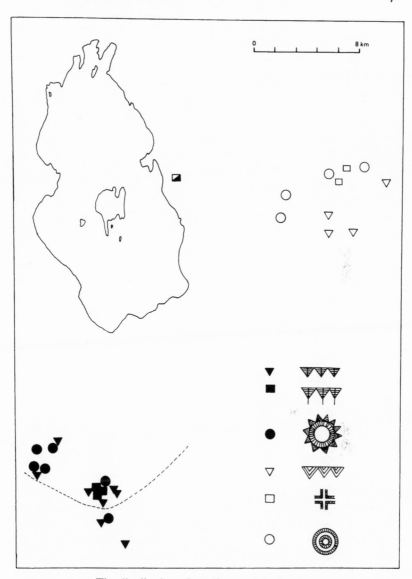

37. The distribution of motifs on calabashes.

sense of group purity and group boundaries. In the Baringo region it is the Njemps who are most concerned, despite variation at different borders, with their overall ethnic identity. They are the minority group, surrounded by expanding neighbours, many of them hostile, and the Njemps are attempting to expand themselves. They are enclosed within a smaller area and assert their identity more forcefully than, for example, the Tugen (more traits move from Njemps to Tugen than from Tugen

Table 7. *The frequency of occurrence of different types of design on Njemps calabashes in two border areas*

	Njemps (eastern border)	Eldumē (southern border)	Total
Simple	10	19	29
Pivoted	37	21	58
Total	47	40	87

to Njemps; Hodder 1977a). They may have a greater concern with group purity than their neighbours and may see a greater significance in surrounding food and drink containers with decoration, in much the same way as do the Nuba.

The greater use of zonation in the Njemps calabash decoration than in neighbouring tribes and the lack of floating designs may also relate to a more marked conception of boundedness. The designs are contained within distinct zones in contrast to the freer Tugen and Pokot decoration. The zonation is part of the more constrained outlook and the greater awareness of boundaries around and within the Njemps. This 'meaning' of zonation can be better understood if different border areas are considered. Sufficient data were collected from the Njemps border areas to the east of the lake, and south of the lake in the Eldumē area. The design zoning on each calabash can be described by denoting the type of decoration on the zone nearest the lip as A, the second, moving downwards, A if it is a repeat of the top zone, or B if it is different, and so on. A' indicates the mirror image of design A. For example, if A = ΔΔΔΔ, then A' = ∇∇∇∇ lower down the calabash. Parallel adjacent lines of design were treated as a single zone (e.g. the parallel zig-zag lines and the upright and hanging triangles in figure 36).

The various types of organisation of the zones were classified as follows. (1) Simple, embracing repetitive and alternating designs. A repetitive design is AAAA (figure 35, third from left), and an alternating design is ABABAB (figure 35, fourth from left). (2) Pivoted, either balanced or unbalanced. A balanced pivoted design is ABA, ABA' or ABCBA (or longer runs of the same scheme as in figure 36), and an unbalanced pivoted design is ABAA or ABCAB'. Table 7 shows the frequencies of occurrence of these types of zonation in the two areas compared. A χ^2 test shows that the types of zoning are not randomly distributed between the two areas (significant at $P = 0.05$). The more complex pivoted designs are more common on the eastern Njemps borders.

As has been noted in chapter 2, those living in the southern Njemps borders (Eldumē) experience greater economic and social tension and competition than in the areas to the east of Lake Baringo. It is tempting to relate the more frequent use of the more complex pivoted designs in the eastern area to the relative lack of tension and the decreased concern with boundaries. In the southern area the greater constraints restrict the number of dimensions that are incorporated in design organisation. So both at the local scale within the Njemps, and at the regional scale between the Njemps and the Tugen, the use and type of zoned designs appear to relate to the degree of constraint and the individual's conception of boundaries. In the silent discourse of the women, the special constraints experienced to the south of the lake are represented in the more constrained zonation.

4.3 *Conclusion*

The relatively simple links that were set up in the previous chapters between material culture patterning and human behaviour now seem more complex. In chapters 2 and 3 it was possible to suggest direct relationships between scarce resources, competition between ethnic groups, and distinct material culture boundaries. But that relationship is now seen to be more complicated because of the part played by social strategies. In the discussion of the calabashes, as for the spears, the spatial patterning of styles has been related to the adaptive social strategies of subgroups within the Baringo tribes. Younger men and women, in their relations with the dominant older men, utilise material symbols which disrupt the dominant social order. It is not possible to set up a general predictive relationship between resources, competition and ethnic distinctions in material culture without also involving aspects of social organisation. The particular relationship identified in Baringo could not be used as a model for societies which are organised in different ways. It remains possible, then, to retain the 'reflective' hypothesis described in chapter 1 only if the social context is incorporated into our predictive models.

In addition, the non-passive nature of material symbols has been further emphasised. It has been suggested that in the Baringo area there is a continual tension between boundary maintenance and boundary disruption; the one exists in relation to the other. And it is the material symbols which actively constitute the different emphases and which have to be continually brought in to justify and support the differing strategies of the subgroups within societies.

The discussion so far has led to an awareness of the importance of social organisation in answering questions concerning ethnic and material differentiation. In chapter 5 more information on social relations and strategies will be presented. The additional social data will also allow consideration of broader topics that have been left unexamined up to this point. Why is it that the borders between the tribes are maintained at all? And why is boundary maintenance particularly associated with older men? We have seen that as competition between groups increases in the Baringo area, so overt tribal dichotomies become more marked. But why is it that stress is channelled into boundary maintenance? In view of the massive movement and interaction between tribal groups that was described in chapter 2, why is it that boundaries have been maintained? The material culture distinctions may justify between-group negative reciprocity, but why do the groups exist at all as separate entities in Baringo? In answering these questions, it is necessary to consider in more detail the internal age and sex divisions within Baringo societies.

5

Within the boundaries: age, sex and self-decoration

In the preceding chapters the notion that material culture reflects behaviour was examined with reference both to the interaction hypothesis and to the relationship between scales of production and distributions of artifact styles. In these cases the relationships between material culture, social and economic behaviour and resource distributions (see chapter 1) are complex because material symbols play an active part in the social strategies and intents of subgroups within the Baringo tribes. The symbols are manipulated and negotiated in particular ways that depend on the local social context and on the specific meanings that are given to the symbols in that context. For example, the particular meaning associated with spears in the Baringo district has been connected in this analysis to the mobilisation by young men of common support against and in defiance of the elders. The calabash decoration allowed women silently to disrupt social control.

In the Baringo context a major component of the strategies of groups in relation to the maintenance of regional material culture boundaries remains to be discussed. What are the internal tensions between age and sex divisions within the societies concerned? How are these tensions manifested in material culture? How do they lead to a better understanding of the manipulation of material items at tribal boundaries? And why do those boundaries continue to exist?

5.1 *The dominance of older men*

In the discussion of the spears in chapter 4, certain tensions between young and old men were identified in which these material symbols played an important role. An understanding of these tensions is necessary in order to answer the questions in the preceding paragraph. Spencer (1965) has discussed forces at work within Samburu society which are relevant to the Baringo area because the Njemps are in part an offshoot of the Samburu. The Samburu and the Njemps have comparatively high rates of polygamy and an age-set system which rigidly prevents men from marrying before they are fairly old – 30 amongst the Samburu. A system

75

like this necessitates strong social pressures and controls on individuals. For example, the adverse effects of public opinion discourage a man from marrying at an early age which would deprive older men of additional wives. There is a great deal of pressure on the young men to conform and accept this situation.

On the other hand, it has been suggested that the young men, the *moran*, express an independence and defiance as warriors. But this world view or 'ideology' of the young men in their warrior role is many-faceted. Through it the young men express independence but it is also the means by which the young men show prowess and readiness for adulthood. The system also has advantages for the older men. In many areas, the cattle raiding of the *moran* has only a slight economic pay-off for a tribe (the failed raid noted in chapter 2 is in fact quite common), so that it is possible to see the warrior activities as having to do partly with internal strategies in Baringo societies. If the older men are to maintain their right to young wives and thus to build up their own familes and herds, it is to their advantage that the young men go through a long period of 'preparation'. During the time when the young men compete and display their prowess in raiding, they are prevented from marriage. Thus the older men encourage a world view in which there is warring and conflict involving young men and tribal boundaries.

So in answer to the question 'Why do the regional material culture boundaries exist?', reference must be made to a strategy of the older men and to a related world view within the tribes according to which it is seen as acceptable that there should be overt spatial categorisations into 'us' and 'them'. The between-tribe distinctions are maintained through material culture as part of within-group tensions.

We have seen that competition and material culture distinctions are more marked in areas of higher density and in more degraded environments. While cross-border raiding in such areas may come to have a real economic purpose in the search for scarce resources, the link between external environmental pressure and between-group competition may be more complex. Depleted grazing lands and increased scarcity of the cattle resources needed in bridewealth payment aggravate the tensions between young and old men. The dominance of the older men is maintained by further restricting the rights of the young, by showing the need for more cattle from raiding, and by involving *moran* to a greater degree and for a longer period in tribal fighting and protection. Material culture is used in such contexts as part of the same ideology in which the 'us'–'them' dichotomy becomes naturalised and accepted. The dichotomy appears overtly, repeated in many spheres of activity, justifying and naturalising the social order and the protective, competitive function of the young men. Ultimately and less obviously, the material dichotomy also supports the dominance of the elders.

The maintenance of between-tribe material culture differences is

Table 8. *Njemps and Tugen approximate age-sets, with average ages for those age-sets for which there is sufficient information*

Njemps (men)		Tugen (men)		Tugen (women)	
Ririmpot/Ilkereu	—	Nyongi	—	Cheparkamai (Chelemai)	64
*Ilnapunye/Ilkaricho	—	*Chumo	55		
*Seuri	—			Chepungwek	48
†*Ilkitoip	41	*Sowe	44	Chesiran	36
†Ilmedoti/Ilbaricho	30	Korongoro	29	Kimasinya	29
†Iltapunye/Ikeyepo	22	Kipkoimet/Kaplelach	26	Chesur	23

* = men wearing metal clasps
† = men wearing upper ear beaded decoration

linked to the relations between age groups. It is now possible to examine how material culture is used within the tribes to support the strategies of men and women of different ages, and to show how the material patterning varies in areas with different degrees of ecological stress.

5.2 *Age symbolism*

Throughout the tribes studied in the Baringo area, individuals are strictly categorised into age-sets. All males circumcised within the period of a named age-set may call each other by the name of the age-set, thereby setting up an immediate bond between complete strangers. The age-set system is thus a mechanism for tribal-wide links. But it is also the framework within which older generations maintain control over younger generations.

Table 8 gives the average age in 1976–7 of Tugen and Njemps men in the different age-sets. Some difficulty was encountered in identifying the Njemps age-sets since local names and subdivisions occur. Table 8 thus gives only a broad outline.

As has already been noted, spears play a part in symbolising younger men in contrast to their elders. Traditionally both Tugen and Njemps *moran* wear dress very different from older men. For example, Njemps *moran* wear long hair, ivory or white plastic rings in their lower ear lobes, rods extending from the upper ear and small versions of the women's upper ear decoration (figure 5). Older men shave their hair and wear only small metal clasps in their ears. Table 8 shows the age groups in which these metal clasps are worn by Njemps and Tugen men, while the small upper ear decoration is worn by the younger Njemps age groups. In their opposition to the older men the juniors not only disrupt the material culture boundaries (as has been shown in relation to the spears),

38. The C-type of ear-flap decoration worn by a Tugen woman.

but they also set up symbolic oppositions to their elders in items of dress. But the symbolic differences are also maintained by the older men since, as has been shown, their very domination depends on an unbalanced access to resources (in this case women, their sons and the cattle wealth that the marriage of their daughters will ultimately provide), and since they wish to encourage the competitive opposition of the *moran*.

Table 8 also provides a broad outline of the age-sets of Tugen women. Njemps women, on the other hand, take their age-sets from their husbands so that the age-set is not an indication of age. To allow comparison between Njemps and Tugen age symbolism amongst women it was necessary to use the real ages of women. These ages were obtained by direct questioning always corroborated by the assessment, independent of decoration worn, of the field worker and his guide. This procedure is likely to be inaccurate, but it is sufficiently precise for the broad 10 year age-categories which have been used. The ages of women are symbolised in many subtle aspects of dress, only two of which are to be considered here – ear-flap decoration and the number of necklaces worn.

39. The B-type of ear-flap decoration worn by a Njemps woman.

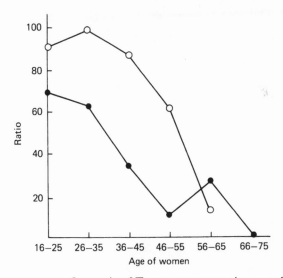

40. ○ = ratio of Tugen women wearing type C as opposed to type B ear-flaps at different ages. ● = ratio of Njemps women wearing type A as opposed to type B ear-flaps.

Both Tugen and Njemps wear leather straps through the lower lobes of their ears. The forward-facing surfaces of these flaps are covered in coloured beads which comprise a pattern that usually conforms to one of three types of decoration. Each woman makes her own ear-flaps. Types A and C are worn fairly exclusively by the Njemps and Tugen respectively (figure 38), and as the map in figure 3 shows these traits are amongst the most distinctive of these tribes. Type B is mainly worn by Njemps (figure 39). It is an older style which was copied by several Tugen women living near the Njemps.

Table 3 shows the frequencies of Njemps and Tugen women at different ages who were found wearing these three types of ear-flap. What is of interest in these figures is the *relative* number of women in each age group in each tribe wearing a given type of ear-flap. These relative numbers are shown graphically in figure 40. Although the sample is small, it is clear from the graph that the nature of the differences between young and old women in the two tribes is similar, at least in terms of ear-flap decoration. However, the Tugen show a greater range of variation with very few young women wearing the B-type. This may be partly because they denote age differences less in other aspects of dress than do the Njemps women. For example, Tugen women make less use of necklace symbolism.

Tugen and Njemps women wear varying numbers of necklaces, each necklace being a single strand of coloured beads (compare figures 4 and 5). The number of necklaces worn varies with tribe and age, but also with occasion (whether dressed to go to market or dancing), with task being performed, and with whether one is the first, second etc. wife. Therefore, although age symbolism is an important factor in the number of necklaces worn, we can only consider some broad aspects of this component of the patterning. Figure 41 shows the average numbers of necklaces worn by Tugen and Njemps women of different ages. While there is little evidence that Tugen women of different ages wear different numbers of necklaces, the Njemps pattern shows considerable variation with age. However, there is no steady decrease in the number of necklaces worn with increasing age. Rather, there are three levels which I shall call 'young', 'middle-aged' and 'old'. Young women, after circumcision and in the early years of marriage (16–25) wear large numbers of necklaces, middle-aged women (26–55) wear rather fewer necklaces, while there is a marked drop in the number of necklaces worn by women over 55 (see also ear-flap decoration, figure 40).

Why should these three levels be so clearly expressed? It is suggested here that they represent the three main stages through which an Njemps woman passes. In the Njemps world view, each stage is separate, associated with different rights. When young, a woman's role is to demonstrate submission and conformity to Njemps life, so that she can obtain a large dowry for her family from a wealthy husband. As a young wife she is a symbol of the husband's wealth and standing. In a patrilineal, virilocal society, at marriage she moves as a stranger into a world dominated by her husband and the male members of his family. Her links with her own family may be physically distant. In her loneliness she has to demonstrate that she is a hard and willing worker to the group which has provided the resources for her bride-price. They wait to see

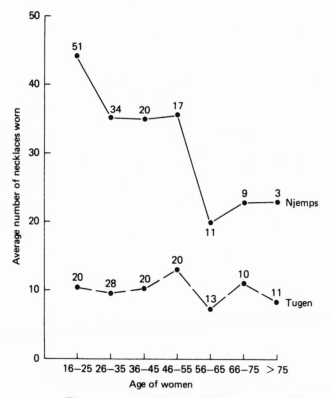

41. The average numbers of necklaces worn by Njemps and Tugen women of different ages. Sample sizes are provided for each average.

if she will quickly repay by producing male children. There are thus considerable pressures on young women and she uses her dress as a way of expressing her willingness to be incorporated.

In middle age, a woman has more independence as a child producer and rearer and she achieves a certain respect in her new environment because she has children. She feels more at ease. There is less pressure on her since she has been able to demonstrate her child-producing abilities. She thus sees herself as different from young women who are as yet unproven and who remain simply objects in exchange relationships.

By her mid fifties, a woman will probably have married sons or *moran* sons approaching marriage. Her position in life again changes. She has achieved her major role and is now able to command a certain amount of respect and attain some standing. She is able to do this because she now has a stronger voice, through her adult sons, in the patrilineal society in which she lives. She may encourage her sons against her husband in their competition for wives and other resources and she may thus receive

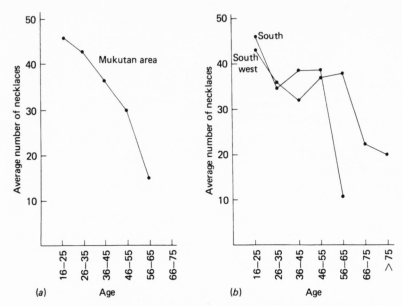

42. The number of necklaces worn by Njemps women at different ages. (*a*) = in the Mukutan area. (*b*) = to the south and southwest of the lake.

reciprocal support from them. A woman with married sons has an honoured position in her sons' compounds and is respected for her seniority and looked after by their wives. An older woman sees herself as different from the less powerful middle-aged women and this difference is outwardly expressed.

We have seen how, in a society in which most rights and positions are attained with age, Njemps women categorise themselves into distinct groups and overtly express the relationship between these groups in terms of self-decoration. However, within this overall pattern there is room for variation. Sufficient data were collected from three Njemps border areas to allow the numbers of necklaces worn by different age groups to be assessed. To the south and southwest of the lake, in the areas of greatest conflict between Njemps and Tugen, we see the same pattern (figure 42) as in the overall scheme discussed above. Numbers of necklaces worn do not decrease gradually with age, but show marked plateaux and kinks. In the Mukutan area, however, there is a smooth decrease with increasing age (figure 42).

Why should these two very different patterns occur? In both, strong constraints are imposed. The age restrictions on access to rights is a dominant part of the society, and the differences in the number of necklaces worn relate to this. But there are considerably fewer constraints in the Mukutan area than to the south and southwest of the lake. In

Mukutan, women may feel less need to express clearly the three age groups, there is a gradual fall-off with age and less marked distinctions between ages. In this area, as we have seen (chapter 2), there is lower density of occupation and less socio-economic stress. It may be reasonable to see this as relating to less competition between age groups than in the high density areas to the south and southwest of Lake Baringo. In the latter areas more strains are placed on the age organisation.

In the age symbolism, as with the material variation between tribes, there are more distinct differences between groups, and less blurring of the cultural patterning, as socio-economic stress increases. But in all areas in the Njemps, the symbolic marking of age differences does more than passively mirror age variation. Rather, the material symbols play a part in forming particular clusters of individuals of similar ages with similar social and economic rights. The members of the age clusters express their common attitudes and expectations and in this expression they manipulate the material symbols to their own advantage and in the manner most appropriate to their positions and roles within society. Similar arguments may be found relevant for overt symbolic differences between the sexes.

5.3 *Sex symbolism*

In different types of social and economic systems there may be more or less conflict between male and female rights and the degree of difference in their roles may vary. The outward expression of the male/female dichotomy may, therefore, not remain constant. We can monitor the distinctiveness of male and female associated artifacts in relation to socio-economic changes. In the Baringo area, the overt male/female dichotomy is exceptionally marked and the status of women is especially low. This is at least partly because of the strong patrilineal and poly-gamous aspects of social relations and the relatively minor economic role in these pastoral systems of women, who can only obtain rights through the male world into which they marry or through sons. As well as the marked differences in dress between men and women (e.g. compare figures 6 and 7), I have shown (Hodder 1977a) that females demonstrate more conformity in material culture than males. This is the result, not only of the male demand for female submission, but also of the general sympathy and mutual support among women. Their depressed status puts them at a disadvantage, but by helping each other in difficult moments, they can at least improve their position a little. Their silent disruption of social control was discussed in chapter 4.

The greater conformity shown by women is one aspect of a world view which is forced on them in a male-dominated society. The overall difference between male and female has been well summarised by Spencer (1965, 231) in a passage dealing with the Samburu but which applies well to their relations, the Njemps.

On the whole I found women were quite ignorant of many aspects
of the total society and usually unhelpful as informants. Outside the
affairs of their own family circle they often showed a certain
indifference. They were less inquisitive than the males and less quick
to grasp situations. They found it harder to comprehend my remarks
and questions. I had the impression that they had never been
encouraged to show much initiative of their own and this was a
quality which they simply had not developed; any inborn tendencies
to this had been baulked by the strictness of their upbringing. Their
demeanour was sometimes listless and frequently sour. They often
lacked the general conviviality and warmth that typified the adult
males, and it was only with the ameliorating circumstances of
middle-age that they tended to acquire it – and many never did.

The Njemps still practise some agriculture and the female role in this
gives a woman greater independence than in Samburu society. Nevertheless the above description, although coming from a male anthropologist who would have been given an impression different from that given
to a female colleague, could be applied to many young Njemps, as well
as Tugen, women.

Although the dress and other differences between men and women in
the Baringo area are marked, it is a curious fact that the small upper ear
beaded decoration worn by young Njemps men is clearly a version of the
female upper ear decoration. Similarly, on the Leroghi plateau (chapter
6) both young men (*moran*) and women wear small white rods in the
upper part of their ears. Why should there be these common symbols
between women and young men? In Samburu society (Spencer 1965,
229) both women and *moran* sing songs which imply a certain rebellion
against the established order. This order is maintained by the older men
to their own advantage and, as we have seen, mothers may unite with
their sons in order to win some influence in this system. A woman's
influence is attained through her sons, and a *moran* is allotted cattle from
his mother's herd and otherwise attains resources from his elders with the
help of his mother. Young men and women have certain common
interests in opposition to elders and this dichotomy is supported and the
common rebellion emphasised in the overt expression.

5.4 *Boundary maintenance and disruption*

Regional material culture tribal boundaries in the Baringo district are
maintained and re-enacted from day to day in the trivia of pots, trinkets,
stools, eating bowls and cooking hearths. This repetitive symbolic action
constitutes and reconstitutes the regional dichotomies where interaction
between tribes is frequent and the movement of people across borders
common. But the reconstitution is also in relation to other forces
disrupting the boundary distinctions, particularly those associated with
young men and women in their opposition to the elders. The opposing

forces of maintenance and disruption involve the continual reproduction of cultural distinctions and cultural similarities. New styles, such as the A-type of ear-flap discussed in chapter 2, come into being to reconstitute the boundary disrupted by the diffusion of the old B ear-flap style (p. 34).

One aspect of the maintenance and disruption of the material culture boundaries which has been discussed above concerns the internal strategies of younger and older men in their competition over resources and women. The material culture acts as part of an ideology of control whereby the dominance of the older men is supported and justified. The authority and rights of the elders and the restricted power and long preparation of young men become acceptable and have meaning in terms of the competitive regional divisions, naturalised in the mundane aspects of daily life.

So, whether an artifact does or does not 'reflect' a particular type of interaction or information flow depends on how it comes to be used as part of the strategies and ideologies of particular groups. Individual artifact types may be used to emphasise or deny, to maintain or disrupt, ethnic distinctions or networks of information flow.

One cannot, therefore, analyse the maintenance of material differences between ethnic groups solely in terms of the degree of interaction between groups. The internal organisation of a society, and the symbolism of objects in that society, need also to be considered. Thus, when discussing both regional distributions of material items in Baringo (chapters 2 and 4) and age group differences in this chapter, greater between-group stress has been related to more marked material boundaries. But these examples cannot be built into a general predictive model for the relationship between stress and material culture dichotomies, since the type of relationship noted depends on the particular nature of societal organisation in the Baringo tribes. In other societies, with different types of social organisation and with different meanings attached to material symbols, there may be no relationship between inter-group competition for scarce resources and marked material boundaries. Some examples of these different types of societies will be examined in the chapters which follow.

More generally, some limitations of the idea that material culture variability reflects societal patterning are beginning to be identified. The main difficulty is that because of the ideological and symbolic components of material items, artifacts are *actively* manipulated in social strategies. I have, up to this point, not moved away from a concern with ecological adaptation and functional relationships. It would still be possible, given the views presented so far, to set up 'reflective' links between material culture and human behaviour. But we now see that those links must have social and ideological dimensions. Our predictive models must be both complex and broad. The need to incorporate the organisation of beliefs and ideas into our interpretive models will become clearer in chapter 8 and will finally lead to a need to reconsider more radically the 'reflective' nature of material culture. But for the moment further examples of material culture patterning at tribal boundaries will be examined in order to demonstrate the active manipulation and negotiation of symbols in social strategies.

6

Hunter-gatherers and pastoralists on the Leroghi plateau

In this chapter the formation and development of Dorobo groups and their relations with the Samburu on the Leroghi plateau, Kenya, are studied with the aim of determining the part played by material culture in these processes. Thus we must examine whether the use and manipulation of material culture in the expression of identities further reveal as problematic the links that have been made in prehistoric archaeology between human behaviour and material artifacts.

Dorobo (or Wandorobo, Ndorobo) is a Maasai word meaning 'poor man' or 'person without cattle'. It is used to refer to hunter-gatherers, bush and forest dwellers (Blackburn 1974; Dundas 1908; Hobley 1906; Huntingford 1951). In Kalenjin, the equivalent word is Okiek. The Dorobo consist of small separated bands of several hundreds of people in Kenya and Tanzania who have often developed close relationships with neighbouring pastoralists and agriculturalists; their distribution in the Samburu area is shown in figure 43. These groups are not part of a unified 'tribe'. 'The looseness of the term "Dorobo" is illustrated by the oft-heard expressions "living like a Dorobo" for anyone who tends to dwell in remote places or to depend partly on foraging or who is expert at collecting honey, and "turning Dorobo"' (Sutton 1973, 9). Failure of crops or loss of cattle through disease, drought or war would from time to time cause small numbers of Kalenjin, Maasai or Kikuyu to seek refuge and alternative livelihoods in hills and forests – either as 'temporary Dorobo' or perhaps by joining up with longer established 'true Dorobo' (Spencer 1973). However, it is by no means certain that an aboriginal stock of 'true Dorobo' hunter-gatherers ever existed.

The small Dorobo bands often adopt the language and cultural traits of the agriculturalists and pastoralists with whom they have most contact. There is considerable intermarriage between many Dorobo groups and the host tribe. Those in Samburu areas speak Maasai and share many Maasai customs and beliefs. In recent years these groups have been confined to certain reserves and have been encouraged to take up cattle husbandry (Spencer 1965, 281).

Most of the Dorobo locations shown in figure 43 are subdivided into

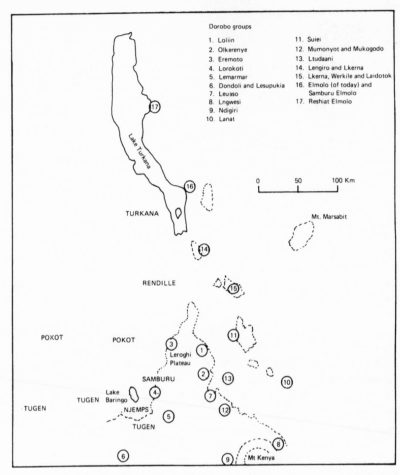

Dorobo groups

1. Loliin
2. Olkerenye
3. Eremoto
4. Lorokoti
5. Lemarmar
6. Dondoli and Lesupukia
7. Leuaso
8. Lngwesi
9. Ndigiri
10. Lanat
11. Suiei
12. Mumonyot and Mukogodo
13. Ltudaani
14. Lengiro and Lkerna
15. Lkerna, Werkile and Laidotok
16. Elmolo (of today) and Samburu Elmolo
17. Reshiat Elmolo

43. The distribution of Dorobo groups in 1900. The edge of
higher ground is dotted. *Source*: Spencer 1973.

areas owned by agnatic groups. Amongst the acephalous Dorobo, closest
social ties are with bilateral kinsmen. Unlike the Samburu, clan exogamy
is not strictly adhered to, and there are also fewer restrictions on marriage
within the age-sets which are superficially similar to those of the Samburu.
Also, by comparison with the Samburu, Dorobo men tend to have fewer
wives, so that young men can marry as soon as is practicable after
circumcision (Spencer 1965, 284).

The Samburu are a Maasai-speaking tribe of some 30,000 people
(Spencer 1965: 1973). They are nomadic, relying on cattle, sheep and
goats. Clan exogamy is practised, and the clan is the most important level
of the segmentary descent system. Although clans are dispersed, clansmen
tend to cluster together into local clan groups. Cross-cutting this descent
system is an age-set system. The *moran* warrior age-set consists of young

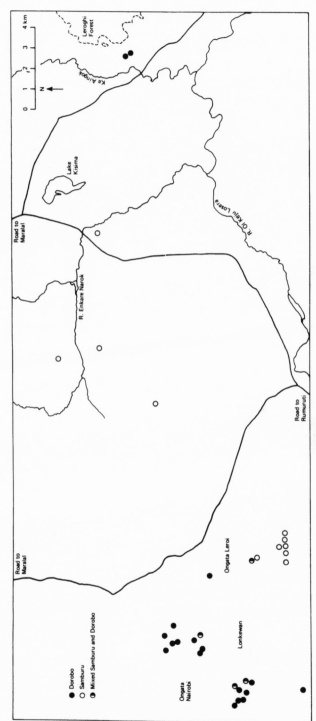

44. The location of the Dorobo and Samburu compounds studied.

men who are not allowed to marry until they are replaced by a new age-set. Control over the *moran* is in the hands of the elders. There are no traditional chiefs and influence is achieved with age. Nowadays older men are elected to act as 'chiefs' in the local administration.

Thirty-two Dorobo and Samburu compounds were studied on the Leroghi plateau to the east of the Rift Valley, beyond the Laikipia escarpment (figure 44). The altitude here is around 1830 m as compared to 975 m in the Baringo area. Consequently the environment and vegetation are richer, and game is more plentiful (although this is partly due to the propinquity of game reserves). Equally, however, there has been greater colonial impact in this area as a result of the presence of European farms. The main group of Dorobo studied (figure 44) inhabits a wooded area called Lonkewan. The Samburu are found to be north and east of this area on the flat and open grasslands, although some Dorobo have now also moved into this environment. To the east, a small group of Dorobo were studied on the edge of the forest at Kisima (figure 44). The method of study in the field was identical to that described in chapter 2.

6.1 *The Lonkewan Dorobo and Samburu*

Evidence was collected concerning the economic and marriage patterns of the two groups. The Samburu practise no agriculture. Today they occupy their compounds in the Lonkewan area for up to eight or nine years, although movement may have been more frequent in the past. They have goats, sheep and donkeys which are grazed locally, while the cattle are either also grazed in Lonkewan all the the year round or are taken by the *moran* in the dry season to Wamba (100 km to the east) and elsewhere. The Dorobo have gradually acquired cattle. They used to live by gathering and by hunting elephants and other wild animals, and many still hunt and keep honey. However, the basis of their livelihood is cattle, with some sheep and goats. The cattle are grazed all year round in Lonkewan or taken in the dry season to Amaya to the west. In both the wet and dry seasons Samburu and Dorobo herds graze together at Lonkewan. Unlike the Samburu, most Dorobo have small fields for the cultivation of cereals and vegetables.

Because of government controls of cattle on the Laikipia (Spencer 1973), the custom of keeping and giving cattle to 'cattle friends' is weakly developed in comparison to the Baringo area. Few Dorobo have any cattle exchange friends, and those that do have both Dorobo and Samburu partners. Samburu cattle exchange friends tend mainly to be Samburu.

Table 9 shows the numbers of marriages, recorded in 1977, between Dorobo, Samburu and Maasai in the last 25 years, 25 to 50 years ago, and more than 50 years ago. It is clear that Dorobo and Samburu men

Table 9. *The numbers of marriages recorded on the Leroghi plateau between the different tribal groups*

Female	Male		
	Dorobo	Samburu	Maasai
Dorobo			
1952–77	25	10	12
1927–51	24	0	5
Before 1926	0	0	1
Total	49	10	18
Samburu			
1952–77	12	20	1
1927–51	0	7	4
Before 1926	0	1	0
Total	12	28	5
Maasai			
1952–77	2	0	2
1927–51	3	0	2
Before 1926	0	1	0
Total	5	1	4

Table 10. *Intermarriage of Dorobo groups*

Tribe or Dorobo group of wife	Dorobo group and generation of husband				
	Leuaso Dorobo		Mumonyot Dorobo		
	Present	Past	Present	Past	Total
Same group as husband	44	17	46	10	117
Neighbouring Dorobo group	9	4	19	10	42
Distant Dorobo group	6	9	1	2	18
Neighbouring pastoralist tribes	10	5	5	5	25
Others and unknown	1	4	1	1	7
Total	70	39	72	28	209

Source: Spencer 1973, 207.
This table gives the marriages made by the present living generation of the Leuaso and Mumonyot Dorobo and by their fathers.

and women prefer to marry within their own tribes, and that cross-marriages between Samburu and Dorobo are mainly confined to the past 25 years. Little evidence was found of intermarriage before this and, in general, most Dorobo and Samburu, when asked, said they had no relatives in the other tribe. A similar pattern is suggested amongst other

Dorobo groups in table 10. However, marriage ties have been maintained between the Lonkewan Dorobo and the Maasai (table 9), and Maasai men may marry Dorobo women as one mechanism by which they can ultimately move into the Dorobo reserve.

In the past there used to be a considerable amount of intermarriage between the two Dorobo groups in Lonkewan and Kisima, while table 10 shows that Dorobo marriages with other Dorobo groups are more frequent than marriages with neighbouring pastoral tribes.

Thus, although Dorobo prefer to marry other Dorobo in their own or other groups, recently there has been a considerable amount of inter-marriage with Samburu and Maasai. The economic pattern of collective grazing of cattle also emphasises the recent high degree of contact between the different tribes.

6.2 *Artifact types*

Figure 45 summarises the distribution of the artifact types studied in Dorobo and Samburu compounds or parts of compounds. These types are described below.

A   A skin dress with bead decoration used in circumcision and other ceremonies. The distinctive zig-zag decoration is confined to the Dorobo.

B   A distinctive leather bag (*ilbene*), decorated with beads or cord (see figure 46).

C   A large beaded ear-ring with an arm extending from one side (figure 46). This ring is attached through a hole in the top of women's ears.

D   Leather flaps which are worn in the extended lower lobes of women's ears. The forward-facing flaps are decorated in two designs, one of which is worn on the left, and the other on the right ear (figure 46).

E   Bead necklaces worn by women. The necklaces are grouped into flat plates and sometimes sewn onto a leather backing.

F   An ear-ring identical to C but without the extended arm.

G   A wide-mouthed cooking pot with two handles and a linear decoration of finger-impressed cordons. In the area studied, all such pots are made by Dorobo potters, and mostly by one woman potter at Kisima. When visited in 1977, this woman was about 40 years old and had been making pots since she got married. She had not learnt potting from her mother, who was not a potter, but from other potters in neighbouring districts. She obtained her clay from the Dorobo forest adjacent to her home and made the pots by a process very similar to that followed by the Kokwa potter (chapter 3). (Dorobo methods of pot manufacture are discussed by Blackburn 1973, 66–7.) She said she often made thirty pots

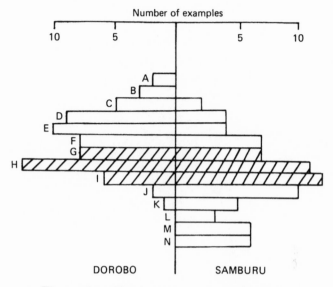

45. The number of Lonkewan compounds of Samburu and Dorobo with objects of type A to N. For types see text and figure 46. Shaded bars indicate more utilitarian items.

Table 11. *The mean dimensions (in cm) of Dorobo and Samburu pots*

Owned by	Mean rim diameter (N)	Mean height (N)
Dorobo	15·4 (6)	21·5 (6)
Samburu	17·9 (12)	22·4 (12)

a month and sold them mainly to people who came to her. She also sold pots in markets. The potter claimed that she was able to make a 'rich' living out of her craft. However, her husband, a stoolmaker, also collected honey and used to hunt. Pot making was only one of their sources of income. No potters were found or recorded in the Lonkewan area, and the Kisima potter provided pots for Dorobo in both Lonkewan and Kisima and for Samburu. Although table 11 records a slight difference in size between the pots she made for Dorobo and Samburu, the sample is small and no decorative features distinguished the pots owned by the two tribal groups.

H Wooden four-legged stools. These are very similar in form to those used by the Njemps (figure 14: 5). They are made by Samburu and Dorobo men, although the latter are the more common stool craftsmen

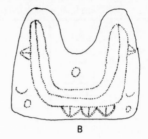

B

C   F   D

G   I

N

46. Some Lonkewan artifact types. Letters refer to descriptions in text.

Table 12. *The percentages of pots, stools and milk jugs owned and made by Dorobo amongst the total of those owned and made by both Dorobo and Samburu*

	Percentage owned by Dorobo (N)	Percentage made by Dorobo (N)
Pots	32 (19)	100 (17)
Stools	67 (33)	82 (28)
Milk jugs (*ilkilip*)	10 (81)	2 (79)

The numbers found are given in brackets. The sample numbers in the two columns do not match because not all information could be collected for all artifacts.

Table 13. *The mean dimensions (in cm) of Dorobo and Samburu stools*

Owned by	Mean seat diameter (N)	Mean height (N)	Mean width of legs (N)
Dorobo	25·5 (22)	18·9 (22)	6·8 (22)
Samburu	25·2 (10)	18·3 (10)	6·4 (9)

For the lack of match between sample numbers in the different columns see table 12.

(table 12). Many Samburu and Dorobo men make stools for the use of their own family, although some specialists do exist. For example, Dorobo carpenters work at Wamba and Kisima. The stoolmaker at Kisima is the husband of the potter discussed above, and he sold a small number of stools to a localised market. Table 13 shows that dimensions of the stools owned by Dorobo and Samburu are closely similar.

I Tall wooden milk containers (*ilkilip*) are made by women for their own use. These are, therefore, common utilitarian items made by non-specialists. Although some are made by Dorobo, most are made by Samburu (table 12). Dorobo who want *ilkilip* often obtain them from neighbouring Samburu. As shown in table 14, *ilkilip* owned by Dorobo are generally smaller than those owned by Samburu. However, relatively few *ilkilip* were found in Dorobo compounds so that the sample is unreliable.

Sendere are honey pots similar to those used by Tugen (figure 14: 1) and are commonly found in Samburu compounds. It is by taking these and calabashes to the Dorobo that the Samburu obtain honey.

Table 14. *The mean dimensions (in cm) of Dorobo and Samburu milk jugs (ilkilip)*

Owned by	Mean total height, including lid	Mean vessel height	Mean width of top of lid
Dorobo	43·8 (8)	28·1 (6)	2·2 (4)
Samburu	49·2 (73)	35·2 (28)	3·8 (50)

For the lack of match between sample numbers in the different columns see table 12.

J A band of beads worn by women across the forehead, often with a small piece of metal attached by a short thread in the middle of the forehead.

K Single necklaces of beads. Unlike E, these are not grouped together into plates.

L Small quadrangular pieces of leather sewn with beads and worn in the upper part of the women's ears. These are very similar in form to those worn by the Njemps (figure 5).

M Small ivory or plastic rods fixed into holes in the top of women's ears and pointing upwards and backwards. These are mainly worn by Samburu women. However, the same rod is worn by both Samburu and Dorobo *moran* (see p. 84 for discussion).

N A distinctive necklace (figure 46) worn by Samburu women in certain ceremonies and by young girls just after marriage. It is made of large numbers of very thin bark strips and zebra hairs bundled at the back into three leather tubes. Some of the individual front strands have single red beads attached on a central axis.

Figure 45 demonstrates that several of the decorative and ceremonial artifact types are largely confined to either the Dorobo or Samburu. It is the utilitarian items (pots, stools, milk jugs) which show greatest overlap between the two tribes. The degree of material culture sharing is increased when it is realised that only selected traits are included in figure 45 and in the descriptions above. The fieldwork was concerned with those traits which allowed any tribal differences to be identified and which would allow the distributional patterning of any such differences to be examined. Many other, especially utilitarian, traits are common to both tribes. For example, both Dorobo and Samburu now live in the same style of rectangular hut with flat mud roof. Also, spears identical to those studied in the Baringo area are made by Samburu smiths for both Samburu and Dorobo.

In general, then, the total material culture assemblages of the Dorobo and Samburu in the Lonkewan and Kisima areas are very similar, as are the dimensions of certain artifact types in the two groups (see, for example, tables 11 to 14). However, a few items of self-decoration and ceremonial use do show differences between the two tribes.

It is of interest to assess to what extent the people studied were aware of any material culture differences between Samburu and Dorobo. In fifteen compounds, groups of individuals were asked if they knew of any such differences, especially in female dress. Indeed, they were aware of *all* the differences for which there is quantitative evidence in figure 45, however slight these differences might be. (No differences in the dimensions of pots and *ilkilip* were mentioned.) Samburu informants most frequently mentioned that they wore numerous single necklaces (K) while Dorobo women more often wore necklace plates (E). They also mentioned differences in the use of the N collar necklace and the M ivory or plastic rods, as well as the differences which appear fairly slight in figure 45. For example, Dorobo women were known to prefer ear-flap (D) decoration and the C ear-rings, and it was realised that the Samburu had copied the latter from the Dorobo less than they had copied the similar F ear-ring. The only decorative trait which appears to distinguish the Samburu from the Dorobo and which was not mentioned by the informants was the J headband.

Utilitarian items were less frequently pointed to as separating the two tribal groups. Both the milk jug (*ilkilip*) and the honey pot were only mentioned once, by Dorobo. Thus, individuals in the Leroghi area would only talk about items of self-decoration and of ceremonial use when asked about tribal differences. Utilitarian items are both less distinctive quantitatively and less frequently mentioned. The reflexive awareness of the significance of symbols forms an essential part in the ability of the individuals in the tribes to manipulate the symbolism of material objects in the course of social action.

Having described some of the present-day material culture patterning amongst Leroghi Samburu and Dorobo, some attempt will be made to understand the factors which have led to the modern pattern. This will involve an outline of how the Dorobo groups have been formed and of the recent relations between the Dorobo and Samburu in the area studied.

6.3 *History and explanation*

The following account of the recent history of the Lonkewan Dorobo is derived from discussion with three Dorobo elders and from the more general studies of Spencer (1965; 1973), Huntingford (1953), Sutton (1973), and Blackburn (1974).

The Laikipia escarpment had originally been occupied by the Maasai, with the Samburu to their north. But in the 1880s, the Purko and

Laikipia Maasai fought, with the result that many Laikipia Maasai lost their cattle. After a meeting of the Laikipia, many decided that they would become hunter-gatherers and bee keepers in bush areas at, for example, Lonkewan and Kisima.

In the forest areas the Laikipia hunter-gatherers came to be called Dorobo. They retained their Maasai costume and culture but changed their economy. In this way they 'became' Dorobo. Those at Lonkewan exchanged honey, stools and pots with the Pokot, Maasai and Njemps, and obtained goats in return. After a time without cattle, the Dorobo began to buy cattle from the Pokot and much later from the Samburu. After 1914 many Dorobo were able to obtain the means to buy cattle by working on European farms.

After 1913, when the Maasai were moved out of the Leroghi plateau, the Samburu moved in. At first they came in only small numbers. These early arrivals exchanged goods with the Kisima Dorobo. Soon, however, the Samburu moved in larger numbers into Ongata Leroi and Ongata Nairobi immediately adjacent to the Lonkewan Dorobo. By this time, in the 1920s and 1930s, the Lonkewan Dorobo said that they had become 'rich' and were selling ivory to the Pokot and Njemps, but not to their enemies the Samburu. Indeed, one of the early material culture distinctions between Dorobo and Samburu was said to be that the Dorobo had ivory ear decoration while the Samburu used wood. With their newly acquired cattle, the Lonkewan Dorobo began moving out of the 'bush' areas into the adjacent plain, in direct competition with the Samburu. Tension increased between the two groups. There was little mixing and inter-marriage 'because it would mean a Samburu could visit a relative and steal cows' (Dorobo informant). Samburu *moran* used to attack Dorobo, including those in the forest, as a sign of bravery and manhood in their 'preparation' for becoming elders. Related to this conflict, material culture differences were marked. Many Dorobo and Samburu informants were insistent that the material culture of the tribes had been more distinct in the past, and that the between-tribe copying was a recent phenomenon.

The history of the Lonkewan Dorobo is complicated by the incor-poration of further Maasai into what became the Leroghi Dorobo reserve. Although the Dorobo and Maasai were separated after 1913, close contact and intermarriage were maintained as is shown in table 9. Of the thirty-two compounds studied, nineteen contained Dorobo families. Of these families, only two claimed to have been in the Lonkewan area for more than two generations, or about 50 to 60 years. The rest consisted of more recent refugees from government restrictions of Maasai in other parts of Kenya. These Maasai had come to Lonkewan in order to 'become Dorobo', and they tended to choose Lonkewan if they had friends or relatives there. If the refugees had lost their cattle, they supplemented their livelihood by hunting, gathering and agriculture as they built up their herds again. Those refugees that brought their cattle with them were especially welcome since the Lonkewan Dorobo as a whole were trying to increase their cattle stocks. The original Dorobo 'tribe' has, therefore, been expanded by later Maasai arrivals and by a few other outsiders such as refugee Tugen. As far as I am aware, there are few, if any symbolic material culture differences between the Maasai and Lonkewan Dorobo. For the Maasai, to 'become' Dorobo means to change name and way of life.

The past tension between the Dorobo and Samburu has recently diminished. This is partly because of the more effective policing in the area than in the Baringo area, related to the large farms on the Leroghi plateau. It is also the case, however, that the Leroghi environment is much richer, and densities of people and cattle much lower, than in Baringo, so that there are fewer possibilities for conflict. Cattle densities were restricted by government grazing schemes (Spencer 1973) which were more successful than those in the Baringo basin.

Thus the present material culture patterning must be seen in the context of good and peaceful relations between Samburu and Dorobo, and of increased intermarriage. The government has recently given the Lonkewan Dorobo and Samburu a common local 'chief', and has encouraged both groups to think of themselves as the same tribe, and this has been largely successful. Some informants even said that the Samburu and Dorobo originated in the same clan and in the same family, so that only the names separate them. We were told of a myth in which two Samburu children became lost in a forest and settled down to form the Dorobo. Nowadays there is no recognised boundary between the Dorobo and Samburu, boys from both groups are circumcised together in the same ceremonies, a member of one group can graze his cattle within the other group without asking permission and, unlike the situation in Baringo, individuals may move to live within the other group without payment. Only the permission of the local chief needs to be obtained. In several instances, unrelated Dorobo and Samburu were found living in the same compound. If one Dorobo compound is attacked by the Turkana, both Dorobo and Samburu *moran* will attempt to retrieve the cattle. Many outsiders, such as Pokot, think of the Leroghi Samburu and Dorobo as being in the same tribe, and the Dorobo are aware of this.

In spite of all this contact and interaction, the two identities are not completely submerged. Some Dorobo, especially the older generation, are contemptuous of the Samburu. On their part, many Samburu feel that the Dorobo children do not adequately look after the cattle and that they do not care properly for their parents. The Samburu characterise the Dorobo as eating rhinoceros and elephant meat, whereas if the Samburu do this their cattle will decrease in number. Differences in the social organisation of the two groups have already been mentioned, and Spencer (1973) adds that individual competitiveness is higher among the

Dorobo. 'The Samburu delight in telling stories of the meanness, the crudeness, the discourteousness, the competitiveness, and the selfishness of the Dorobo' (*ibid.*, 206).

The past tensions between the Lonkewan Dorobo and the Samburu were related to clear material culture distinctions. The recent general decrease in tension is related to large-scale diffusion of material culture traits from one tribe to the other, although some tension remains and the cultural mixing has not been complete. A rather different development is found at Kisima.

The Kisima Dorobo know of no period in which tensions between them and the Samburu were high. From the 1920s, the two groups were involved in peaceful exchanges and had common clans. Indeed, the Lonkewan Dorobo consider the Kisima Dorobo to be weak cowards for having befriended the Samburu. At Kisima, none of the cultural differences noted in figure 45 could be identified, and the Dorobo have a material culture identical to that of the Samburu.

Why should the cultural patterning of the two Dorobo groups in relation to the Samburu be so different? We have seen that in Lonkewan the initial relationship with the Samburu was tense. The exchange of goods such as honey, pots, stools and small stock was initially with the Maasai, Pokot and Njemps rather than with the Samburu. At Kisima, on the other hand, the Dorobo entered into an early symbiotic relationship with Samburu. Honey pots and stools were exchanged for sheep, goats and spears. The Kisima area never became a refuge to the same extent as the Lonkewan reserve. In this symbiotic, non-competitive relationship, there was little advantage in overtly stressing differences with the Samburu. Rather, open acceptance and integration was desired. The cultural differences disappeared. When the government brought pressure to bear on the Kisima Dorobo to move out of their forest, some moved to join oïher Dorobo groups. But many completed the assimilation by becoming fully Samburu. Those that remained with the Dorobo name were those whose livelihood depended on the traditional Dorobo skills. They moved to the forest edge and provided honey, pots and stools for their Samburu neighbours.

Non-competitive symbiosis leading to symbolic material culture integration is evident in a number of other Dorobo groups in Kenya. Elmolo (Spencer 1973, 213–18) is the name of a small group of people (figure 43) living on the southeast shore of Lake Turkana (Rudolf), who differ from the rest of the Dorobo in that their livelihood is fishing as opposed to hunting and honey. In 1958 there were only 143 Elmolo living in two villages. There has often been some raiding between them and the neighbouring Samburu, but in general the relationship is non-competitive and symbiotic. The two groups exist in different niches, the Samburu providing small stock in exchange for leechcraft, cords and ropes, sandals and whips. Related to this non-competitive interaction, there is a long history of cultural borrowing. In the nineteenth century the Elmolo spoke a Cushitic language; today they speak Samburu (Maasai). In the past the Elmolo did not circumcise males or have *moran*, but by 1958 they had begun to adopt both these traits from the Samburu. Some Samburu customs associated with marriage have also been adopted, such as the giving by young men of beads to girls and the form of the bridewealth. Most of the recent cultural borrowing consists of traits involving the younger generation. 'It was as if these younger more impressionable Elmolo were reacting against the scorn that they knew the Samburu had for them by becoming partially Samburu' (*ibid.*, 216). Although Spencer only briefly mentions material culture, it seems probable that many aspects of Elmolo culture are gradually becoming Samburu in form in parallel with a non-competitive symbiotic relationship between the two groups.

Huntingford's (1953) account of the Dorobo of the North Tindiret forest, adjacent to the Kalenjin Nandi, provides a similar example. This group of mainly hunter-gatherers was studied by Huntingford in 1938–9, by which time they had entered into close relationships with their Nandi agricultural and pastoral neighbours. In this exchange the Dorobo obtained iron axes and knives (the Dorobo made the wooden handles), pottery, beads, tobacco, goats and the seed of cereals for planting. In return, the Nandi obtained honey, furs and skins, red and white earth for colouring and for magico-religious uses. Exchange was peaceful and carried out by individual gift exchange. There were no special places or markets for the trade. At the same time there was evidence of increasing intermarriage, and the Dorobo gradually acquired and assimilated much Nandi culture, including language, clan names, agriculture, dress and ornaments. The items of self-decoration which were copied included iron wire armlets, necklaces and married women's ear-rings. Some young men had their hair done in pigtails like the Nandi. Once again a non-competitive symbiotic relationship between groups living in different niches is associated with the borrowing and adoption of material culture traits.

The Lonkewan Dorobo, on the one hand, and the Kisima, Elmolo and Tindiret Dorobo on the other, present two different economic strategies in their relationships with pastoralist and agriculturalist neighbours. In Lonkewan, the Dorobo hunters and gatherers early re-acquired cattle and their numbers were soon swelled by Maasai 'becoming' Dorobo as a refuge. Tensions existed with the cattle-owning Samburu so that the Dorobo identity was stressed in opposition to the Samburu, and material culture was used to demonstrate Dorobo independence. It is only recently that tensions between Lonkewan Dorobo and Samburu have decreased, and intermarriage and cultural mixing increased. The economic strategy followed by the Lonkewan Dorobo was thus initially one of confrontation and competition with their pastoralist neighbours. This pattern was perhaps perpetuated by the creation of a Dorobo reserve. The Kisima and other Dorobo groups followed a different path. Here the economic strategy was one of non-competitive symbiosis and integration. Hunter-gatherer and host tribe exchanged products and became incorporated within one system. Some cattle were obtained by the hunter-gatherers, but the overall result, encouraged by government administration, was a gradual breakdown of cultural and tribal differences by intermarriage and assimilation.

6.4   *The maintenance of overt identities within tribes*

One of the most characteristic aspects of Samburu society is the very strict age-set system by which individuals of particular age groups are assured rights of access to different resources. Spencer (1965) suggests that the whole polygamous structure of this society depends on the older men preventing the younger men from marrying and thus using up the available supply of women. Related to these restrictions, the material culture distinctions between age groups are very clear. Amongst the Samburu (*ibid.*, 173), when a *moran*'s age-set matures he shaves off his long hair and wears his hair short, and he replaces his ivory ear-rings with brass ones. He obtains a longer cloth which can be worn over the right shoulder and which reaches down below the knees. He carries a long heavier staff and stops decorating his head with red ochre except on ceremonial occasions. This change in dress is an outward sign that a man has abandoned his rash youthful behaviour and that he is ready to settle down to elderhood and conform to the conventions of that status (*ibid.*, 205). Similarly, once a Samburu woman has sons who have been circumcised she acquires a special status which is displayed by certain ornaments she wears on her head (*ibid.*, 220). In the Lonkewan survey one Samburu woman said that she wore both a large and a small plate necklace because she had a *moran* son, while another noted that she needed to have an *ilkilip* in order to get married according to Samburu law.

There is less evidence for similar restrictions of artifact types to particular age groups in Dorobo society. Why is this? Spencer (1965, 284), in comparing the Samburu and Dorobo, notes that the strict subordination of young men to old in Samburu society was related to the fairly high rates of polygamy. The older men needed to restrain the younger men from taking up the available supply of women. The high rates of polygamy were, in turn, related to the Samburu desire for economic independence of families and the need for a large labour force of children to look after cattle and pastures. The origins of the Dorobo economy, on the other hand, are in hunting and gathering, which necessitated collective action and the pooling of combined resources. Hunting required the joint efforts of all active males in an area, the older with their skill and the younger with their agility, and food obtained was distributed widely. Dorobo men participated more as equals and reached an earlier maturity. There was less competition between men of different ages, and the gathering activities of women and the lower rates of polygamy may have meant that women of different ages had more equal access to basic rights. The Dorobo economy is gradually changing and becoming more like that of the Samburu, but even today more hunting and gathering, as well as more 'cooperative' agriculture, are practised than amongst the Samburu. Dorobo social organisation involves less competition between individuals of different ages and there is less need for the active involvement of material symbols in the formation of interest groups based on age.

6.5 *Conclusion*

The example of the Leroghi Dorobo demonstrates the way in which individuals, in this case Maasai, may manipulate ethnic identity for their own means. The Maasai 'become' Dorobo in order to escape drought, raiding or government persecution. But, although the Dorobo have a real separate existence in the conscious thoughts of those who call themselves by this name, there is no symbolic expression of any differences between Dorobo and Maasai. Thus the outer surface of being Dorobo has two faces. The verbal signal identifies the Dorobo as being non-Maasai; the material culture signal shows the single identity of the two groups. In the author's view, it is the latter state of affairs which is also the underlying conception amongst the Dorobo. At heart they are Maasai. The Dorobo identity is a convenient front to present to a hostile world.

Amongst the Dorobo on the Leroghi plateau, the two economic strategies of competition and symbiotic integration with the Samburu are related to distinctively different types of cultural patterning (for further examples of these two strategies see Cohen 1974, 92). Relations between agriculturalists and pastoralists in other parts of Africa show that economic symbiosis can be related to competition and cultural distinctiveness as preferential access to restricted and specialised resources is safeguarded (an example is provided in chapter 8). But in some Dorobo groups (Kisima, Elmolo, Tindiret), the particular pathway that is chosen, and the particular type of symbiosis that is found, is non-competitive, involving cultural integration. Another Dorobo group (Lonkewan) had in the past competitive non-symbiotic relationships with its neighbours. It seems that we cannot erect any simple correlations between resource distributions, material culture patterning and degrees of economic competition. Economic competition may encourage cultural distinctiveness, but equally, particular conceptual and social dispositions may encourage particular forms of economic and cultural strategy. The distribution of resources is only one of the relevant variables when the explanation of regional material culture patterning is being considered.

Different groups manipulate material culture boundaries in different ways depending on the social context, the economic strategies chosen, the particular history of the socio-economic relations, and the particular history of the cultural traits which are actively articulated within the changing system.

The fact that the Lonkewan Dorobo are in some sense Maasai affects their relationships with the neighbouring Samburu and the articulation of material symbols in that relationship. The close links maintained with the Maasai and the possibility of reversion to that tribal label discourage absorption into the Samburu. In direct contrast to Cohen's (1974) claim that the history of a cultural trait is irrelevant to its use in a contemporary context, at Lonkewan it is precisely the Maasai origin of the Dorobo traits which is of importance. One factor affecting the maintenance of some overt cultural distinctions from the Samburu, and the very existence of earlier competitive relationships, is the intention of many Dorobo of re-acquiring cattle and once more becoming full Maasai pastoralists.

The other Dorobo groups discussed here (Kisima, Elmolo and Tindiret) have shown a greater degree of adoption of Samburu and Nandi traits. While this is partly related to the economic strategy of these groups in relation to their dominant neighbours, the internal social relations of the interacting groups also play a part. The Dorobo groups have less strict age divisions and separation of rights of old and young men, men and women. The elders have less control over the young men and over women than do their counterparts in the Njemps (chapter 5). The age-set system through which such control could be expressed is not well developed. The elders are less able to emphasise overt cultural boundaries and to utilise the 'us'–'them' dichotomy as an arena for the preparation and involvement of young men. But at the time of study of the Kisima, Tindiret and Elmolo Dorobo, the *moran* system was well developed amongst the Nandi and Samburu and these latter groups might be expected to show less blurring of their boundaries. It is thus of interest that cultural traits move easily from the Samburu and Nandi to the Dorobo groups, but that Dorobo traits are adopted less frequently by their dominant neighbours. In the same way in Baringo, the Njemps with higher rates of polygamy and a more developed *moran* age-set are more closed to Tugen traits than the Tugen, who are less polygamous and have today a weakly developed *moran* system, are to Njemps traits (Hodder 1977a). In both the Baringo and Leroghi areas, it is insufficient to examine solely the relations and interactions between ethnic groups when considering material culture patterning. The intentions of subgroups within societies and the nature of the social organisation also play a part.

7

A state of symbiosis and conflict: the Lozi

In the ethnographic examples examined so far, there has been only slight evidence of a traditional social and political hierarchy. In contrast, the example outlined in this chapter concerns the articulation of material culture in a highly developed kingdom, or 'state' – the Lozi in Zambia. In addition, it will be possible to begin consideration of the use of symbols within sites – a task which will be pursued in chapter 8.

7.1 Introduction

The Lozi occupy the western part of Zambia, centring on the floodplain of the Zambezi. The rich peats of the seasonally flooded plain are largely treeless, while the sands of the surrounding areas (the bush) are lightly wooded. In the rainy season the royal centres and other settlements in the floodplain move to the higher edge of the plain. Many families thus have villages both along the plain's margin and on low mounds in the plain itself. The villages usually comprise the huts, kitchens and stores of an extended family group (figure 47), although larger villages and conglomerations occur, for example, at the royal centres of Lealui, Limulunga, Nalolo and Muoyo. Population density is generally low but settlement is clustered along the plain margin and around the edge of 'dambo' marshes in the bush areas. The economy is based largely on arable farming, with cattle and fish important in the floodplain.

A selection of villages, located in different environments in the heart of the Lozi area, Barotseland, were visited during the 1977 dry season. At its height in the later nineteenth and early twentieth centuries A.D., the kingdom covered perhaps 388,500 km². Within this area lived twenty-five Bantu-speaking tribes, many of whom had their main communities outside the realm (figure 48). Many of these tribes spoke different languages and dialects. For example, Mbunda is different from Lozi (Kololo), while there are language differences between the northern and southern tribes. There are also differences in social system: the Mbunda are matrilineal, have no circumcision and were originally more decentralised than the Lozi.

47. A Lozi village on the floodplain of the Zambezi. For plan see figure 54.

At the heart of the kingdom was the Lozi elite, centred on the capitals at Lealui (with its wet season counterpart at Limulunga) and Nalolo (with Muoyo). The royal family were considered to have divine ancestry. All the royal graves had special importance and were especially guarded. Special accoutrements included royal drums. The state was organised into two sorts of units, one territorial and one only partly so, a pattern most clearly structured in the plain itself.

The territorial unit was termed *silalo* and was made up of smaller units (*silalanda*) and villages. In the village there was one or more, usually related, families. The village head was chosen with the approval of the king from the various family heads in the village. The head of the *silalanda* was the oldest and most influential headman, chosen by the people and approved by the king. This head settled local disputes and organised the cleaning of canals in the floodplain. *Silalo* comprised several *silalanda* under one bureaucrat or administrator, called an *induna*, appointed by the king. He was not necessarily a local man but he was always given a piece of land in his *silalo*. He had a *kuta* (council) composed of village headmen and *silalanda* heads who came together to make major administrative decisions. Each *silalo* had another non-resident *induna* who represented the *silalo* on the national, central, *kuta*. There were also provincial capitals, originally run by distant members of the royal family, but later run by administrators.

Another sort of unit, less territorial, was the *likolo* (pl. *makolo*). These were largely kin groups headed by an *induna*. Originally any royal person

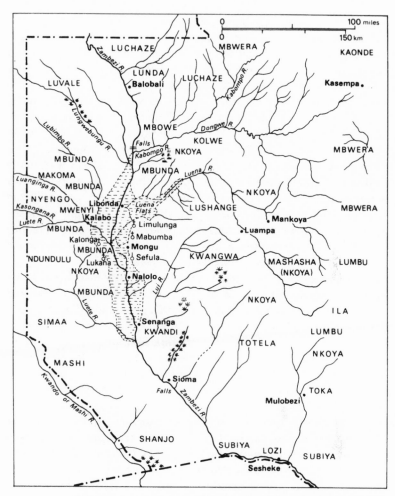

48. Turner's (1952) map of the Lozi peoples of western Zambia.
The shaded area indicates the floodplain.

could create *makolo* and appoint *indunas* to them, a system which guaranteed the royal families resources for labour (for example, in the canals) and military services. But gradually the king took over the sole right to the *makolo*. His capital was divided into *makolo* areas, and visitors to the capital had to stay in their own *likolo* area under their own *induna*. From the *likolo* the king could demand labour or demand that men carry out a raid.

There is some argument about the relationship between the two types of unit. For Gluckman (1941), the two types were distinct. *Silalo* were land units only. Officials in the *silalo* had control over land and land rights. The *makolo* were civil, judicial, political, administrative and military sectors into which one was born, taking one's father's *kilolo*. Tribute was paid via the latter units, but its members were widely dispersed. For Gluckman, two types of unit were needed, one related to the land and the other related to the people moving over the land, in a region where mobility was high.

Mainga (1973) disagrees. She gives the territorial *silalo* more importance, claiming that mobility was not high on the plain. Although there was some dispersal of the *makolo* kin groupings, each *likolo* had a main concentration which could often be related to the *silalo* units.

The Lozi kingdom or state was a large complex system with many levels. To control it, the king needed an ever bigger and more complex central administration. The *induna* administrators were recruited from the population at large. Children were chosen and brought up in the capitals. They were thus personally dependent on the king and they gradually took over control of the regional centres. There was much specialisation of activities within the *induna* bureaucracy.

But to feed and fuel this ever growing administrative machine, the king needed to expand his state in order to obtain control over essential resources such as iron. Some of these essential goods moved to the centre as tribute. In 1887 Coillard saw some of the range of goods which moved as tribute. 'Just now, one sees in every direction long strings of people laden with burdens...it is the king's tribute: honey, pelts, wild fruits, fishing tackle, mats etc. – the produce of the fields, of the chase, and of industry...The whole, brought to the court with great ceremony, is divided among the chiefs of the nation' (Mainga 1973, 138).

Another observer noted in 1895 'certain tribes must annually send the king a fixed impost of canoes, building wood, cattle, grain, milk, wild honey, fish, game, skins, iron spearheads, etc....' (*ibid.*). Archaeologically, it is of interest that most of the items moving to the centre are perishables. The main non-perishables, including pottery, are not redistributed in this way. There were no markets and pots could not be bought and sold in central fora. The greatest exchange of such items was reciprocal, at the local level.

Some of the tribute was usually redistributed to *indunas* who passed it on to their followers and dependents. The king's allocation of tribute to individuals was an important source of his power, while it also meant that he could redistribute localised commodities to areas in need. In addition, the king had a monopoly over long-distance Arab and European trade goods, which he redistributed in the same way.

However, certain goods were reserved for the king and royal family. Sanctions existed to ensure that the royal family was the wealthiest in the kingdom. It had a monopoly on all lion and leopard skins, certain parts of animals, including hippopotamus, one tusk of each elephant killed, and eland tails. The king could also demand free labour for personal and national projects.

Thus, around the Lozi plain there was a circle of conquered tribes paying tribute. Outside this was a further zone of tribes whom the Lozi raided and traded with. These provided important sources of slaves, for labour, and cattle. For example, thousands of cattle and slaves were taken from Ila and Toka. Gradually these tribes were brought into the inner sphere of regular tribute payers as the state expanded outwards. The Ila and Toka in the southeast and the Lunda and Luvale in the north were won over, and people from these areas came to live in the centre while Lozi villages were planted in, for example, Ila areas. The degree of political control decreased outwards. In peripheral areas there was less interference in local affairs, and all the surrounding areas became depleted, weakened and had relatively decentralised governments.

But what was the relationship between the different tribal groups as they came under the aegis of state control? There is evidence that distinct tribal territories became blurred with spatial mixing of villages belonging to different tribes. Also, cultural differences became less distinct, with much copying of Lozi face marks and cultural items (Hodder 1981). The widespread copying of the elite's language in the short period of Kololo domination of the Lozi in the mid nineteenth century is perhaps another example of the ease with which traits could be adopted. There was much exchange of products between tribes enjoying a symbiotic relationship in which there was little concern with the maintenance of distinct identities. The state encouraged everyone to think of themselves as Lozi and tried to give them equal economic and political opportunities. For example, the Mbunda began moving into the state in the early nineteenth century in small separate groups under the leadership of chiefs Mwene Kandala and Mwene Ciengele (Mainga 1973, 64). The king tried to absorb the Mbunda as Lozi and gave the two chiefs equal status as Lozi princes. They were given positions in the *kuta* and had their own royal residences, similar to the Lozi palaces. The Mbunda followers were allocated to *makolo*. However, we shall see that, more recently, there has been a reassertion of Mbunda separateness.

In the twentieth century, the organisation of the Lozi kingdom gradually changed. When a British Protectorate was established, the king gave up his rights to try theft, murder, witchcraft and some other offences, and later serfdom (1906) and tribute (1925) were abolished and royal officials were paid by the British authorities. A new centre, Mongu, developed as the commercial and administrative hub of the province and is now the provincial capital in western Zambia. Yet the royal centres remain, and remain important.

What is the modern relationship between tribes in the Lozi kingdom? The true Lozi are the Kwandi, Mbowe and Kwangwa. Closely allied and assimilated tribes are the Nkoya, Nyengo and Shanjo, while members of the Ila–Tonga group (including the Ila, Toka, Tonga, Totela and Subiya) also sometimes call themselves Lozi. In the past, the first three

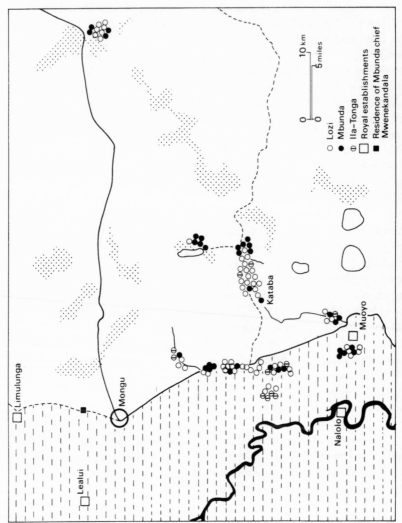

49. The distribution of Lozi, Mbunda and Ila—Tonga villages visited in the Mongu district. The seasonally flooded plain and *damboes* are dotted. *Source:* Hodder 1981.

tribes were not subject to raids by the Lozi but the Ila and Tonga were. Old Mbunda who immigrated from the west earlier in the nineteenth century have become largely assimilated and may at one time have thought of themselves as Lozi, but newer Mbunda arrivals, together with Luvale, Luchazi, Lunda and Chokwe, would never describe themselves as Lozi, to whomever they were talking. All the latter immigrants (called *wiko* by the Lozi) are termed Mbunda here, with a subdivision made between Old Mbunda and recent Mbunda, the second group being those who moved into the area less than two generations ago. Problems in the identification of the 'tribes' will be discussed below.

The field method used in studying these groups and their symbolic expressions was similar to that outlined in p. 18. Visits were made to 107 villages (figure 49), and drawings made and measurements taken of a representative range of cultural items. In each village, information was collected on the tribal affiliation of the inhabitants, the length of time the family had lived in the locality, the economy of the village, and marriage patterns.

Having previously worked in the Baringo area, I was struck by the fact that individuals in Zambia often seemed vague and ambivalent about their 'tribe'. In Baringo, people might change tribe, but at any one time there could only be one answer to the question, 'What tribe do you belong to?' In the Lozi area, on the other hand, individuals could at any one time claim to be members of either their mother's or father's tribe (although the latter was more common), and they could claim to be, for example, either Kwandi or Lozi. Some, I fully believe, were unsure of the tribal subgrouping (Kwandi, Toka etc.) of their spouses. Numerous different subgroupings were often represented in the same village and there was much intermarriage within the major Lozi grouping. The subdivisions have little importance today. It is this very weakness and fluidity of the tribal concept amongst the Lozi which is especially interesting, and it will be discussed further below.

In view of the difficulties in assigning individuals to tribes, it is the major division between Lozi and non-Lozi (Mbunda) which is used here, with a subset of the Lozi, the Ila–Tonga group, considered for comparison. There was never any confusion or uncertainty about whether a person was Mbunda or not, and this is the one division on which one can rely. In the frequent cases where mixed villages occurred at this more general level, the tribe of the village headman was taken in assigning tribal labels to the villages. This system provides the tribe of the central and main part of the village and the tribe of the majority of the occupants.

7.2 *Present-day cultural patterning*

A detailed analysis of the material culture of the modern Lozi is provided elsewhere (Hodder 1981). It is sufficient for our purposes here to make

Table 15. *The percentages of the artifact types owned by the different tribal groups*

	Lozi	Ila–Tonga	Old Mbunda	Recent Mbunda	Total
Village percentages	56·1	12·1	15·9	15·9	107
tubana	71·0	0·0	28·0	0·0	14
spoons	68·0	21·0	5·0	5·0	19
D baskets	67·0	12·5	11·5	9·0	24
mukeke wa kota	64·0	6·0	14·0	14·0	48
A stools	64·0	11·0	17·0	5·0	34
A, B, C pots	63·0	13·0	13·0	9·0	44
A baskets	62·0	10·0	12·0	15·0	58
chika	57·0	10·0	13·0	18·0	134
E pots	57·0	0·0	14·0	28·0	14
D, F pots	52·0	9·0	28·0	9·0	21
knives	45·0	19·0	15·0	19·0	86
B stools	44·0	9·0	18·0	27·0	43
spatulae	43·0	12·0	16·0	27·0	96
B baskets	36·0	0·0	17·0	45·0	74
C baskets	5·0	0·0	5·0	88·0	17

50. Artifacts from the Lozi area. Wooden bowls (*mukeke wa kota*), spatula (foreground) and spoon (centre), knife, A basket and B pot.

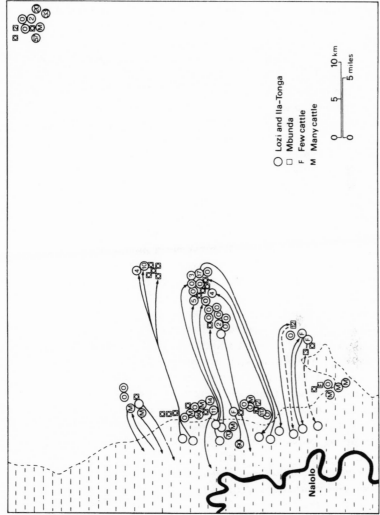

51. The numbers of cattle said to be owned by the villages visited, and recorded instances of movements of Lozi (solid lines) and Mbunda (dotted lines) cattle between bush and plain. The lines do not indicate precise routes. *Source:* Hodder 1981.

Nalolo

○ Lozi and Ila-Tonga
□ Mbunda
F Few cattle
M Many cattle

0   5   10 km
0   5 miles

a few general comments. Table 15 shows the percentages of a range of different artifact types found to be owned by the major tribal groups (some of the artifact types are shown in figure 50). The percentages of villages visited in these groups is also provided for comparison. Overall, there is clear similarity in the artifact types owned by the different tribal groups. Similarity is also found in the sizes and dimensions of several locally made items.

In explaining this general cultural similarity between the tribes, it is initially considered to be of interest that there is a marked symbiotic economic relationship between different groups in the Lozi kingdom. Many of the tribes have craft and economic specialities and are dependent on each other.

This exchange and symbiosis especially exists between the floodplain and the bush. For example, cattle are moved from the plain in the wet season, and then down into it again in the dry season (figure 51). In the dry season the cattle on the plain are looked after by friends and relatives of those who remain in the bush. In the wet season the cattle are taken back to their owners in the bush or to friends and relatives of those owners who remain on the plain margin. In exchange, the cattle provide manure for the fields. Their milk, however, is the property of the owners. Even people who do not own cattle can be involved in this cattle system.

Other specialities of the plain are maize and sweet potatoes and these move to the bush in exchange for cassava. Also, the plain produces good potting clays and the best pots, while the trees in the bush mean that the tribes there are the main producers of baskets and wooden containers. Gluckman (1941, 72) has catalogued the numerous specialities of the different tribes. For example, the Nkoya supplied beeswax for repairing wooden utensils, the Kwangwa provided hoes, fish spears, spears, axes, adzes, mats and baskets, the Lunda dugouts, and the Totela iron implements and honey. Generally there is little past or present evidence of conflict between the tribes within the kingdom, or of competition over resources. In the past, the presence of the king also helped to remove competition by providing an economic, administrative and juridical umbrella.

It is suggested here that, since each member of each tribe is involved in an exclusive symbiotic and non-competitive economic system, there is little need to express tribal differences symbolically. Rather, there is an advantage in demonstrating symbolic and cultural similarity with others in the same system. Thus the various Lozi and Ila–Tonga tribes are indistinguishable culturally and their tribal identities have become blurred. As already noted, many people were unsure of their tribal subdivision (Kwangwa, Kwandi etc.) within the Lozi and Ila–Tonga groups. There is also complete spatial mixing of villages of different tribes, and families of different tribes may live in the same village. Thus, in general in the Lozi kingdom, a symbiotic interdependent economic relationship in which there is little conflict of interests is associated with cultural blurring and similarity.

However, while this is true of most of the tribes in the Lozi kingdom, it is less true of the immigrant Mbunda. At present, the Mbunda *are* aware of their tribal affiliation, and they would never call themselves Lozi. Mbunda villages can be distinguished in that they more commonly have certain artifact types (the B and C baskets in table 15) and B baskets which occur in Lozi villages are smaller than those in Mbunda villages. In addition, Mbunda rarely own the 'spoons' (table 15). But such differences are not a result of a lack of awareness of each other's items. The symbiotic relationship results in intense interaction between Mbunda and Lozi. While Mbunda know of Lozi spoons, can describe them and could easily make them, 'they are Lozi objects and we do not have them'.

Why then, while most tribes have become culturally assimilated in the Lozi kingdom, have the Mbunda retained a certain distinctiveness? It is suggested here that the Mbunda are more 'visible' archaeologically because there *is* some degree of conflict of interests between Mbunda and Lozi. The interaction is competitive and the competition has three main sources.

1. The numbers of cattle owned by each village were assessed in the fieldwork. Although it is extremely difficult to obtain such information, it is quite clear (figure 51) that Lozi have large numbers of cattle compared to the Mbunda. There is some evidence that Mbunda are sometimes involved in the cattle system in that they look after Lozi cattle and use them to manure their fields but the important distinction is that Mbunda rarely own cattle. Cattle are an important source of wealth and the Lozi have always had a cultural and economic concern with them (Prins, pers. comm.). The inability of Mbunda to obtain this cattle wealth is the first conflict of interests.

2. One reason why the Mbunda do not have access to cattle is that they are not allowed to own the rich grazing lands on the plain. The Lozi in that area can control how many Mbunda cattle are allowed to graze there and they can thus determine how many cattle are owned by Mbunda. In more general terms, the plain provides a more productive, although riskier, soil than the bush. Thus the second source of competition between the Mbunda and the Lozi and Ila–Tonga is that access to this land is restricted to the latter two groups.

3. A third conflict of interests concerns iron. The areas with iron ore are confined to the bush. Iron is essential for working the matted peat in the plain (Prins, pers. comm.) and so was essential for the Lozi. Also, the restricted distribution of this resource gave the Lozi elite an opportunity for centralised control. The ore mining and iron production (for example, at Kataba) were controlled by the king. Individuals obtained metal by working for it in the iron production centres or by

exchange of goods at these centres. Mbunda were often involved in this work as skilled smiths, but the resource remained under the control of the Lozi elite.

It is to support and justify this present conflict of interests over cattle and land, and in the past over iron, that Lozi and Mbunda have retained a cultural distinctiveness more than other tribal divisions. The pattern of the cultural differences between the tribes relates, not to the intensity of interaction between them, but to the nature of that interaction and to the degree of economic competition. The competition and strain between the Lozi and Mbunda *wiko* (a pejorative term used by Lozi to describe Mbunda) is especially marked nowadays because of the relative weakness of the royal elite. As the modern Zambian administration gradually replaces the royal power, a few subject tribes have tended to assert themselves against the Lozi for political ends. Some tribal identities are more strongly felt (Turner 1952, 39). The Lunda and Luvale (both 'Mbunda' tribes) have been granted independence, and the Nkoya have made similar demands.

The distinctiveness of the Mbunda is also seen in the marriage pattern that was recorded during the fieldwork. Most individuals in the Mbunda group, whether Luvale or Chokwe, marry other Mbunda. Most people in the Lozi and Ila–Tonga groups marry amongst themselves, but seldom marry Mbunda. It is difficult to see these marriage patterns as the cause of the cultural patterning. Individuals *can* marry across tribes, and one Lozi man may marry both Lozi and Mbunda women. The marriage pattern is seen here as expressing the same underlying world view as the material culture distributions. This is a world view which contrasts Lozi and Mbunda and in which the uneven access to resources is justified.

Gluckman (1949) has provided a clear example of how this Mbunda–Lozi dichotomy can play a part in a wide range of activities. Gluckman discusses a Mbunda circumcision ceremony in the Lozi area. The ceremony is concerned with the 'rite of passage' to manhood. Throughout, material culture plays a symbolic role. For example, 'men dress as women to assert their common loving care for the children' who are to go through the pain of circumcision (Gluckman 1949, 160). After the circumcision, 'the fathers gave spears, symbols of manhood' to the novices who 'buried their skirts, sticks and head-dresses under water' (*ibid.*, 159). Masks and fibre dresses are worn by the males involved in the ceremony.

Although the circumcision ceremony is about the 'coming of age' of young men, Gluckman shows how it is transformed into symbolic acts expressing the dominant conflicts in society. In particular, the tensions between male and female are played out. But also, the ceremony plays a part in supporting Mbunda (*wiko*) opposition to other Lozi tribal groups who do not practise circumcision. The ceremony takes place in a 'lodge'.

> What was very marked was the hostility of the *wiko* in the situation
> of the lodge to their Lozi and Kwangwa neighbours...the true
> uncircumcised (*Banjenje*). Here the lodges definitely assert *wiko* pride
> and culture against the dominant people among whom they have
> settled. One song went: 'the Lozi come today, men seize your guns'.
> The men delighted in threatening...Lozi with 'cutting', and told
> us stories of how they had frightened Lozi intruders into tears. Twice
> I saw *wiko* fiercely threaten with axes Kwangwa passing on paths
> near the lodge...In Barotseland the *wiko* circumcised probably
> glorify the lodge additionally against the uncircumcised foreigners
> because they live amongst those who despise them (*ibid.*, 152).

Thus even a circumcision ceremony becomes significant as a 'tribal'
symbol because it is the ethnic boundary which is one of the dominant
tensions in *wiko* and Lozi society.

There is thus intense interaction between the Mbunda and Lozi. Many
Mbunda look after Lozi cattle in the bush in the wet season, and the
Mbunda craftsmen make many pottery (E, D and F pots), basket (A
basket), wooden (B stools, *chika*) and metal items (knives) for the Lozi
(Hodder 1981). There is continual daily contact. Yet we cannot use the
interaction hypothesis here and assume that all material culture traits
will reflect the intensity of information flow. The competition and
restriction which lie behind the interaction involve each side in a
rejection of the other and in a conception of difference which is
maintained and constituted in some aspects of material culture.

A fuller understanding of the role of material culture differences in the
relations between Mbunda and Lozi can be obtained by comparing the
present with the past. It has already been suggested that in the nineteenth
century, and especially at the height of Lozi expansion, the king
encouraged Mbunda to think of themselves as Lozi and gave them
certain rights and privileges. But the basic restriction in access to
important resources (cattle, the better land and iron) that has been
described above has long existed. There is some evidence (Hodder 1981)
that in the past the material culture differences between the Lozi and
Mbunda were less marked. This similarity in the past relates not only
to the adaptive decision of the Mbunda to integrate into the Lozi society
and economy, but also to a strategy of the Lozi elite involving masking
and hiding of real differences in access to rights. The material similarities
between the Lozi and Mbunda were manipulated ideologically by the
elite. More recently, with the decline of the elite's power, material
differences have been stressed as part of a different ideology which is
concerned with reinforcing tribal rights and justifying between-group
tensions. We cannot examine the material culture patterning in the Lozi
area simply in terms of degrees of interaction or degrees of between-group
competition since social and ideological factors also play a role.

Apart from the interaction hypothesis, another theory that came to be
criticised as a result of the Baringo work concerned the relationship

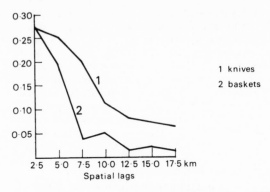

52. Values of spatial autocorrelation (I) at different spatial lags (distance bands) for (1) lengths of knife handles, (2) widths of baskets of B-type. *Source*: Hodder 1981.

between the scale of production of craft items and the distribution of the styles of those items. Further support for those criticisms comes from the Zambian work.

7.3 *Production and distribution*

As we saw in chapter 4, a number of archaeologists (e.g. Phillips 1975; Whitehouse 1969), including this author (Hodder 1978), have assumed that the nature of localisation of the production and dispersal of cultural items is related to stylistic variation. Thus it is often supposed that great stylistic variation over space reflects dispersed small-scale production and dispersal, and widespread conformity indicates specialised and centralised production.

This relationship was first examined for the Lozi data by assessing the degree of spatial autocorrelation in different traits. If nearby values of some variable are more highly correlated than distant values, there is said to be spatial autocorrelation. The I coefficient was used to assess autocorrelation for measurements of several artifacts in table 15. The most significant results (under the null hypothesis of randomisation) were for the lengths of knife handles and widths of B baskets (see also p. 115). However, the fall-off in spatial autocorrelation with increasing distance is more gradual (and bell-shaped, see figure 52) for the knives than for the baskets. It is of interest therefore that, while many knives are made and obtained from outside the village of use, nearly all B baskets are made in and remain in the same village. However, this clear relationship between the scale of production and dispersal and stylistic variability is disturbed by the A baskets. These exhibit significant evidence of spatial autocorrelation at $2 \cdot 5$ km (lag 1. $p = 0 \cdot 05$) and yet they are mainly obtained from travelling hawkers and from outside the village of use.

Spoons and spatulae are usually made and used in the same village and their distributions indicate localisation of traits on these items. *Chika* (grain pounders) are both made for village use and are widely exchanged and they show localised styles. *Mukeke wa kota* are widely traded and show widespread similarities. However, the E type of pot which is frequently exchanged between villages also shows style localisations.

The Zambian evidence thus supports the Kenya results (chapter 4) that preferential movements of traders and localised consumer demands *can* lead to localised stylistic traits on widely traded items. Equally, in certain social contexts, localised village-based manufacture and on-site use can produce widespread conformity in styles. In the Lozi context it has been suggested that there is generally little competition between most tribes. As a result, the styles of most items do reflect the nature of their production and dispersal. Few constraints are in operation which might disturb this relationship. In a more highly constrained context in Kenya the relationship is more frequently and clearly broken. Locally produced items show great conformity over wide areas. It thus becomes very important for the archaeologist, working back from the cultural evidence to the society which produced it, to compare the spatial pattern of stylistic variability of items with independent evidence for the scale of their production and dispersal. If the archaeologist wishes to examine social and economic constraints on individuals and groups, he cannot assume that stylistic patterning reflects either the nature of production or of interaction in any simple way.

7.4 *Status symbolism*

Ethnic groups may have a high intensity of contact, but the nature of that contact may be very competitive. Certain cultural items may be used to support and justify the identity differences. In figure 53*a* are schematically depicted three social groups in competition for scarce resources, with distinct cultural differences and with internal mechanisms leading to boundary development and within-group conformity.

We have seen that the presence of a strong and fully developed state umbrella over such groups may be associated with a lessening of overt between-tribe differences. The umbrella of the state encourages coexistence and a decrease in open conflict near its centre, and material culture is involved ideologically in masking or hiding inequalities and tensions between tribes (figure 53*b*).

In addition, conflict may be redirected as the dominant tensions in society change. The economic and political tensions in a highly centralised political system often involve conflict between levels and elitism as much as conflict between tribal groups and ethnicity. This is shown diagrammatically in figure 53*c*.

Certainly the Barotse elite maintained control of a range of basic

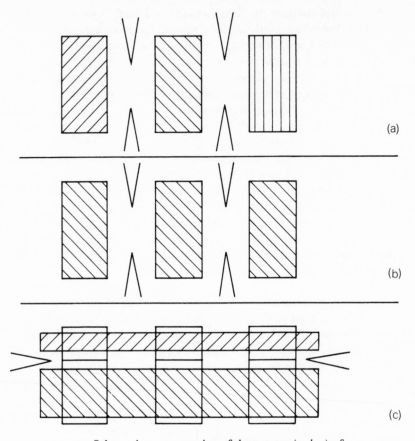

53. Schematic representation of three types (*a, b, c*) of
relationships between different groups. Very marked cultural
distinctions are shown by different types of shading. Arrows
indicate major loci of competition. *Source*: Hodder 1981.

resources. For example, in the past they controlled iron deposits, had legal
control of all land, controlled large herds of cattle, and controlled much
of the long-distance trade. The elite's unequal access to limited resources
was symbolised and reinforced by a series of distinctive cultural traits.
For example, double clapperless bells (*ngongi*) are awarded by the king
and queen of the Lozi to Lozi and Mbunda statesmen, royal hunters,
blacksmiths and so on. These objects are handed down within families
long after the death of the individual to whom they were awarded. They
are most frequent in villages near the royal centres.

Other artifacts such as feather crowns, eland tail fly-switches with
specially carved ivory handles, and in the past ivory wrist bangles, were
also the property of particular sets of high status or wealthy individuals
in the kingdom. In addition, special gifts such as elaborate painted pots
were given by the king and queen to specially honoured subjects.

But how does this patterning change as tensions decrease and increase between hierarchical levels? As King Lewanika's kingdom expanded in the later nineteenth century, tensions built up between the king, his elite, and the rest of the population. As the kingdom expanded and became more complex, it became more and more important for the king to stress his status and rights. He became ever richer and more distant, and more and more symbols were used to characterise him. For example, Coillard in 1895 writes (Mainga 1973, 140) that at the royal court 'for three days they discussed the question of stools, and of certain ivory and bead ornaments which the people have had since Sipopa's death...Lewanika confiscated and forbade them, except for the use of the royal family'. It was decided that only the royal family could use the stools. This is a good example of the way in which material culture distinctions may become more clear-cut, and the dominant tensions in society more 'visible' to the archaeologist, as those tensions increase (see also chapters 2 and 5). 'The more pronounced the social and political stratification in any kingdom, the larger the number of ways it is expressed materially, to preserve, reinforce and legitimate the distance between upper and lower groups' (Dalton 1981). Dalton lists some of the ways this is done in Africa – size or shape of houses, fences of distinct shape or materials (the Lozi palace compounds are easily identifiable by pointed stakes placed in the perimeter fence), type of weapon, hair style, scarification, jewellery, metal collars, the carrying of batons, the wearing of official green or red, the king's messenger carrying a rooster or wearing a state sword with a golden hilt. The Lozi example shows how the dominant group may consciously and carefully manipulate material symbols in order to justify and legitimate its power.

But is it the case that elites are always reflected in material culture as in the Lozi example, and is Dalton right in making direct behavioural links between stratification and material differentiation? It seems not, since elites may manipulate and negotiate the use of material symbols in many subtle ways. For example, under a different ideology of legitimation which denied the real power of the elite, material differences might be played down and decreased as social stratification increased. Turner (1969) gives examples such as that of Gandhi where political power is associated with the use of symbols of humility and non-differentiation. I will discuss further aspects of the relationship between ranking and material culture in chapter 9, but for the moment it is sufficient to note that we should not be led by the Lozi and some other African examples to assume deterministic and direct links between status and material symbols. Clear 'reflections' are often found, but as with the relationship between interaction, competition and regional cultural differentiation, the nature of the link between material and social ranking depends on the local historical context and on the attitudes and intentions of those involved. In the Lozi case, the intentions of the elite were to legitimise their power by emphasising the material differences. In this way the special right of the royal family to power, and their divine ancestry, became more acceptable and 'natural'.

7.5 *Within-site patterning*

The importance of attitudes and intentions in the relationship between material culture patterning and social relations is also seen in a very different sphere amongst the Lozi – in the styles of pottery made and used in the villages. The Longacre–Deetz–Hill hypothesis that matrilocal residence of female potters leads to localised pottery designs within sites has been widely questioned (e.g. Allen and Richardson 1971; Longacre 1981). Certainly, in a Lozi village, the continual reuse of huts and the changing occupants would blur any original pattern. But how is learning carried out, and if localisations within villages occur at any one time, are they the result of residence rules and learning networks?

Only one village could be examined in sufficient detail and had sufficient pots to allow such patterning to be studied. In the village in figures 47 and 54 three women who make pots for their own use were interviewed. The Subiya wife of the Nkoya headman living in compound 1 had been taught by her mother before moving to the village. She made several pot forms including B-type jars, all painted, and with width and height measurements shown in figure 55. Her daughter-in-law living in compound 2 (figure 54) made similar jars. They were of similar dimensions (figure 55), were also painted, and used the same distinctive and unique motif of scatters of isolated red-painted triangles. However, she had *not* learnt potting from her mother-in-law. She had learnt before coming to the village, but had obviously copied, or been copied by, her mother-in-law.

A reverse pattern is found for the woman living in compound 3. Married to the brother of the headman, she *had* learnt to make pots in the village by watching the other two. Yet her pots were different – unpainted and slightly different in dimensions (figure 55).

Thus, at the time the village was visited, two different style groupings occurred. These groupings are not the result of matrilocal residence (residence here is virilocal) nor are they the result of the learning network used. So why did the woman who had learnt from others in the village make different pots, while the women who had learnt potting in different outside villages made similar pots? In the village studied there was a noticeable degree of antagonism between the oldest man – the headman – and his brother (the husband of the woman who made unpainted pots in compound 3). This antagonism was reflected in bad relations between his wife and the two other women. Indeed, north of the headman's house (1) and that of his favourite son (2) we always met considerable resistance so that it was never possible to visit houses 4, 7 and 8. This situation had

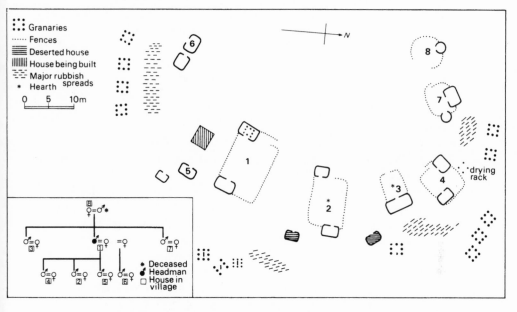

54. Plan of a Lozi village in the Zambezi floodplain (see figure 47). The numbers refer to the individuals in the inset diagram. *Source*: Hodder 1981.

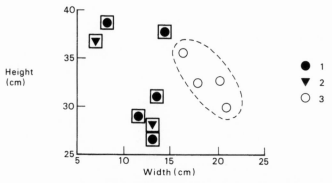

55. Widths and heights of pots from the village in figure 54. Numbers refer to houses in the village. Symbols in squares represent painted pots. *Source*: Hodder 1981.

occurred because our initial contact had been made with the other, southern, half of the village. Related to this antagonism within the village, the woman in house 3, although she had learnt to make pots by watching women in the southern half of the village, made them differently. The friendship and common feeling between the women in the southern half of the village was supported in the similar pots they made even though they had learnt the craft in widely separated villages.

Thus, even at the local within-village scale, it is not possible to discuss stylistic variability without taking into account the individual's perception of social relations and tensions, and the symbolic nature of material culture. Styles will only reflect learning networks and interaction patterns in certain forms of context, and in the particular instance described here styles contradict the learning networks. As was noted at the end of the last two chapters, symbols play an active, not a passive, role in social relations.

At both the village and the regional scales, Lozi material culture patterning relates not so much to degrees of interaction as to the adaptive strategies of economic competition and restriction of access to rights and resources. But it was shown in chapters 5 and 6 that the type of adaptive strategy chosen by ethnic units does not simply correlate with the pattern of available resources or the pattern of economic relationships. Internal social strategies also play a role, as is again evident in the Lozi example. The presence of the royal elite affected the adaptive strategies chosen by the Lozi tribes in that they were persuaded towards non-competitive economic and social integration. But the way that material symbols are involved in such strategies partly depends on the ideological context and on attempts made to justify or to hide the nature of the relationships between groups. At the height of Lewanika's reign, material culture similarities were used to mask the restricted access to rights of the Mbunda group while, at the same time, material culture differences were used to naturalise the elite's superordinate position. Today, with the decline of the elite, the various Lozi tribes use material symbols to support their economic interdependence and to reinforce and justify the competition with the Mbunda. Within a Lozi village, pottery styles justify and support the family tensions and relationships. In all these instances, ideologies can be seen to play a part in determining the relationship between material culture and adaptive strategy.

8
Dirt, women and men: a study in the Nuba Mountains, Sudan

The preceding ethnoarchaeological studies have shown how overt boundary maintenance between tribes, status levels, age-sets, sexes and families plays a part in economic dependencies and social interactions. For example, in certain contexts, increased competition between groups for scarce resources is associated with more distinct cultural boundaries. But it has also been suggested that the reason why tensions are channelled into boundary expression at all may derive from the internal organisation of societies and the attitudes and intentions of the interacting groups. In the Baringo example (chapter 5), the concern over boundary maintenance can be related to the internal tensions between old and young men and between women and men. The internal organisation of Lozi society, on the other hand, encouraged in the past fewer examples of spatial, ethnic dichotomies and many of the overt differences concerned 'vertical' status dichotomies.

In chapter 1 it was suggested that one of the reasons for the adoption of the view in prehistoric archaeology that material culture reflects behaviour lies in a trend towards interpretations which refer to function and adaptation. Material culture is seen as functioning between man and his physical and social environment, so that predictable links can be set up between behaviour and material residues. So far in this book interpretation has mainly concerned adaptation and function. Within such a framework, it is now clear that if predictable links do occur between material culture patterning and social and economic behaviour they are very complex because of the ideological manipulation of material symbols. In all the ethnoarchaeological examples, material culture reinforces, emphasises or masks certain aspects of information flow as part of ideologies which support, justify, legitimate or disrupt the adaptive strategies of groups within societies. An adequate notion of the role of material culture in adaptation must integrate ideologies.

Realisation of the importance of ideology in interpreting material residues immediately seemed to suggest further questions. After the ethnoarchaeological studies described above, a major aspect of material culture patterning remained unexamined. If so much depended on ideas and ideologies, what determined the form of those ideologies, and what determined the way in which they were integrated into social and ecological relationships? Might not the ideologies actually play a part in forming the adaptive strategies?

A lack of interest in form is evident throughout most of the preceding chapters, although in the discussion of the Baringo calabashes (chapter 4) this further dimension of symbolism was recognised. Why is it that calabashes are decorated in the first place? A symbolic principle concerned with purity and pollution was suggested as being of relevance. But why are other artifact types not decorated in the same way? Hearth positions vary from tribe to tribe in the Baringo area (chapter 3), but why are hearth positions used to mark ethnic differences whereas the shapes of the hearths are not? And how are the particular hearth positions (left, right, centre) chosen in each tribe? From such questions it can be seen that two problems concerned with material culture form have remained largely neglected in the studies so far: first, why are particular artifacts chosen to symbolise one thing rather than another, and second, why does a material culture trait (hearth position, calabash decoration) have a particular form within the constraints of its utilitarian functions?

Attempts have been made to answer the first question by reference to the history of the artifact. Through time a trait comes to have a particular significance which affects its later use (see, for example, the Maasai traits used by the Dorobo (chapter 6), and the Baringo spears copied by the *moran* (chapter 4)). But such an answer is unsatisfactory in that it merely pushes the problem back in time. How did the trait come to have that history at all? I have also tried to answer the first question by noting the use of items as symbols in the strategies of groups and individuals within societies. Thus the reason why spears are used to disrupt the Baringo boundaries is that they are associated with young men (chapter 4). But again, such an answer shifts the focus of the question without really answering it. We are still unclear as to why spears were given their symbolic significance by young men in the first place, in the same way that we are unclear about why hearth positions are used in boundary maintenance and not hearth shapes.

The questions 'Why decoration?', and 'Why this or that position of a hearth in a hut?' require fuller answers than that the traits are used strategically in internal and between-group relations. It is necessary also to examine symbolic principles which lie behind the production of material traits. It is the additional problems posed by these two types of questions which will be examined in this chapter. It will be found that, in answering the questions, discussion will be led into a reassessment of the viewpoints that material culture patterning 'reflects' human behaviour and that the patterning can be adequately explained in terms of the adaptive strategies of social groups. In the ethnoarchaeological studies

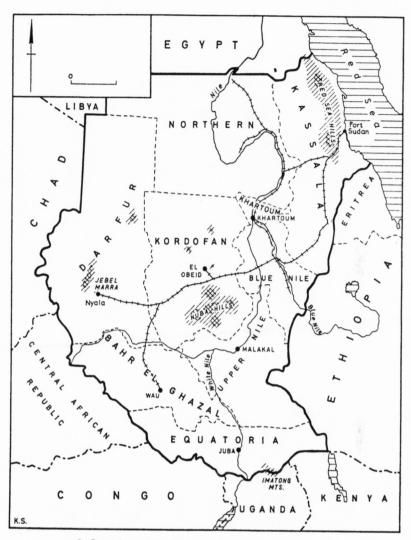

56. Location of the Nuba in Kordofan, Sudan.

so far, too much emphasis has been placed on the 'ecological' relationships between individuals, groups and societies.

8.1 *The Nuba*

The Nuba Mountains are isolated massifs standing above the plains west of the White Nile (figure 56). The basically negroid people inhabiting these hills consist of numerous loosely related 'tribes' and tribal sections. Although there has been a considerable amount of recent migration down from many of the hills (Roden 1972), the Nuba are traditionally

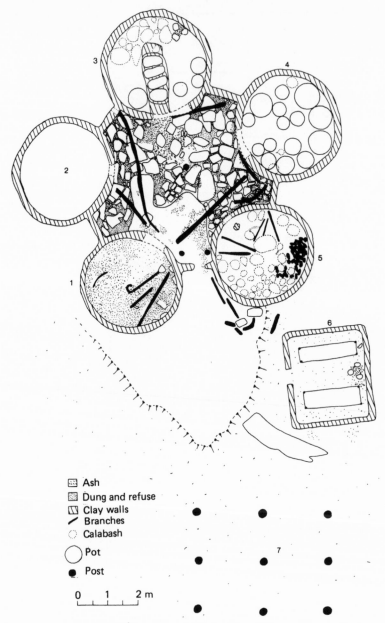

Ash
Dung and refuse
Clay walls
Branches
Calabash
Pot
Post

0   1   2 m

57. Mesakin Qisar compound (Reikha); 1 = previously a
sleeping hut; now often used for keeping chickens. 2 = granary.
3 = grinding hut with four stone querns set in a clay support;
pots and calabashes. 4 = pots and a few calabashes for the
storage of water, alcohol and sesame seeds. 5 = previously a
granary; now used for storing calabashes, baobab fruit, and
female items of personal decoration. 6 = sleeping hut for men.
7 = raised platform for drying sorghum, beans and hay.

associated with isolated hill-top communities, and it is these latter groups which are discussed here. The hill refuges were sought as a result of raids on the Nuba by Baggara nomads and Mahdist armies. Each major hill holds a dispersed hill community, the individual house compounds being scattered amongst the terraced fields. These hill communities are divided into named sections but the main unit of social and economic life is the compound – a cluster of individual houses (sleeping, storage and work huts) belonging to one family (e.g. figure 57).

The economy of the Nuba is based on hoe agriculture in which both men and women play a part. The main crop is sorghum and the farmland can be divided into three types (Nadel 1947). Near the compound are the terraced 'house farms'. Here is grown maize, millet, early maturing sorghum, as well as melons, gourds, cucumber and tobacco. On the lower slopes of the hills, the 'hillside' farms, also terraced, are used for late maturing sorghum and sesame. Three to five miles from the compounds, out on the plain, the 'far farms' exploit the black clayey 'cotton soils' which are deep and self-mulching. Here is grown early and later maturing sorghum, sesame, groundnuts and cotton. Beans are sown everywhere with grain. Although there is some shifting cultivation, especially on the hillsides and plain, most fields are now used and inherited within families over long periods. The house farm fields are regularly manured with cattle and pigs and are kept permanently under cultivation. They are mainly the concern of women. The far farms are worked by both sexes but the men play the larger part.

The yearly cycle involves fairly continuous labour, carried out by group work of family, friends and neighbours, with the host for each day, on whose farm labour has been concentrated, providing *marissa* beer (made from sorghum) as 'payment'. The main rains (average annual rainfall is 700–900 mm) fall from late April to mid October, and this is the time of the main planting, weeding and early harvesting. Harvesting, threshing, winnowing and storing take up the remainder of the agricultural year though work is lightest from January to March, the period of the major dancing, feasting and wrestling matches.

The Nuba also keep cattle, pigs and goats. Cattle are looked after by young men between puberty and 22 to 27 when they build their own homes and enter into full marriage. The young men, who do little work in the fields, take the cattle down into the plain in the rainy season although some families give their cattle to nomad Baggara during this period. Amongst the Mesakin Nuba, Nadel (1947, 67) recorded individual properties of two, three, five, ten, twenty and thirty head of cattle. Cattle are only killed for meat in major ceremonies, especially funerals (see below), but they are handed on as part of kinship obligations as in the paying of bride-price in certain tribes. Pigs remain around the compound throughout the year and are largely cared for by women. The same is sometimes true for goats, but these may also be taken with the cattle.

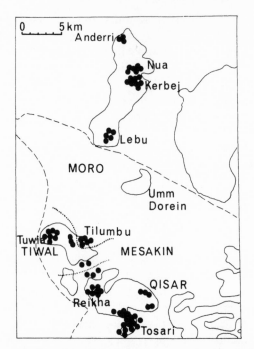

58. Location of the house compounds visited on the Moro and
Mesakin hills. Dirt roads (dashed lines) and divisions between
tribes (dotted lines) are shown.

The Nuba do not form a homogenous unit. There is great diversity
from tribe to tribe, and from community to community in language
(Stevenson 1962; 1964), social structure (Nadel 1947), degree of acceptance of Islam and Christianity, details of economic practice, and
material culture. The work to be described here concerned three tribal
groups among the southern Nuba, southeast of Kadugli – the Moro,
Mesakin Tiwal and Mesakin Qisar (figure 58).

The Moro, numbering about 20,000 in 1940 (Nadel 1947) and more
than 30,000 in 1971 (Roden 1972, 80) inhabit three large hill ranges
rising 400–600 m above the plain. The westernmost range examined in
this study runs north–south and is cut by a series of high level valley-like
depressions running east–west and cutting the range into blocks. The soils
in the hills are variable, often rocky and poor but sandy loams in the
depressions.

According to oral traditions this westernmost Moro hill range was the
first to be inhabited, with the village at Lebu (figure 58) being the
original home. Linguistically, Moro is attached to the large group of
Koalib–Moro speakers which occupies the central spine of the Nuba
Mountains (Stevenson 1957). However, the Moro have little sense of
tribal unity and until recently they had no common name for themselves;

59. View of a partially deserted village in the Moro hills.

60. Part of a Moro village with a compound of huts in the foreground.

Moro is an Arab name. Individuals consider themselves primarily to be 'Lebu' or 'Nua', that is, members of a named hill community. But, nowadays, neither Moro nor Mesakin are ever ambiguous about the tribe to which they belong.

Each hill block is densely settled with dispersed compounds and

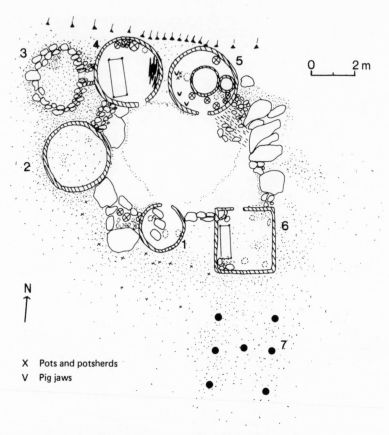

61. A Moro compound. For symbols see figure 57. Unlike many
Mesakin compounds the interior of the Moro compound is clean
except for small scatters of broken calabashes along cracks in the
rock and around the edge of the courtyard. The entrance to the
courtyard is across the wall between huts 1 and 6: 1 = grinding
hut containing three saddle querns. 2 = disused hut, previously
for sleeping. 3 = pig pen with an opening leading under hut 4.
4 = hut containing bed and clay hearth with pots on stands on
either side of the hearth. 5 = granary containing one large and
one small silo. Pig jaws are hung in the roof. 6 = hut containing
bed and corner hearth. 7 = posts for a 1.70 m high platform on
which beans are dried.

terraced house farms (figures 59 and 60). Although these communities
are divided into individually named sections, each forms a continuous
area of dense settlement approaching 'villages' or even 'hill towns'. The
northern villages, and in particular Anderri, have been affected by down
migration. Lebu, however, has been little affected by such desertion
(Roden 1972).

Each Moro hill community comprises numerous patrilineal exogamous

62. A Mesakin compound (foreground) with covered central
courtyard, similar in type to that in figure 57.

clans. Most marriage is monogamous, and since sons build their houses
near their fathers, clans are localised. Until the development of the official
system of *meks* and local *sheikhs*, there were no acknowledged tribal
leaders.

The Mesakin, numbering about 8,000, live in lower hills (rising 200 m
above the plain) to the south of the Moro. Scattered amongst these rolling
hills are very extensive and dispersed settlements. Because of the lower
relief, less effort needs to be placed in terracing of the house and hillside
farms. The Mesakin again have no clear sense of tribal unity and they
have been divided into two named groups by the Arabs – the Mesakin
Tiwal (meaning the high or long Mesakin) and the Mesakin Qisar (short
Mesakin). While linguistic differences between the two groups are fairly
marked, other distinctions are less clear-cut (see below). The Mesakin
Tiwal are divided into an eastern half (the 'upper' Tummi) and a 'lower'
western half called Tuwia. Each half speaks with a slightly different
accent.

Mesakin Tiwal and Qisar compounds form tighter clusters of houses
than the Moro (figures 57, 61 and 62), but the compounds themselves
are much less densely packed and agglomerated in the landscape. Living
in each compound is a man, his wife (or wives) and either their unmarried
children or the children of the husband's sister. Men often adopt and
bring up the children of their sisters rather than their own children as
part of the matrilineal system. However, this rule is flexible, and many
families retain their own children. Mesakin clans are no longer exogamous.

Traditionally, chiefs had little importance, although today these largely acephalous groups have an imposed system of government-appointed sheikhs who carry out judicial and administrative duties.

8.2 *Regional patterning in material culture*

Seventy-three compounds were visited amongst the Moro, Mesakin Tiwal and Qisar (figure 58). Information was collected on the manufacture, distribution and ownership of pots, calabashes, baskets, spoons, spears, knives and items of self-decoration. Details of the painted decoration of houses were collected as well as data concerning the function and inhabitants of the different parts of the compound. Questions were asked concerning eating habits and avoidances, the dispersal of refuse, and burial practices. In addition, cemeteries are visited, recorded and plans made (figure 63). The nature and organisation of the subsistence economy in different areas were examined, and the nature of inter-tribal and inter-community relations, exchange and intermarriage was assessed.

Houses

Each compound of houses is used by a man and his immediate family, although often a separate compound is built for each wife. In all three tribes the compound consists of a ring of houses joined together by connecting walls. Amongst the Moro these connecting walls are low and of stone, with a brush fence along the top. It is thus easy to see into a Moro compound from the outside. This is not the case amongst the Mesakin Tiwal and Qisar. These build 2 to 2·5 m high clay link walls and place a roof of branches over the central compound. The Mesakin houses themselves are built largely of clay, 0·3 m thick at the base and thinning towards the top. Often the base of the wall is built of dry stone and this tendency is more pronounced in the higher and rockier Moro hills where much or all of the house walls may be built up in stone blocks. Amongst the Moro the houses are often built above pens and tunnels for pigs. One section of the central courtyard is built 0·5 to 1·5 m below the main surface. From this the pigs are able to run through tunnels underneath the courtyard into pens beneath the houses (figure 61).

The composition of the Moro compounds is highly variable and it is difficult to identify a common scheme. An example is provided in figure 61. The central courtyard, entered through a simple break in the circuit fence, is the main eating, cooking and living area and is kept clean. Where there is a lower pig section within the courtyard this is usually between the houses to the left of or opposite the compound entrance. The number of houses in a compound varies from two to seven. In the case where there are only two huts, one is a granary where the wife sleeps and in which there is a small area for grinding grain into flour on hollowed saddle

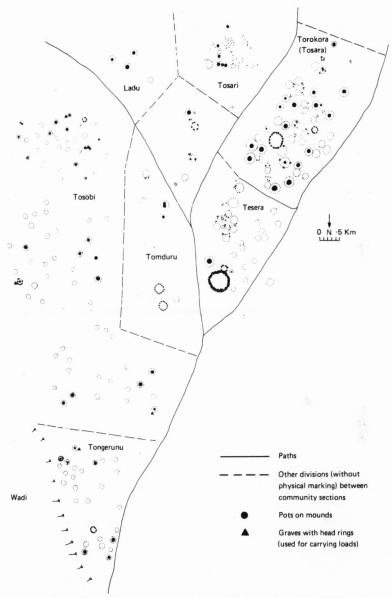

63. Mesakin Qisar cemetery at Tosari. Dotted lines define grave mounds.

querns, the other is for the man and perhaps the children. As the number of houses increases in a compound, so the number of granaries increases, while separate huts may also be built for grinding and for the wife to sleep in. One compound with six huts contained two granaries, one grinding hut, one sleeping hut, one cooking hut, and one hut for the calves. A

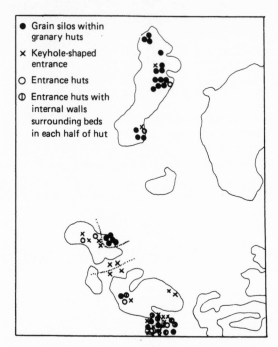

● Grain silos within
  granary huts

× Keyhole-shaped
  entrance

○ Entrance huts

◑ Entrance huts with
  internal walls
  surrounding beds
  in each half of hut

64. The distribution of compound construction traits.

compound with seven huts contained a wife's sleeping hut, a man's and
his son's hut, a granary hut in which goats were also kept, two further
granaries, a lower hut for pigs, and a grinding hut. However, the function
of huts is continually changing (cf. David 1971) in relation to the
changing size, wealth and age of the family.

The Moro, unlike most other Nuba tribes, store their agricultural
produce for more than one year. Large silos are built within the granaries
which can hold the grain for four years (figure 64). Each silo is a cylinder
on clay feet, covered at the top except for a small entrance which is
usually plugged with a pot. The major, central, silo in each granary is
for sorghum while there may be up to three smaller silos at the back of
the granary for beans and sesame.

Grinding is done on stone querns set in clay in the hut floors. Where
the grinding is carried out in the granary, the quernstones are set near
the entrance within a cleaned area marked by slight clay ridges.
Sometimes small separate grinding huts are built in which is found a row
of three or four quernstones (cf. figure 61: 1).

The compounds of the Mesakin Tiwal and Qisar show less variation
than the Moro. Unlike the Moro, who sometimes attach compounds into
larger agglomerations, the Mesakin compound is always isolated and
tightly closed. The main forms are shown in figure 65. The A-type with
five huts and a simple keyhole-shaped entrance through the linking wall

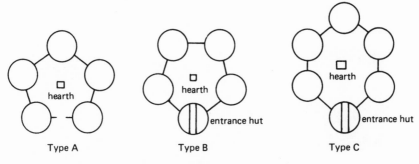

65. The main types of Mesakin compound.

is by far the most common. In addition, there is evidence of a development from the B-type to the A-type since several B examples were found in which the outer wall into the entrance hut had been closed off and a new entrance cut through a connecting wall. Although the A-type normally has five houses, cases with four or six also occur. In addition to the ring of huts there is sometimes an extra hut outside the main entrance and usually used as a man's sleeping hut.

The entrance huts, like the entrances through the connecting walls, have keyhole-shaped entrances to the exterior and interior. A passage leads through the centre of the hut with beds for guests, women and children on either side. These beds are sometimes enclosed with high clay partition walls and in some cases there is a roof hung from the partitions (figure 64). The interior walls of the entrance huts of the Mesakin Qisar are often covered in isolated panels of geometric decoration. The exterior of the hut is brilliantly painted on the wall facing into the courtyard and there is often some decoration on the outside wall.

The Mesakin granaries rarely have any interior silos. Rather, the granaries are simple huts with clean floors and extremely small circular entrances (30–35 cm across), 1·2–1·5 m above the ground. The grain is simply piled on the floor. Grain is also stored in large pots in the storage hut (figure 57:4). This hut has clay rings around the edges of the floor on which stand pots, often sealed, for keeping water, sorghum gruel, sorghum beer and grain. There is a remarkable uniformity in the relative placing of the pots in the storage huts. In particular, the first pot on the left on entering a Mesakin Qisar hut is a small-mouthed water jar behind which are arranged large wide-mouthed storage bowls.

The Mesakin grinding huts are considerably more complex than their Moro counterparts. Running diagonally across the centre of the hut is a raised clay platform into which is set a row of three to five saddle querns (figure 57: 3). Between this platform and the entrance is a further stand for a water jar and the oval entrance itself also includes a pot stand on its lip (figure 66a). The flour is placed in pots, but is also piled against

66. House front decoration. (*a*) = Mesakin Qisar. (*b*) = Mesakin Tiwal. (For the distributions of these two types see figure 69.) (*c*) = decoration around a shower in Mesakin Qisar. Other panels of decoration (Mesakin Qisar) are shown, not to scale.

the interior hut wall. The wall above the piled flour is burnished blue-black and surrounded by an arc or rectangle of raised cordon decoration (figure 67).

Each Mesakin compound normally contains two granaries, one storage hut, one grinding hut and one sleeping hut. Some regularities in the relative positioning of the huts in the most common A-type compound are suggested in figure 68, in spite of the fact that huts are continually changing in function. There appears to be a trend in which grinding huts

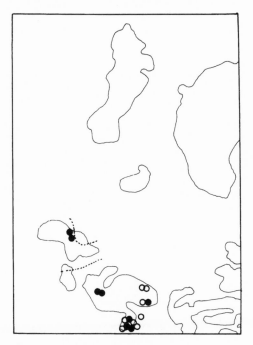

67. A distribution of compound construction traits: ● = the depiction of breasts on house fronts. ○ = grinding hut with band of repoussé decoration surrounding an area of burnished wall. These features occur where the flour is placed against the wall.

are found farthest from the entrance towards the back and right of the compound. Huts for sleeping are more common near and to the left of the entrance. Between these interior and front sections, the middle section contains most of the storage huts. Granaries can be found in any position. Thus, moving from the bottom left to top right in figure 68, three sections seem to occur. But there is also a cross-cutting division between the top left and bottom right halves. Almost without exception, one granary occurs in each half. One of these granaries is associated with the male, the other contains the grain which has been allotted to the wife. The man and the woman's granaries face each other across the courtyard. Of all granaries in the top left section, 75% belong to the man, while 82% of the granaries in the bottom right belong to women. Similarly, when men and women eat together in the courtyard they eat off separate plates in the separate halves. It is of interest that spears are always stood against the connecting walls in the left, 'male', half of the compound, while the shower (see below) always occurs in the 'female' section (figure 68). This type of division of settlement into male and female halves is recorded by Nadel (1947, 323) for the Tullishi Nuba whose village contains a male (east) and female (west) section. Children and young men are forbidden

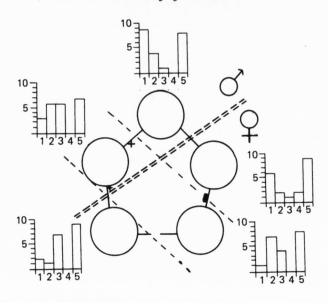

1 = grinding hut
2 = storage hut
3 = sleeping hut
4 = goat hut
5 = granary

68. The frequency of hut positions in the Mesakin compounds.
Vertical axis of graphs = frequency of huts. Horizontal
axis = type of hut. Crosses mark the places where spears are
usually stood, and the position of the shower is shown by a filled
rectangle. For the division of the compound into male and female
see text.

to cross the Tullishi boundary and people from the eastern section must
walk clockwise round a certain hill standing on the boundary, while
people from the western section will walk round it anti-clockwise. It will
be shown below that similar symbolic expressions of the male–female
symmetry occur in other aspects of Mesakin material culture.

The central, covered courtyard is surrounded by decorated walls.
Amongst the Mesakin Tiwal this decoration consists of raised cordon
decoration with zig-zag incisions or rows of finger impressions in the
cordons. The Mesakin Qisar, however, often paint the walls facing into
the courtyard in brilliant red, black, blue and white designs (figure 66).
These occur chiefly in panels above and to the side of the hut entrance.
The panels are bordered by cordon decoration containing wooden pegs
above the entrances on which are hung a bewildering array of personal
items, pots, calabashes, animal jaws, digging sticks and so on. The pegs
represent horns and are sometimes replaced by them. Within the

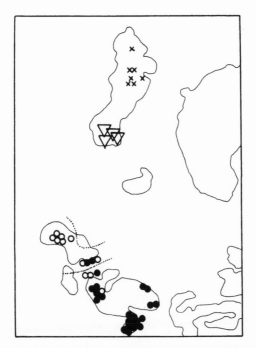

69. The distribution of compound construction traits: ∇ = roof apexes surmounted by ceramic collars with small protuberances on the handles. × = forked stick roof supports. ● = painted house decoration (as in figure 66*a*). ○ = repoussé decoration on houses without painting (as in figure 66*b*).

decorated panels and immediately round the entrance hole is an expanse of dark blue burnishing. This glaze is achieved by rubbing clay and graphite on the wall with the fingers.

The house construction, the plastic decoration and the blue burnishing are carried out by men. The painted designs are done by young men and girls. Nadel (1947, 179) records how painting the granary amongst the Heiban Nuba occurs when the granary has been successfully filled, and it certainly seems to be the case that the Mesakin painting is concerned with fertility symbolism within the context of the male–female relationship. The only decorative motifs in the area of blue burnish around the hut entrances are frequent depictions of human breasts (figure 67). Yet the symbolism in the panels which surround this central female area is explicitly male. The designs are those which are found painted and scarred on male bodies only. The markings found on women's bodies never occur painted in the panels, even though this painting is often done by women. Symbolically, then, male symbols enclose the female area around the entrance to the huts. Further aspects of the symbolism of the wall decoration will be discussed below.

Between the huts, isolated panels of geometric decoration usually occur on the link walls, sometimes with depictions of animals, birds, men and, rarely, aeroplanes. One of these panels usually has especially complex decoration, including cordons surrounding two cattle or antelope horns set into the wall and holding a wide-mouthed bowl or calabash. When the receptacle is filled with water and tipped forwards, this feature acts as a shower (figure 66c). The shower is located to the right of the compound on entry, between the two huts nearest the entrance (figure 68).

The distributions of certain compound construction traits show marked localisations. For example, the apexes of the roofs are sometimes covered by a multi-handled clay collar. But only in the southern Moro at Lebu are the handles of these pottery collars covered with small protuberances (figure 69). On the other hand, forked sticks placed in the wall exteriors to hold the roof struts are found only amongst the northern Moro (figure 69). Various motifs of wall decoration are also fairly localised amongst the Mesakin (figures 67 and 69), while the building of partition walls around the beds in the entrance hut is only found frequently in southeast Mesakin at Tosari (figure 64). Wider distributions occur for keyhole-shaped entrances (mainly found amongst Mesakin) and for silos within granaries (mainly found amongst the Moro) as is shown in figure 64. Thus many of the traits connected with compound construction do not occur in distinctly separate areas – there is overlap at both local and regional scales. That this spatial variation may have a temporal aspect is suggested by Nadel's (1947, 181) record that entrance huts are normal amongst the Moro. Figure 64 shows that today entrance huts are largely confined to the Mesakin, especially to the southeast Mesakin. It is possible that the change from the use of entrance huts has gradually diffused through the area over the last forty years.

Pottery

Three functional classes of pottery are found in the areas studied. (1) Globular narrow-mouthed jar (figure 70: 2) used for water carrying and storage. These pots are also sometimes used for mixing water with flour. (2) Wide-mouthed bowls. Larger examples are used for storing grain and *marissa* beer. The smaller are used for cooking and as 'showers' in the compounds (figure 70: 1). (3) Necked pots with everted rims (figure 70: 3) are used for storing beans and sold to the Baggara Arabs. The Baggara are known to prefer this form of pottery and the Nuba often make pots specially for them. Despite this general classification, pots may have multiple uses and be reused in different ways.

In the tribes studied, all potting is by women, using the abundant local clays. However, the degree of centralisation in pottery manufacture varies from tribe to tribe. For example, in Mesakin Qisar, of the forty-one pots for which the information could be collected, thirty-six had been

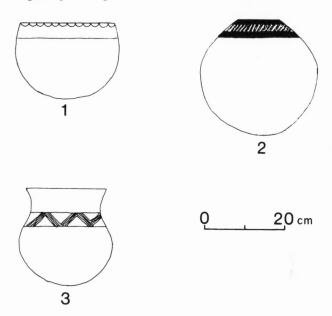

70. Pottery types: 1 = wide-mouthed bowl. 2 = globular jar of Kaji type. 3 = necked vessel.

made by a woman living in the compound in which the pot was kept and used. Only five had been obtained from women outside the compound or from outside the community. In Mesakin Tiwal, comparable information could be obtained for fifteen pots. Only two of these had been made by a woman living in the same compound, the rest having come from elsewhere in the community or from other tribes such as the Moro (Lebu) and Baggara. Amongst the Moro, six pots had been made by women in the compound and twenty-one from outside the compound in the same hill community. Only one case was found of pot exchange between Moro hill communities, further emphasising their isolation.

The more dispersed nature of production in Mesakin Qisar is also seen in the location of potting hollows. These are small smooth depressions used for moulding the base of the pot and as a support for the pot construction. Amongst the Moro they occur in groups in clay surfaces which form part of 'workshops' 30–80 m from the compounds. Groups of women work together in these workshops and provide most of the pottery for at least part of the hill community. But amongst the Mesakin Qisar, the individual hollows are dispersed, located between and near the houses.

The greater degree of centralisation of pottery production amongst the Moro may occur because the higher concentrations of Moro population made specialisation in pottery production more viable. In view of the different scales of organisation of pottery production amongst the Moro

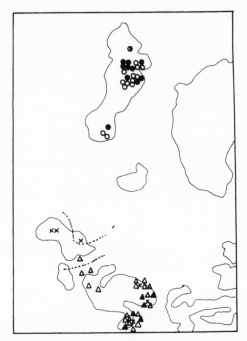

71. The distribution of types of pottery. ● = the Kaji type as in figure 70: 2. ◐ = as the Kaji type but without central band of cord decoration. ○ = pot form as a Kaji type but with only one zone of burnishing around the rim. △ = wide-mouthed bowl with decoration as in figure 70: 1. ▲ = as figure 70: 1 but with a line of arcs added below the straight incised line. × = plain wide-mouthed bowl with two opposed lug handles on rim.

and Mesakin, the archaeologist might have expected greater stylistic uniformity in those pots produced as a result of the centralised Moro system. Unfortunately such patterning does not occur.

Pots from the two tribes were measured. The distribution of a Mesakin type of cooking pot decorated with an incised wavy line around the rim above a continuous straight line (figure 70: 1) is shown in figure 71. For the Moro, a type of water jar with a band of cord decoration between two bands of burnish around the rim (the Kaji type to be discussed below and illustrated in figure 70: 2) is shown (figure 71). The standard deviations for the mouth diameter, height and maximum body width (cm) are 3·16, 2·88 and 3·92 for the Mesakin type ($n = 20$), and 1·60, 3·79 and 3·61 respectively for the Moro type ($n = 33$). Thus the detailed measurements are not consistently more varied for dispersed production than they are for more centralised production.

A similar conclusion is reached if the design distributions are examined (figures 71 and 72). There is a certain amount of clustering of designs in closely spaced hill communities, these designs being found less

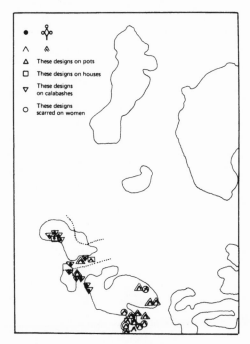

72. The distribution of design motifs.

frequently with greater distances between communities. There are no sharp boundaries and the distributions do not always respect tribal borders. The scale of style clustering is similar in both Moro and Mesakin Qisar. Thus, the scale of production and dispersal, and the organisation of potting is difficult to trace from stylistic studies. The localised distributions of pottery styles may help to reinforce feelings of community identity, but the relative lack of contact between communities (see p. 152) may also be a significant factor. A Mesakin Tiwal potter said that she was ignorant of the decorative traits on Moro pots.

In the adjacent Kerbej and Nua communities amongst the Moro, two separate workshops occur at about 80 m from the nearest of the scattered compounds. During the period in which one of these workshops was studied (December 1978) three old women made pots there. At other times in the year, when there is less work in the fields (January to March), they are joined by other women. No work is carried out in the rainy season. The potters informed us that young girls may start to make pots before they are 10 years old by watching women in their own and other families. The mothers of potters are often not potters themselves, and generally there is no restriction on who makes pots and on who may watch and copy a potter at work.

At the Moro workshops pots are not made to order, but are made in sufficient numbers to supply the needs of the customers who come to the workshops. Some types are put aside for Baggara (p. 142). A very large storage pot is sold for 50 piastas (about 50p) and a small pot for 10 piastas. Alternatively, one to three baskets of grain may be exchanged for the pots.

Potting clay is obtained from near the workshop, especially from ant hills. The red clay which is used to provide a fine red coating to many of the pots is also obtained from preferred localities near the workshop. The clay is pounded and mixed with water and grass. Thin clean grass is then placed in the base of a potting hollow and the sides of the pot built up from the original clay lump with the aid of a pebble. After drying, further building up of the walls produces a regular spherical form. After decoration and burnishing, the pots are left out to dry fully in niches between rocks, in hollows or under trees. Firing occurs in a bonfire 20 m from the workshop.

The decoration for water pots preferred by the leading Kerbej potter (Kaji) at the workshop visited is uniformly used by her associates. Two lines of burnishing near the rim are separated by a band of cord impressions (figure 70: 2). The latter are made with a string wrapped in a spiral around a small stick which is pressed into the clay. All the women in Kaji's workshop, as well as all the other potters in the Kerbej–Nua agglomeration make the same general design (figure 71), but there is some minor variation. For example, one woman in Kaji's workshop applies horizontal cord decoration, while another prefers an oblique arrangement. But, on the whole, there is a remarkable lack of interest in attempting new designs and ideas. We showed Kaji alternative designs which she said would be 'better' than her own and she said that she would attempt designs if they were shown to her by another woman. But she was not willing to experiment herself. Similarly, she was aware that other hill communities made different designs but she was not willing to copy them.

The general sense of community conformity in pot styles seems to occur even when designs do change. About 5 to 10 years earlier Kaji *was* asked by men and women in the community to change the decoration 'since the previous design was considered old'. In such a context she *did* change the details of her decoration and all the other potters in the community immediately and abruptly followed suit. It is of interest that such conformity occurs even though there are no sanctions on which women make pots. The corporate identity is spontaneously expressed.

As potting is exclusively the work of women, so it is women who mainly use the pots in cooking, storing and carrying water. A man living on his own may have no pots 'because he has no wife'. In parallel with this association with women, the decorative symbols on the pots are often explicitly female. Distinctively male symbols never occur. For example, as suggested in figure 72, a design found scarred on women's bodies (figure 73: 6) amongst the eastern Mesakin Qisar is frequently found on pots. Since pots are associated with women, care must be taken that pots

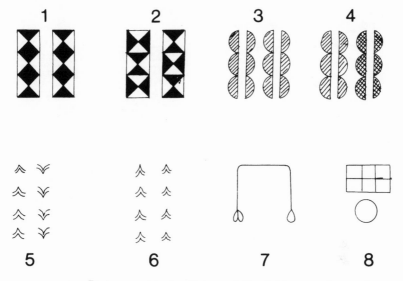

73. Designs used in the Nuba and Cambridge experiments (see text).

do not become 'polluted' (see below). Thus women do no potting during menstruation.

Broken sherds have long and multiple uses as, for example, pot covers, water containers, feeding receptacles for chickens and pigs, props to support the roof. So larger sherds (greater than 10–20 cm across) are kept within the compound in convenient corners for long periods of time in case there may be some use for them. It is only the smaller sherds (averaging 3–9 cm across) which become incorporated into general household rubbish inside (Mesakin) or outside (Mesakin and Moro) the compound. As already noted (p. 137), many pots have fairly fixed relative positions within the compound. When a compound is deserted, many pots, especially the larger ones set on stands, are left where they are and are not removed by human scavengers. Their ultimate within-site distribution provides an accurate representation of their positioning at the end of the compound's life.

Calabashes

Two types of calabash container are found in the area studied. The first is an open bowl used for eating sorghum gruel and beans (figure 74: 2 and 3). Deeper 'bottles' are used for drinking *marissa* beer and water (figures 74: 1 and 75). Designs are incised and burned on both forms.

The majority (70%) of decorated calabashes are made by men – usually men less than 30 years old. The greater the degree of decoration on calabashes, the more explicitly are they made and owned by men. Especially at major feasts, the men are 'served' by the women, the food

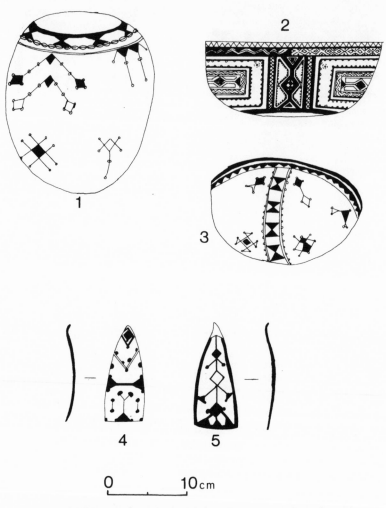

74. Decorated calabash drinking bowl with a line of cowries below the rim (1), calabash eating bowls (2 and 3), and spoons (4 and 5).

and drink being brought in the calabashes. The women may also use them to take food and drink to men working in the fields, living in the cattle camps or participating in the wrestling and stick-fighting. These highly decorated calabashes may take 5 to 10 days to make. Many of the less decorated bottles and bowls are made by women. In any case, the line of cowrie shells, beads or buttons is usually placed around the rim of the calabashes by women (figure 51: 1).

Many decorated calabashes are given by male relations and friends to younger men and women on marriage and some are exchanged as gifts between young men and women before marriage. Thus the majority of

75. A calabash 'bottle' of the Mesakin Qisar.

76. Calabash spoons of the Mesakin Qisar.

calabashes are involved in young male–female interchange – either as gifts at or before marriage or in some form of 'serving' of young men by women. This role of calabashes as part of male–female play is seen in the calabash designs which often clearly show sexual acts. However, all the geometric designs on the calabashes are 'male' in that they are the same as those found scarred on mens' bodies.

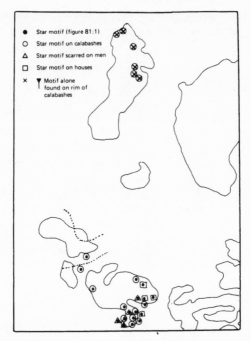

77. The distribution of design motifs.

Calabash spoons (figures 74: 4 and 5 and 76) are highly decorated with
the same male motifs as are found on the calabash containers and male
bodies. These highly decorated spoons only occur amongst the Mesakin
(figure 78). Over 90 % are made by men – usually by youths in the cattle
camps. They are used by both men and women for eating. A young man
will either retain the spoon he makes or give them to girls and future
wives. Thus a girl may receive many spoons before marriage.

The distributions of calabash designs (figures 72 and 77) show
localisations within the tribal areas. Many of the informants were
conscious of the fact that certain motifs were distinctive of certain village
communities or sections of those communities. However, the data show
that most of the localised motifs are copied peripherally so that there are
no clear boundaries around the communities. The same movement of
calabash styles occurs at tribal borders. In the village of Tilumbu in
northern Tiwal (see p. 153), the western half is Mesakin Tiwal and the
eastern half Moro. But certain very distinctive traits occur on calabashes
in both halves of the community. The scale of style localisation in figures
72 and 77 relates to the degree and scale of cooperation and dependence
in community labour. Even in divided Tilumbu, individuals from the two
tribes cooperate in the fields.

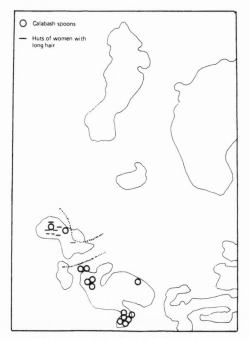

78. The distributions of calabash spoons and long, shoulder length hair. See figure 74: 4 and 5 for spoons.

8.3 *Explanation of regional patterning*

The main characteristics that can be identified in the regional distributions of the cultural traits discussed above are localised and overlapping spreads with neither clear nor congruent boundaries. Traits are frequently concentrated and sometimes restricted to one hill community or to neighbouring hill communities. This is especially clear in the distributions of design motifs (figures 72 and 77), the same localised motifs occurring on pots, calabashes and scarred on bodies. Within communities, neighbouring compounds are more similar than distant compounds. The same scale of localisation as noted for the trait distributions discussed above occur in other distributions, including some hair styles of women (figure 78). Men and women wear metal rings in different positions in their noses (including the central nasal spine) and ears. The lower lips of older women are often perforated. Many of these items of self-decoration show great spatial variation and some clear localisations. For example, the placing of large numbers of small rings in the outer margin of the ears of young women is especially common in Tosari in southeast Mesakin Qisar. The material culture localisation and variability relates to the high degree of linguistic variation (Stevenson 1962; 1964).

In attempting to understand the observed pattern, the nature of the contact and interaction between communities must first be considered. In general there is much less movement between hill communities in Moro than in Mesakin. In Moro, all informants had been born in the hill community in which they now lived. This was true of both men and women, and only one person knew of another individual who had not been born in his hill community. This isolation is due both to the abruptly sectioned terrain and to the sense of stability and continuity amongst local patrilineal Moro groups cooperating through time in intensive agriculture. However, it will be shown that most Moro would be willing to accept other Nuba into their society. In addition out migration has led to the movement of young people down onto the plain rather than across between the hill communities.

Nadel (1947) notes that the adoption of wives amongst the Moro is partial and incomplete, further indicating the sense of separation of patrilineal groups. The degree of isolation is demonstrated by the fact that most informants had no acquaintances in neighbouring hill communities and had never travelled out of their own hill range. It was rare that Moro had ever visited Mesakin.

Amongst the Mesakin, on the other hand, a third of the informants knew of individuals in their community from another Mesakin community. Yet the actual number of these moves of habitation remains small. There is less down migration and the terrain is less rugged than amongst the Moro, and this may partially account for the greater inter-community movement. It is also possible that matrilineal descent associated with virilocal residence leads to greater movement and wider networks. But at death, wives that have married into a community are sent back for burial in their own community. This custom emphasises the isolation of matrilineal groups and the temporary links that are established between them.

The variation in material culture within the area examined may thus relate to the relative lack of contact between the different communities. Yet since there is *some* contact, this hypothesis seems insufficient. If there was a social and ideological need for between-group, 'tribal' conformity, there is sufficient contact to allow the diffusion of traits. That the traits do not diffuse despite contact – however limited – suggests that feelings of identity and opposition may exist at the scale of the hill communities. Nadel (1947, 244–6) has demonstrated that Moro stick-fighting occurs between hill communities and sections. In the past there was real warring between the communities. The lack of a sense of tribal unity, and until recently the lack of tribal names, suggest that identification is mainly with the hill community and it seems that some slight competitive feeling exists today at this scale. The localised cultural patterning may reinforce the sense of local community coordination in intensive agricultural labour. But the scale of between-community competition over resources, especially agricultural land, is not high, and the cultural boundaries or discontinuities between localised groups are not exceptionally marked; there is much overlap and blurring.

Whereas the pattern of movement within tribes indicates slightly more flux in Mesakin than in Moro, an examination of between-tribe relations suggests the opposite. The Mesakin feel significantly more closed to Moro newcomers than do the Moro to the Mesakin. All Moro informants agreed that Mesakin would be welcome to come and live in their hill community. The sons of Mesakin men who had lived amongst the Moro and married a Moro woman would be considered Moro. On the other hand, only one Mesakin informant felt that Moro would be welcome in his community. If the Moro do move into the Mesakin hills, they usually move as a block, forming an enclave on the edge of the hills (as at Tilumbu, see below), and are not considered Mesakin by the Mesakin. Questions were also asked as to whether men from other tribes could be buried in a community's cemetery. Again, all Moro replied that Mesakin could be buried in their cemeteries and that they would be accorded the traditional rites of the Moro community. The Mesakin were equally adamant that Moro could not be buried in their cemeteries. The Mesakin are thus much more closed to tribal outsiders. This difference perhaps relates to many aspects of the beliefs and world views of the two tribal groups to be discussed below, as well as to differences in the compound forms. The Mesakin compounds are tightly clustered with high walls. There is an emphasis on entrance into the compound with special entrance huts, decoration around specially shaped doorways, and enclosed courtyards. The Moro, more 'open' and less concerned with tribal outsiders becoming insiders, have simple entrances (small gaps in the light surrounding fence), low walls and less 'closed' courtyards.

The Moro and Mesakin tell of nineteenth-century wars and raids between them (cf. Nadel 1947, 259). Such a level of aggression no longer occurs. The present relationships between the two tribes are perhaps best exemplified by the Tilumbu community in the Mesakin Tiwal hills. The Moro inhabitants came to their half of the community in about 1962 from Umm Dorein, attracted by the soils and the availability of land for fields. Until recently Moro family groups from the same community at Umm Dorein continued to arrive at Tilumbu.

Up to 1978, six Moro men in Tilumbu had married Mesakin women from the other, Mesakin, half of the community (although no Mesakin men had married Moro women), but five of these marriages had ended in separation, the women returning home. This pattern may be the result of an incompatability between the matrilineal and patrilineal systems of the two tribes. While the Moro would allow Mesakin women to be buried in their cemetery (each half of the community having its own cemetery), the Mesakin would not accept that their women be treated in a similar way. In life the claims of the matrilineal descent group of the wife would be in conflict with the patrilineal claims of the Moro husband.

Stick fights occur between the Moro and Mesakin at Tilumbu and there is some stealing of goats across the community boundary. Generally, however, economic cooperation in the fields is high. Moro and Mesakin work together throughout the year in the changing agricultural tasks. Dances are held together and the Moro inhabitants of Umm Dorein now call their offshoot 'Mesakin'.

There is little evidence (figures 64, 67 and 69) which indicates a clear material culture difference between Mesakin Tiwal and Qisar. For example, the distribution (figure 69) of types of house decoration shows a gradual and broad overlap. But some traits do show a distinction between Mesakin and Moro. No Moro houses have painted or relief decoration in the central courtyard, and decorated calabash spoons do not occur amongst the Moro. Even at the local level at Tilumbu, the Moro/Mesakin material culture distinctions are maintained in certain traits (figures 72 and 78). However, some designs on calabashes are common to both halves of the community and the youth of Tilumbu are now bilingual. Many of the most rigid and distinct differences between Moro and Mesakin, both at Tilumbu and on a wider scale, concern traits related to different attitudes to pigs and cleanliness in the two tribes. Amongst the Moro, jaws are hung out of sight of the central courtyard; they are openly displayed amongst the Mesakin. Moro compounds are clean with the pig pens placed beneath the courtyard. Mesakin compounds are often dirty with the pigs and other domestic animals free to move around within the circle of huts. Resistance to the between-tribe diffusion of traits associated with pigs, cleanliness, women and purity will be shown in the sections that follow to occur because a range of traits are embedded within the different conceptual schemes of the Moro and Mesakin. We cannot fully understand the lack of movement of traits until these conceptual structures have been examined.

In discussing between-tribe relations it is also necessary to examine the contacts between the Nuba and the Baggara Arabs. Raiding between these two groups on the plain was one reason for their initial flight into the hills. These wars are remembered by the Nuba especially since there continues to be a certain amount of competition between them and the Baggara nomads for land on the plain. Several Nuba informants complained about the way Baggara herds harmed their crops. Despite this competitive relationship, a few Baggara shops have now appeared on the margins of the plain selling sugar, salt, oil etc. In addition, some Nuba give their cattle to Baggara on the plain in the rainy season. There is also a considerable exchange of Baggara metal items (knives and spears) and pots for Nuba sorghum, sesame, beans and groundnuts. It has also been shown (p. 142) that Moro produce specially shaped pots for the Baggara. In spite of this flow of goods and the symbiotic economic relationship, there are clear barriers to the flow of stylistic traits. House types and pottery forms are kept rigidly distinct. Nearly all Nuba were

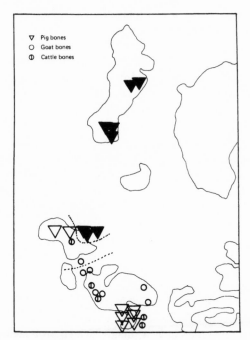

79. The distribution of compounds containing the jaw or skull bones of pigs, goats and cattle. Filled symbols = the placing of bones inside the granary. Open symbols = the placing of bones outside the granary.

adamant that Baggara should not live in their community, nor build Nuba houses, while burial in a Nuba cemetery was impossible. Only one instance of a mixed marriage was recorded. Baggara–Nuba relations in the area studied are thus symbiotic but competitive (contrast the situation described in chapter 6). There is some economic interdependence and a movement of traded goods, but less movement of distinctive stylistic traits.

8.4 *Within-site patterning: bone refuse*

In all three tribes, animal bones are often thrown outside the compound to the dogs. The only bones in the compounds are jaws and skulls of pigs in the Moro and jaws and skulls of pigs, goats or cattle amongst the Mesakin (figure 79). In the Moro the head bones are hung from the roofs inside the granaries, usually near the door, or placed under the eaves of the roof above the granary entrance. In both cases, the bones are invisible from the centre of the Moro compound. But amongst the Mesakin, the jaws and skulls are hung openly in front of the granaries (usually the granary of the owner of the animal) on the rows of wooden hooks on which many personal items are displayed. The head bones (rarely replaced by other parts of the skeleton) thus look into the compound, although in a few cases they are hung on the outside wall of the compound. This difference in the visibility of the head bones relates to the greater emphasis on display in Mesakin society, as is seen in the decoration of the houses, the decoration of the self, and the exhibition of personal items on the hooks above the hut entrances.

Various verbal justifications were given for the retention of animal head bones within the compound. Several wives said that they did not throw out the head bones with the other bones since the pigs would start eating them and then 'eat live chickens and goats'. Other informants stated that it was disrespectful to throw away the skull, and that keeping the head bones ensured that another pig would be obtained. It was frequently claimed that the skulls commemorated the special events at which the animals were killed.

The hanging of skull bones could simply be interpreted as a display of wealth and of the generosity inherent in the giving of feasts at which animals were killed. But this explanation cannot account for the close association between head bones and granaries, nor for the fact that the Moro jaws are extremely difficult to see at all. Several informants noted that the pig or cow jaw bones have a 'magic' which protected the grain in the 'holy' granary. In fact there seem to be a number of rites concerned with the granary entrance, such as pouring *marissa* beer over it or hanging up plants with magical properties above it. The successful storing and reproduction of the grain is a major concern in these intensive agricultural societies. The jaws are part of the ritual protection of the grain and they also encourage future fertility. More generally, amongst the Nuba, the boundary surrounding an area or object over which there is great concern is 'ritualised' with signs of death, generosity and wealth, the better to preserve it.

Similarly, men and women cover themselves with ash at various stages in the harvesting and handling of sorghum grain, while the young men paint themselves in ash during the Mesakin harvests. In these cases, ash is used explicitly to ensure the fertility of the grain and to prevent spoiling or 'pollution'.

Amongst the Moro, pigs play an important part in a man's marriage payment. He will often pay two or three pigs as part of his dues, while amongst the Mesakin, cattle and goats but *never* pigs are paid. It is of interest, then, that the Moro hang up pig bones (figure 79), while the Mesakin also hang up cattle and goat skulls. Cattle feasting plays an important part in burial ceremonies (see below).

Meat-eating and particular bone refuse thus mark conceptual boundaries both in space and time. In space, the jaws are placed at the boundaries around the grain, and in time, the yearly festivals associated with grain are the occasions of the main pig and cattle feasting.

But the interpretation of the head bone distributions as guardians of the grain is incomplete because there is also evidence that the relations between men and women are involved. In both Moro and Mesakin societies there is a strong sense of purity and cleanliness. One of the major sources of impurity is conceived of as menstrual blood and great care is taken that women do no work and handle no food during menstruation. In some Moro clans the first menstruation of girls is marked by a five day seclusion (Nadel 1947, 198). More generally, there are severe eating taboos between men and women, husband and wife, and husband or wife and their respective parents-in-law. Amongst the Moro a woman may not eat with her husband and his brothers until the ceremonial first meat-eating. Amongst the Mesakin, the restriction on men and women, husband and wife eating together may be retained throughout their lives. But even amongst the Moro, a man will always eat first and out of a separate bowl, and the husband and wife often eat in their own halves of the compound or in different huts.

The uncleanliness of women is reinforced by their association with pigs, which are considered dirty. Women look after pigs, including those of their husband. Amongst the Moro women may eat in or near the pig pens. Yet women also play a large part in the production of grain, and they carry out all the processing and cooking. It seems probable that the ritual and concern surrounding grain partly relates to fear of impurity through contact with women. The skull bones on the granaries may act to prevent spoiling and to ensure future fertility. It will be shown below that aspects of compound decoration, including male sexual symbols and recognisable 'bogeys', have a similar significance – to ward off the effects of female impurity. In one Moro compound pig skulls were found in a hut other than the granary. The husband claimed that the bones had been put there 'because his wife cooked in it'.

It is of interest that the grain is symbolically protected both by symbols of male purity and strength (cow skull bones; see below) and by the bones of pigs which are clearly associated with women and with dirt. Purity and fertility can be assured either by safeguarding the entrance to the granary with the clean, or by confronting impurity with the unclean.

This pattern becomes clearer if other aspects of bone refuse are examined amongst the Mesakin Qisar. In this group, while younger men eat cattle meat and drink milk, it is only older men who eat pig meat (the discussion being confined to traditional non-Muslims). There is an absolute distinction between pig and cattle meat, especially amongst men. The unmarried men who spend much of their time in cattle camps or with cattle cannot eat pig 'otherwise their cattle will die'. This prohibition on pig-eating continues into the early years of marriage, often until two or three children have been born. After this time a man may begin to eat pig and will stop drinking milk.

During the time of absolute prohibition on pig-eating, the wife is able to eat pig but not at the same time as she drinks milk, and she eats pig apart from the men and probably away from the compound. However, she cannot drink the milk of her husband's cows nor of her own cows nor of her own families' cows. She drinks the milk of other families' cows and if milk is brought into the compound and she drinks it, she then refrains from eating pig for a short period. The Mesakin have a feeling of disgust and repulsion at the very thought of letting women milk goats or cows. Men think that their teeth will fall out if they drink milk from cows which have been milked by women (Nadel 1947, 61).

When an older man begins to eat pig, the distinction between the products of cattle and pig is retained. This can be seen by following through the process of killing, cutting up, eating a pig and discarding the bones.

The pig is killed by being stabbed under the left foreleg. Because many pigs are eaten in the dry season (from February to May) when the cattle are kept near the compound, pigs usually have to be killed away from the compounds. This is also the case for the next stage – burning off the hair on a fire, opening the stomach and cleaning and eating the intestines. However, these activities may be carried out in the compound if the cattle are far away.

The pig is then cut up and boiled, again well away from any possible contact with cattle. If the pig is to be eaten by the family it is cut into five portions if it is small and seven portions if it is large. The five sections are obtained by removing the head and dividing the body longitudinally into three portions – the vertical region or 'back' and the two sides with attached limbs. The 'back' is then divided into two to produce five portions. The seven portions of a larger pig are produced by further dividing the vertebral region. If the pig is large and guests are present, then portions are produced by cutting the vertebral region into three and separating the limbs from the side sections. There is no indication that different parts of the carcass are reserved for particular individuals. For example, meat from the head and jaws can be eaten by anyone. The fat is mixed with beans and sorghum and eaten with the meat.

As already noted, the head bones are hung up on pegs outside granaries. Since pigs are only eaten by older men, the archaeological assemblages of bones in the compounds will vary with the age of the husband at the time of abandonment. In older men's houses in which both cattle and pig are eaten, the skull bones will usually be hung in separate places.

The remaining pig bones are thrown outside the compound if they are quickly removed and eaten by dogs and if there is no chance of their having contact with cattle. However, in order to ensure no contamination of cattle by pig bones, the bones are often stuck in crevices 40 m or more from the compound. Equally, since pigs are always present around compounds, the cattle bones are also placed out of their reach in the same way. But the cattle and pig bones have to be placed in separate locations.

So the bone refuse pattern of the Mesakin Qisar is distinctive. Within the compound are found only skulls and jaws. These occur in association with the entrances of granaries but pig and cow skulls are found in different places. There are no other bones within the compound. Outside there is a low density of bone refuse except in localised clusters at some distance from the compound. These clusters consist of either pig or cow bones, but not both.

The whole sequence described above appears to concern a fear of ritual pollution of cattle and cattle milk by contact with pig products and bone residues. It seems that this is a symbolic expression, played out in domestic animals, of the fear felt by men of pollution by women. Cattle are looked after by men and are clearly associated with male power. Milk is regarded as essential for building up the strength of young men for tribal fighting (Nadel 1947, 65) and the milk is made into a sort of butter which decorates mens' bodies. Pigs, on the other hand, are associated with women and the domestic world. Faris (1968, 50) notes that amongst the southeast Nuba, while most animals are regarded as 'male' property, pigs are 'female' property. But pigs are also unclean 'because they eat animal excretions'. In the same way that men cannot eat out of the same plate as women because women are dirty, so cattle and their pure milk cannot be allowed to come into contact with polluting pigs.

The fear of ritual pollution by pigs takes a rather different and more direct form amongst the Moro. Here there is not the distinction between cow and milk consumption and the eating of pig meat. Contamination from pigs is prevented simply by building the compounds in such a way that contact between man and pig can be avoided. The Moro put a large amount of effort into building pens and passageways *beneath* their homes (see above, p. 134). The men eat and live at the upper level, while the pigs exist in a complex world beneath them. It is the task of women to care for the lower level.

Amongst the Mesakin Qisar, this physical division does not exist. Pigs live and excrete in the courtyard where women cook and where men and women eat. Since cattle and goats also excrete here, the eating area is remarkably unpleasant. The Mesakin Qisar males achieve their sense of freedom from pollution by a more ritual and less practical division between them, their cattle and women and their pigs. While the Moro build a separate domain for pigs in the real world, the Mesakin Qisar emphasise the symbolic separation of the domestic animals associated with the two sexes.

The main concern of the analysis of Nuba bone refuse has been to demonstrate that bone distributions must be seen as part of conceptual and symbolic schemes working within broad environmental constraints. These schemes, as in the case of the Nuba, may be directly identifiable in the surviving archaeological evidence. If the archaeologist finds analysis of cognitive schemes in refuse difficult, it is not so much because of bad data but because the relevant models have not been developed. These models must relate attitudes to refuse to broader concepts within societies. In the example from the Nuba Mountains, some models suggested by Douglas (1966) may be relevant.

The evidence describes a particular use of domestic animals to symbolise male anxiety about pollution by women. Mary Douglas has made some interesting generalisations about such forms of sex pollution.

> When male dominance is accepted as a central principle of social organisation and applied without inhibition and with full rights of physical coercion, beliefs in sex pollution are not likely to be highly developed. On the other hand, when the principle of male dominance is applied to the ordering of social life but is contradicted by other principles such as that of female independence, or the inherent right of women as the weaker sex to be more protected from violence than men, then sex pollution is likely to flourish (1966, 142).

When women have particular rights or abilities to contradict male dominance and physical control, then ideas of pollution of the male by the female come to the fore.

The Mesakin Qisar, who have the stronger sex pollution concepts, are certainly within the category of society in which there is a contradiction between male dominance and female power. Descent is matrilineal, counted through the female line. A woman has certain rights over the grain in 'her' granary although she cannot own fields. Some animal stock may be owned by or linked to women. A wife is always ready to move back to her own family, taking or joining her children who may live with her brother. All these aspects of Mesakin society indicate the independence and strength of women. But, there are also some bilateral aspects to this mainly matrilineal society. Children often live with their father rather than with their mother's brother, and there is frequent competition between husband's and wife's families over the care of the children. Despite the matrilineal system, some inheritance does pass from father to son (see p. 169). In this type of context dominance by men of women and offspring is frequently ambiguous and contradicted by the female line. It may be for this reason that concepts of sex pollution are so clearly demonstrated in a wide range of symbolic relationships.

Amongst the Moro, on the other hand, the role of men and women is less ambiguous since the patrilineal system allows more direct dominance of the female by the male. Thus there is less evidence of clear concepts of sex pollution. However, a slight bilateral aspect remains in the society. Nadel (1947, 213) records the various ways in which maternal and paternal relations are balanced against each other. For this reason, expressions of fear of female impurity are seen in customs such as eating avoidances and in the physical separation of the pigs in the compounds.

Studies of bone refuse in archaeological bone reports have been produced by separate specialists and packaged as a different sphere of study. Archaeologists studying the economy through bones appear to assume that their evidence of relative proportions of animals, butchering practices, age distributions, herd control and so on are somehow free of all symbolic content; theirs is supposed to be a practical, rational, scientific world. But meat-eating, the division of the carcass and the dispersal of the bones must always have a symbolic content behind which there is a conceptual order. Beyond the functioning of 'the economy' is a conceptual scheme and meaning. Until this is accepted and the relevant models developed, the archaeologist will remain unable to provide a complete interpretation of his 'economic' evidence of the past.

8.5 *Other aspects of refuse*

Amongst the Moro, refuse apart from bones is thrown directly over the compound fence into the adjacent garden plots. The approach to the compound is often 'dirty' (figure 61) while the interior is relatively clean. The opposite pattern frequently occurs amongst the Mesakin. Here, while compound interiors may be clean, they are frequently covered in a thick deposit of the excretions of cattle, goat or pig, together with straw, pieces of calabash and general household rubbish (figure 57). In contrast, the area immediately outside the Mesakin compound is usually kept clean. In fact the Mesakin Tiwal often build a low wall around the compound and about 1 m distant from it. The enclosed circuit separates the compound from the fields and provides an area which can be kept clean, especially near the entrance. It should be emphasised that in both Moro and Mesakin compounds cooking and eating take place most commonly in the central courtyard, amongst the refuse in the Mesakin case.

Ideas of sex pollution may be as relevant to these rubbish distributions as to the bone refuse. The Mesakin place a great emphasis on the ritual and symbolic prevention of female pollution as is seen in the distinction between cow and pig products. But also it is the Mesakin, eating and living amongst the dirt of animals and humans, who decorate the insides of their compounds with complex plastic and brilliantly painted decoration (figure 66). Many of the designs in the paintings can be seen to be explicitly male since they occur in male scarification, and are explicitly meant to frighten or ward off. For example, snake designs occur on granaries while there are also depictions of aeroplanes which have been a tribal bogey since the punitive expeditions. It has been suggested that animal skulls may be placed in order to prevent grain from pollution. Several Mesakin informants hinted that the complex panels of decoration in their compounds were also related to the fear of female pollution.

It is difficult to interpret the compound decoration simply in terms of display, since the designs inside the dark and enclosed compounds are much more complex, colourful and frequent than the few white and red lines which sometimes occur on the exterior wall. The main decorated wall surfaces surround female cooking activity in the courtyard and the eating of food by men and women. Nadel (1947) notes that decorative painting among the Nuba may have a ritual and symbolic content. It is perhaps not unreasonable to suggest that the painting and plastic decoration symbolically purify or protect the compound interior and the female preparation of food in that area. This suggestion is perhaps supported by the distinct relationship between the cleaning of the body in the 'shower' area and the location of the most complex decoration around the 'shower'. (I am grateful to L. Donley for pointing out an association between complex wall decoration and toilet areas in Islamic houses on the East African coast.) But perhaps the clearest indication that decoration is used to keep things clean is seen in the Mesakin grinding huts (p. 138). Here a cordon of decoration surrounds the part of the wall against which the flour is piled 'because the flour is clean'.

Amongst the Mesakin, then, activities in the courtyard are ritually or symbolically 'cleaned', and the activities themselves can in practice be carried out amongst dirt. The food can be prepared and eaten amongst the animal detritus because the whole scene is encircled by the purifying designs. The emphasis is on the decoration of the compound boundary and on keeping the area around the boundary clean. Amongst the Moro, on the other hand, the appearance is given of a more practical and internal solution in many aspects of refuse disposal. There is no painting of the boundary around the compound interiors. The inner courtyard floor is itself kept clean, pigs are placed in their own pens, and cattle and sheep are kept outside. The sense of cleanliness is safeguarded directly while the surrounds of the compound can appear dirty to the outside world. This 'more practical' solution appears to be associated with a less developed fear of pollution and less emphasis on surrounding boundaries with ritual and display.

It was shown above that the Mesakin are more closed to outsiders such as the Moro than are the Moro to the Mesakin. It has also been noted that the Mesakin live at lower altitudes where they are involved in closer relationships with the wider, larger and dominant Baggara Arab society. In her study of Gypsies in Britain, Okely (pers. comm.) has shown a strong sense of purity in a minority group whose economic basis is dependent on the wider non-Gypsy society in which it lives. Similarly, the sense of purity and boundedness in Nuba groups, but perhaps especially amongst the Mesakin, may be related to this minority, competitive but dependent position. It has already been suggested (chapter 4) that the status of the Njemps in Baringo and their conceptions of boundedness may be of an equivalent kind. But there is no deterministic one-way relationship between the interactions of minority and dominant groups and conceptions of purity. The existence of a sense of purity amongst the Mesakin becomes contradicted by close relationships with outsider Baggara Arabs. There is a concern with the contradiction, and symbols and rituals of purity are emphasised. The competition does not cause the sense of purity although the former may be consistent with, and be given meaning by, the latter. Other factors are involved, such as the greater ambiguity in Mesakin male–female relationships. There are many complex inter-connections and no simple causality can be assumed.

8.6 *Burial*

In general, a Mesakin and Moro burial is a major event on which much effort and resources are expended. The most marked characteristic of the burial rite is the degree of variation from community to community. But some common features can be distinguished. Burial involves inhumation in single graves (although collective, family burial was recognised amongst the northern Moro, and Seligman (1932, 405) mentions the same practice in southern Nuba groups), which are dug into the ground in the shape of inverted funnels. Very narrow entrances (30 to 55 cm across) lead into a chamber that widens out towards the bottom where it is broad enough to lay an extended corpse. The body usually faces east and in some areas objects are placed with the deceased. The chamber entrance is sealed with stones and then covered with a small mound (up to 80 cm high) and sometimes surrounded by a circle of stones. Personal items, often broken and smashed, are usually displayed on the top of the mound (figure 80), the number and type of these varying with age, sex, wealth and standing. For example, young men have more fighting sticks and signs of contrast. Older men have often acquired more dependencies and will have more items placed on their graves, especially if they have achieved high standing and wealth. Thus the number of items on graves partly relates to the quantity of people who had obligations to the decreased.

Graves occur in cemeteries (figure 63). Up to six of these may be associated with one hill community (e.g. Kerbej). In Moro, the cemeteries are located around the edge of the relatively compact communities, up to $1\frac{1}{2}$ km from the edge of the community. Amongst the more dispersed Mesakin, the different cemeteries are placed around and within the hill communities, sometimes immediately adjacent to the houses. The cemeteries are not bounded by physical limits except for the paths that often run through and around them (figure 63). Each cemetery contains the dead from one or more community sections, and a person is buried near his immediate family. Informants could always point to their father's or mother's grave and in some cases to the graves of the grandparents. The informants always knew in which cemetery and in which area of the cemetery they would ultimately be buried. It has already been noted (p. 153) that wives are frequently buried in the

80. A Mesakin Qisar grave with pot placed on top of the small mound and broken through by walking sticks. A circular band for carrying head loads (see also figure 82) and a calabash are hung on the sticks.

cemeteries and parts of cemeteries of their own family rather than that of their husband.

In all three tribes funerals are the main occasions at which large numbers of cattle are killed. Relatives and friends may sacrifice up to twenty head of cattle each, depending on the closeness of their relationship with the deceased. Seligman (1932, 405) records mainly relatives attending funerals, all of whom, with the exception of the spouse, eat the cattle meat. In the case of important men these feasts are continued two or three times at yearly intervals.

But, as already stated, it is difficult to generalise. In particular, there are only a few tribal-wide customs which distinguish between, for example, the Moro and Mesakin Qisar. These differences will be mentioned below, but the more distinct community to community variation can be assessed by accounting the information gained from each hill community.

Moro

Lebu. Men and women are buried extended on their right sides (although there are clan and section preferences for women to lie on their left side) with the heads facing east 'so that, if the body leaves, it goes in that direction, towards the house of god'. Sorghum and sesame are placed in the grave before the body. Pots are also often put in the graves. Clothes, shoes, pots, tools are placed on top of the grave.

Kerbej. Six cemeteries occur around the community. The cemetery visited was $\frac{1}{2}$ km from the edge of the community, overgrown and difficult to see. An informant, however, was able to identify the graves of his mother and father, and to outline the area where his grandfather, brothers and sisters were buried – the area where he also would be buried. Male and female bodies are laid extended and looking towards the east. The covering mounds are very low so that the main mark of the grave is the kerb or circle of stones. Pots and beds are placed on top of the grave or in the surrounding trees. Even very young children are accorded burial similar to the adults (a 5 month old female internment was witnessed). The child's covering mound is smaller in diameter and there are no grave goods except the shawl placed around the body.

Nua. Men and women are buried on their left sides, either crouched or extended. Nothing is placed in the grave with the body, but clothes, shoes, pots, calabashes are left on top.

Anderri. Men are buried extended on their left sides, women on their right. If the grave does not collapse between internments, brothers and sons may be placed in the same grave. The two cemeteries visited were located immediately adjacent to the compounds amongst the nearest fields. The graves are usually surrounded by a circle of stones with a mound only 10 cm in height. Where the mound and entrance had collapsed inwards, it could be seen that the grave chamber was shaped like an inverted cone or beehive. Objects placed on top of the graves include broken pots and sherds, calabashes, knife blades, dented and misshapen teapots (teapots being considered signs of status and wealth).

Some common differences between Moro and Mesakin rites are as follows. Firstly, the covering mounds are less substantial amongst the Moro. Secondly, only the Mesakin place thorn brushwood over the grave mound while spears and shields rarely occur on Moro graves. Finally, the Moro generally place fewer items on the graves than do the Mesakin. None of these differences shows a marked boundary between Moro and Mesakin.

Mesakin Tiwal

Tuwia. Individuals (both male and female) are buried extended on either right or left side depending on locality within Tuwia. Two or three people from the same family are sometimes placed in the same grave. The entrance to the burial chamber is explicitly compared to the small round entrances to the granaries in Mesakin compounds. A man is buried with cooked meat in a pot, together with sorghum, water and alcohol, also in pots. A woman or young man would be buried in a similar way but a woman would also have her bead decoration and a young man would have the painted body designs that he had used in life. The entrance is sealed with clay and an earth mound is built over it. A man's spears and tools are placed on the mound, while walking sticks and straw head rings (for carrying pots) are placed on a woman's graves together with some of her pots broken on the burial mound. All the remaining pots of a woman are often broken and put in caves or shelters in the hills.

Mesakin Qisar

Reikha. Men and women are buried extended on their right sides looking east 'because that is where the sun rises'. Food, including groundnuts, beans and sesame, is placed in pots in the grave, with ornaments, clothing and field tools. The mound above adult burials is 50 to 80 cm high, covered with thorn brushwood and surrounded by a stone kerb. Placed on top of the mound over a male burial are broken spear shafts, calabashes and fighting trophies. In addition, sesame seeds are sometimes placed in the grave mound so that sesame stalks are seen growing on the mound and immediately around the grave. Sesame is also placed in women's graves. Objects placed on top of a woman's grave include adzes, walking sticks, calabashes, head rings, water pots, and the flat shell used to harvest sesame. The items placed in or on a grave may vary according to the age of the deceased but only inasmuch as different objects are used at different stages during a person's life.

Each family has its own burial area within one of the cemeteries located around and within the dispersed community. These cemeteries may be as near as 50 m from the nearest compound. At the funeral feast attended by relations and friends, large numbers of cattle are killed outside the house of the deceased. At the first anniversary of the death, a second feast is held at which more cattle are killed and sword fights take place between the younger men.

Tosari. Men are buried on their left sides (but on their right in some sections), women on their right, extended and looking east. The body lies on its side with one hand under the head. The orifices of the face are sealed with wax and the body laid out in the shroud, with body ornaments, in the grave chamber. Sorghum flour and seeds, sesame seeds, alcohol, water and meat may be placed in the grave. The objects used during life (spears, walking, dancing and fighting sticks, pots, calabashes, shields, head rings) are placed, often broken, on the grave. The number of these items depends on the age and status of the deceased. The mounds are up to 80 cm high and often are covered with thorn bushes. A richer man is given a larger mound or a larger circle of stones around the grave. A distinctive feature of Tosari burial is that very large storage jars are upturned on the grave mound with spears and other items stuck into the mound through the broken bases of the pots. These large pots often cover smaller narrow-mouthed water jars.

Several cemeteries for the different community sections and families are found at Tosari. The largest of these cemeteries (figure 63) contains clusters of graves belonging to different families (clans) and sections, including the burials of members of offshoot communities. While these sections are to some extent visible in the clustered distribution of graves, they are often bordered by paths, as is shown in figure 63. The burial areas belonging to different community sections or families were identified by informants. There are minor differences in burial rite in different parts of the cemetery. For example, the mounds are appreciably smaller in the Tongerunu and Tosobi sections, and it is only in these two groups that head rings are placed on the graves (figure 63). The largest graves occur in the Tesera and Torokora (Tesara) sections. In each of these sections there is also a major 'chief's' circle. That only one such grave occurs in each of the two sections suggests that these may not only be the graves of successful individuals but also the founders of the local community. Male and female graves could be distinguished with the aid of informants and on the basis of the items (shields, spears) placed on the mounds. No spatial separation between male and female graves could be identified. Variations in the 'wealth' of items placed on the grave mounds were recorded but were not subjected to analysis since the amount of material visible on the mounds is severely affected by survival factors. It is clear, however, that in Tosari, the main cemetery clearly maps out the pattern of local dependencies and ties in socio-economic relations.

At the funeral feast the cattle of the dead man, his brothers and friends are brought together in the absence of women and children. Those men who wish to kill some of their cows mark them with a triangular-ended beater covered with ash. The flat triangular end is made of cow hide, which is also used to cover the wooden shaft. The son and brothers' sons of the deceased then kill the marked beasts with spears. Up to thirty or forty animals may be killed in the case of the death of an important man and larger numbers were also mentioned. The meat is prepared and cooked by women (sisters and daughters of the deceased) but the immediate family of the dead man is not allowed to eat the beef. However, they can join in the feasting at the first or second anniversary.

The first feature of the burial evidence to be considered here is the presence of agglomerated and separate cemeteries near or in the hill communities. Where access to land rights is through lineage ties, links with the ancestors, with earlier owners of the land, often become of importance (Meillassoux 1972). Most land amongst the Nuba is passed down from father to son or from mother's brother to sister's son. The burials in community and community section cemeteries, and in family clusters within those cemeteries, stress the links through time with the land. The community at any one time depends on the communal labour invested by the ancestors, labour invested in terracing, well-digging, clearing fields of stones, manuring, building threshing floors and so on.

It is thus of interest that the second burial feature to be considered here is the clear relationship between death, grain and fertility. As noted, sorghum and sesame seeds and flour or gruel are often placed in the graves. There is also a clear and explicit similarity between the form of the graves and granaries – they have equally small round entrances and deep dark chambers within. Pots, originally used for storing grain and grain produce as well as water, cover the entrance to the grave in the same way that they cover the small entrances at the top of the Moro grain silos. Seligman (1932, 409) records that amongst the Dilling Nuba the dead are thought to be present at harvests. He also notes (*ibid.*) that on Jebel Kawerma the body was wrapped in the skin of a pig. The clear association between grain, granaries and pigs has already been described (p. 156). The jaw bones and skulls, signs of pig death, 'guard' the purity and fertility of the grain. The pig skin may similarly protect the body in death.

The association of death with fertility is also seen in the covering of mourners with ash and in the frequent use of ash during the burial ceremony. Before they marry, young men smear themselves with ash at wrestling matches and at points during the harvest. Ash is intimately associated with fertility and strength, and it is as a symbol of strength and continuity that it is placed alongside death at burial. These various emphases on fertility at death suggest a fear that the misfortune in death may adversely affect the fertility and continuation of the crops and of the family and society. The Nuba sense of cleanliness and their fear of impurity (p. 160) are well-developed, and the burial ritual provides further evidence for this.

The frequent breaking on the grave of personal items – the items which 'are' the deceased – removes the impurity and ill-effects of the dead. In both Moro and Mesakin the dead person's spears and other personal items which are retained by the family are ritually purified before they can be reused. Similarly, the personal items may be placed aside for one year before use. The general emphasis on maintaining purity and fertility relates not only to the long-term communal investment of agricultural labour, but also to the nature of Nuba male–female relationships and to relationships with Baggara Arabs as has been shown. The discussion of burial allows a further aspect of the purity and fertility concepts to be identified – the inheritance of goods.

The structure of Nuba inheritance is the third feature of Nuba burial to be examined here. Goody (1962, 416) has suggested 'that many of the most important differences [in burial rites] result from the inheritance system'. Before we can examine the relationship between inheritance and ritual for the Moro and Mesakin, we need to know something of the patterns of inheritance.

Amongst the patrilineal Moro it is sons who inherit most property. 'Far farms' go to the eldest son but he is expected to allot parts of the land to his younger brothers. House farms and the compound are inherited by younger brothers. The property of women (personal, household, and the pigs which formed part of her dowry) goes to her sisters. However, wills are sometimes made which may change these rules and can add to the severe disputes which often develop over the division of land.

Although the Mesakin nominally have a matrilineal descent system, property may go to both sons and sisters' sons. Far farms, house farms and the compound itself go to either the son or the sister's son, depending on which has been brought up in the compound of the deceased. Livestock, money, guns, spears, spades, knives and ornaments go mainly to sisters' sons but each son must also receive spears. Usually, a man will have explained to his wife and/or brothers what is to be done with his property after death. But once again disputes are common.

It is mainly the inheritors who are concerned with making sacrifices at funerals. Amongst the Moro, it is the son who is seen as giving the cattle feast so that he can take over the belongings of his father. Amongst the Mesakin, it is again the inheritors who are most concerned with the main death ritual and feasting. Usually it is the brother of the deceased who decides how the personal items are to be divided, how many are to be given to sons, sisters' sons, and how many to be put on the grave. If all the brothers are dead, the old men of the family and locality make the division of items. How many objects go on the grave and how much is distributed to each person depend on the wealth and standing of the deceased as much as on age and sex. As already noted (p. 168), the number of cattle killed at funeral feasts depends on the wishes of family and friends, with sons and sisters' sons being closely involved.

It is possible to suggest that many of the funeral rites are concerned with making an offering or sacrifice in return for inherited wealth. Because there are frequent disputes over inheritance, an inheritor openly and perhaps competitively demonstrates his gift to the dead. It is the open and public sacrifice of cattle and broken items which 'allows' the inheritance. Thus, more items are placed on top of a richer man's grave partly because more people inherit and more demonstrate their worthiness to accept. That the part of the inheritance which is placed on the grave is often symbolically broken emphasises the sacrificial and absolute nature of the gift. The break 'releases' the rest of the inheritance.

In Mesakin there is greater competition over inheritance since the matrilineal system contains certain patrilineal elements, for example, the frequent inheritance by the son rather than by the sister's son. The greater display of goods on Mesakin graves, relating to the greater emphasis on body display and display in the compound (the objects placed on the graves correspond closely to those hung up in front of houses, p. 140) and to the greater fear of pollution, also relates to the greater ambiguity of inheritance.

The emphasis on grain ritual in the burial rite is related to another aspect of inheritance. Agricultural land is the main commodity about which there is competition between heirs. Nadel (1947, 37) notes that most Mesakin house farms are obtained by inheritance (as opposed to purchase or clearance of virgin land), as are many far farms. This is less the case amongst the Moro, but in both tribes a major part of inheritance concerns agricultural land. The grain and granary symbolism relate to a general concern about the continuity and fertility of the crops and more specific concerns about individual rights to the land and its produce.

Thus, Nuba burial is about the handing on of Nuba assets within family lines. The continuity of the society is stressed not only in the inheritance procedures and in the grouping of graves into community cemeteries, but also in the rites concerned with the fertility of grain. To any such conception of continuity and fertility, death is a threat – the reversal of sequence. The threat is removed by purifying or breaking the items associated with the dead, by sacrificing in order to remove the guilt of inheritance from the dead, and by confronting and surrounding the dead with symbols of grain and fertility.

8.7 *Aspects of design*

Aspects and transformations of the principles seen in settlement and burial can be sought in a very different domain – design. The richest area for design and art is in the Mesakin, especially the Mesakin Qisar. Here calabashes, hut fronts, bodies and fighting-stick handles are richly decorated. It has already been suggested (p. 162) that this decoration may be related to the desire to provide ritual protection and to draw attention to boundaries around the domestic courtyard, the self and the food that enters the body. The decoration is partly naturalistic and representational, and most is geometric. The geometric designs often have a conscious meaning. Amongst the southeast Nuba, Faris (1972) notes the following meanings of designs.

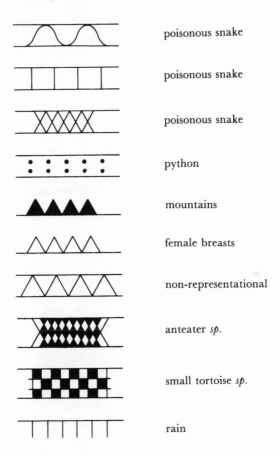

It is of note that even minor differences in designs relate to substantially different meanings. Thus lines of inverted 'V's unfilled are female breasts, while filled they are mountains. Yet an extremely similar design is non-representational.

But for the Nuba, the placing of designs within an overall pattern is as important as the individual designs themselves. In particular, there is a continual emphasis on symmetry and balance. Most Mesakin design arrangements on calabashes and houses are carefully balanced, usually

Table 16. *Links made between designs (for numbers along margins see figure 73) by Mesakin Nuba*

	1	2	3	4	5	6	7	8
1		29 (6)	22 (5)	22 (5)	7 (2)	20 (4)	6 (1)	8 (2)
2			24 (5)	27 (6)	10 (2)	9 (2)	2 (0)	7 (2)
3				30 (7)	17 (4)	11 (2)	9 (2)	2 (0)
4					12 (3)	10 (2)	8 (2)	6 (1)
5						36 (8)	15 (3)	25 (6)
6							19 (4)	16 (3)
7								43 (10)

Percentages of total links are given in brackets
Total number of links = 451

resulting in a careful symmetry. However, much of the balance is achieved without symmetry. Thus, designs on calabashes may be organised into the four quarters of the calabash or into the two halves, and the designs in each section will be slightly different. A similar effect is achieved by having two similar designs juxtaposed which are different in size or shading.

It may be too easy to relate this widespread emphasis on balance and asymmetrical balance to the prominent part that the male–female division plays in society. Many aspects of male–female relationships have been discussed above, including concepts of female pollution and the absolute division of most aspects of life amongst the Tullishi Nuba into east/west, male/female, strong/weak divisions. However, the cognitive pattern behind the male/female division and the major emphases on balance in the art may be related. A more general interpretation will be offered in the conclusion.

That awareness of balance is especially important amongst the Mesakin was examined through a field experiment. Sixty-six individuals of different age and sex groups were given eight slips of paper with the designs shown in figure 73. The pieces of paper were spread face-up but disorganised on the ground and the informant was asked to pick them up in an ordered sequence. That individuals understood to some extent what an ordered arrangement meant is suggested by the non-random results that have been obtained. But it should not be supposed that the Mesakin have great experience with abstract typology and many appeared to find the exercise confusing and difficult. Young women especially often gave the impression of being at a loss although the results of their choices are not significantly different from those of the older women and men. No experiment lasted longer than 1–2 minutes.

Table 16 shows the numbers of times each design was placed adjacent to each other design in the experimental sequences. For example, design

Table 17. *Links made between designs by Cambridge archaeology undergraduates*

	1	2	3	4	5	6	7	8
1		32 (13)	7 (3)	6 (2)	8 (3)	4 (1)	2 (0)	3 (1)
2			12 (5)	7 (3)	4 (1)	7 (3)	1 (0)	3 (1)
3				33 (13)	5 (2)	4 (1)	1 (0)	4 (1)
4					5 (2)	4 (1)	1 (0)	7 (3)
5						32 (13)	7 (3)	6 (2)
6							10 (4)	5 (2)
7								26 (10)

Percentages of total links are given in brackets
Total number of links = 251

1 was most frequently placed adjacent to design 2. From these figures and from an examination of the sixty-six sequences, it appears that the most common arrangement for the eight designs is 1-2-4-3 and 6-5-8-7, while a frequent pattern is 1-3-2-4, again with 6-5-8-7.

The same experiment was repeated on thirty-six second and third year archaeology students at Cambridge University in order to determine whether archaeologists from a non-random subset of western European society might classify and respond to very different aspects of design. The students were asked to spread the designs out in front of them and then put the designs into a sequence. They were asked to do this quickly and the results were collected within 1–2 minutes. The results of this experiment are shown in table 17, and it is immediately apparent that there is less of a 'spread' of responses. The percentage values along the diagonal in table 17 are higher than any of the percentage values in table 16. This may partly relate to the better understanding and greater familiarity with classification amongst archaeology students.

Many aspects of the results from the two samples are similar, in particular the higher values along the diagonals in both the tables. But a detailed comparison of the results shows several differences. For example, the common links made by the Mesakin between designs 5 and 8 and between 1 and 6 do not stand out in the Cambridge results. Also, the most common sequence is 1-2-3-4 and 5-6-7-8. Many of the differences between the classifications made by the two groups relate to different reactions to balance and symmetry. The designs can be divided into those which are balanced and in which the two halves are symmetrical (1, 3, 6) and those which are balanced but asymmetrical (2, 4, 5, 7). Most of the Cambridge classifications are based on design content rather than on symmetry. Thus the pairs 1-2, 3-4, 5-6 are put together because motifs in the designs are similar. Indeed, discussion after the experiment showed that many had not noticed the varying degree of symmetry.

The Nuba sequences differ from the Cambridge classifications in that the balanced assymetry of 2 and 4 are frequently associated while the symmetric 1 and 3 often occur side by side. The close relationship between designs 5 and 8 may have a similar nature. Thus, the Nuba often classify according to symmetry before motif content. Symmetric designs were placed adjacent to symmetric designs, and asymmetric with asymmetric, in only 18% of the links made by archaeology students, and in 35% of the links made by the Mesakin. These percentages are based on designs, excluding the two 'odd' patterns 7 and 8. If the latter are included as asymmetric designs, 34% of the archaeology links are between symmetric and symmetric and between asymmetric and asymmetric, and 46% amongst the Nuba.

The greater awareness of symmetry amongst the Mesakin Nuba partly depends on age. The eleven children interviewed between the ages of 5 and 10 never made links between designs 1 and 3, nor between designs 2 and 4. This difference in the classificatory procedures followed by young and old could result from several factors. It is possible that it is only with maturity that the whole emphasis on balanced symmetry and asymmetry in social relations is fully experienced and participated in. However, it is also possible that an original sensitivity to design symmetry and balance has been 'taught out' by the western European influence in the new schools. Since not all the children interviewed had been to schools, the former explanation is perhaps the more likely.

The Nuba and the British students, after a brief look at the designs, tended to pick out different characteristics. But the Nuba concern with symmetry is evident in their art and decoration. As the analyst, I became aware of the importance of symmetry by looking at the designs themselves. It is reasonable to suggest that the archaeologist, after careful and detailed examination of such designs, would try coding and classifying according to symmetries (cf. Washburn 1978). The Nuba example does not suggest that we must, with empathy, get into 'the minds of the makers' of designs. All it suggests is that variation in emphasis on symmetries can be studied as having a meaningful relationship to other aspects of life (see above and in the conclusion to this chapter).

The logic of design

Most, if not all, the geometric decoration on calabashes, huts and male bodies can be seen to be a 'play' on a particular design – the star of figure 81: 1 (see also figure 82). This motif occurs widely in Sudan, Ethiopia and North Africa. Amongst the Nuba it sometimes occurs in isolation and complete (for the distribution see figure 77), but more frequently the various components are broken down and reassembled to produce new patterns. This is made clear in figure 81, where the relationship of a range of designs to the original star is suggested.

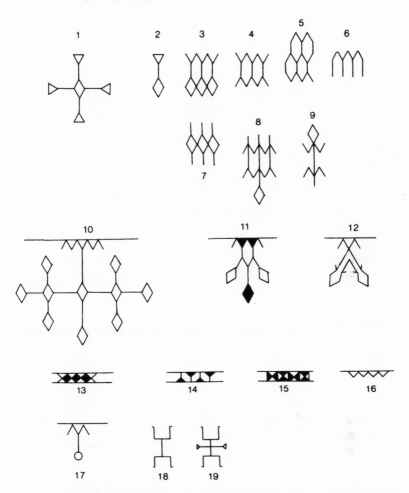

81. The similarity of common Mesakin and Moro designs to the star motif (1).

In the construction of the designs such as those in figure 81, the star may have been used as a source for the two components of the design language – 'words' and the relations between words. The words or elementary units that can be derived from the star are

A B₁ B₂   C

◊ ▽ ∨ and | . The syntactical relational rules which are used to

build up patterns out of these units can also be derived from the star. The most important of these rules is that joins are made at vertices and not along the sides or bases of triangles or lozenges. It is by examining the arrangements that do *not* occur that these rules can be identified. Thus ⋈ on its own, involving a link between two B₁ at vertices is common,

82. A panel of decoration placed above the burnished surround to a hut entrance inside a Mesakin Qisar compound.

83. A Mesakin calabash with a design involving rotational symmetry.

whereas ⬦ on its own never occurs. Similarly, ⬦ is never found whereas ⊠ is, since in the latter case the nodal connecting point is seen as being the central vertex. ◁— never occurs but —◁ is very common. In general, joins at oblique angles are preferred. Thus Y is a very widespread motif, whereas ↓ is not.

Another syntactical rule derived from the star is rotation around a central point, usually in 90° units or multiples. Thus the ▶◀ motif is obtained by rotating the first bow-tie motif through 90° (see figures 75

and 76). ╳ ╳ is obtained by a 180° rotation (see figure 83).

Rotation is often associated with repetition of the same design and with filling in of the motifs. These are further rules which can be derived from the star motif.

The syntactical rules appear to be retained even when the words or elementary units are changed. In a few cases, ⋒ or ⊔ is found instead of Y (figure 82: 17 to 19). The A, B_1 and B_2 words may be changed into circles or squares, but the main components of the relational rules remain constant.

The design language can be used to produce radically different designs. The use of the B_1 unit to produce ▶◀, repeated in a band and then repeated in adjacent bands, gives a tilted chessboard pattern:

Rotated, this produces a normal chessboard pattern which is used as the basis of much panel decoration on calabashes and houses. The rotating circularity of the star design could also be used to build the circle and concentric circle motifs. These occur frequently scarred on male bodies and rarely within designs on other media.

In fact the 'new' composite units produced in these ways (the chessboard square and the circle) are infrequently used alongside the A, $B_{1, 2}$, C words. This is because there is a logical incompatability between the motifs if the relational rules are adhered to. For example, it is difficult to incorporate lozenges and Y patterns with 120° angles into a sequence of squares with 90° angles if the rules involve only rotation, repetition and joins at vertices. Attempts *are* made to use chessboards and A units together, but it has clearly been found difficult to produce a regular pattern in this way. The original units and the 'composite' units derived from them cannot easily be used side by side in an extended vocabulary, but the restriction results from the relational rules rather than from the words themselves.

By examining in this way what patterns do *not* occur, we can begin to understand in greater detail the logic behind the decorative grammar. As is shown in figures 72 and 77, some design configurations are localised within the Mesakin area. Yet throughout the region studied, patterns are generated in the same way, following the same rules and logic. Given a set of units and a set of relational rules, it is clear that a very large number of designs could be built up. By examining those that do *not* occur, we can obtain a better idea of the logic which restricts the range of possible pattern. Thus, (*a*) ⟍⟋⟍⟋⟍⟋ never occurs, whereas (*b*) ⋁⋁⋁ is common. The first design cannot be reproduced by simple repetition (as in the second) nor by rotation since ⟍⟋ rotated and added gives ⟍⟋⟍ . Perhaps another reason for the non-occurrence of the first motif is that, in the star, where the B_2 motifs are rotated through 180° they occur at opposing ends of C links rather than being linked laterally. As a further example of what does not occur, a grid of squares is *always* filled to produce the chessboard pattern. Grids such as ▨ never occur because they cannot be produced by the units and relational statements.

Work of this type on archaeological data could throw light on why particular traits are not adopted in local areas. New motifs may have to be incorporated within the existing linguistic design. Traits may be adopted or rejected depending on their logical compatability with the existing structure and on the degree to which that structure can withstand realignment. This aspect is visible in the Mesakin drawings of animals. Those animals are incorporated into the art which can readily be represented using the available words and language. For example, the tortoise with its chessboard back is frequently depicted, as are snakes with zig-zag body designs and ostriches with long links between triangular or lozenge-shaped entities.

It has been assumed in this account that the rules and words derived from the initial star design. It is equally possible that the star design achieved popularity in the Mesakin area because it could be constructed using existing grammatical rules.

Further examination and more rigorous testing of the logic behind the design language can be achieved by 'programming' the generation of designs. The production of Nuba patterns can be mimicked using the hypothesised grammatical rules in order to test whether the motifs and rules are sufficient to account for all design configurations. The extent to which superficially different designs, and designs using different sets of 'word' units, actually conform to the same logic or syntax can also be examined. The attempt in table 18 to programme Nuba design generation follows the idea suggested by Faris (1972) in his work on the southeastern Nuba.

The minimal rules used in these illustrative programmes show the way in which the Nuba designs can be reproduced. By programming such design generation on the computer it is possible to experiment further with design rules and generative logic. Experimentation of this form may allow comparison of the formal rules behind different sets of designs (on

Table 18. *The operation of various grammatical rules in the construction of Nuba designs*

Instructions

A. Choose object and part of object (calabash, house, etc.).
B. Choose starting element (word unit).
C. Begin design generation.

Moves	Possible operations
1. Move horizontally	At vertices (if possible or oblique angles) CONnect to (R)ight or (L)eft: CONnect after ROTating (in units of $45°$ or $90°$): EXPand size of element: SKIP
2. Move vertically	As 1, moving Up or Down: SKIP
3. Fill	SOLid fill: DESigned fill of the spaces generated in 1 and 2: SKIP
4. Rotate	ROTate whole design so far completed in units or multiples of $90°$ and redraw: SKIP
5. Expansion, reduction	EXPand or REDuce size of whole design so far completed by 'n' units – a unit being the length of the sides of the A and B elements: SKIP
6. Repeat	REPeat design so far completed n times, VERtically or HORizontally, to Right or Left, Up or Down: SKIP
7. Return	RETurn to nth step or starting point

Examples

(a) ▶◆◀

Starting point: Choose B_1, ROT $(270°)$, SOL. (Comment: the left triangle is chosen, and obtained by turning B_1 through $270°$, and filled.)
1. CON (R) ROT $(180°)$
2. SKIP
3. SKIP
4. SKIP
5. SKIP
6. REP (1) HOR (R)
7. SKIP

(b)

Starting point: Choose A, SOL. (Comment: the left lozenge is chosen and filled.)
1. SKIP
2. CON (U) C: CON (U) B_2
3. SKIP
4. SKIP
5. SKIP
6. REP (2) HOR (R)
7. SKIP

Table 18 *(cont).*

(c)

Starting point: Choose A, SOL. (Comment: the central lozenge is chosen
        and filled.)
1. CON (R) C ROT (90°): CON (R) B_1 ROT (90°)
7. RET (starting point)
2. CON (D) B_1 ROT (180°)
3. SOL
4. ROT (180°)
5. SKIP
6. SKIP
7. SKIP

(d)

Starting point: Choose B_2. (Comment: the central V in the top line is
        chosen.)
1. CON (R) C ROT (135°): CON (L) C ROT (45°)
7. RET (starting point)
2. CON (D) A
1. CON (R) C ROT (135°): EXP (2): CON (R) A
7. RET (2)
1. CON (L) C ROT (45°): EXP (2): CON (L) A
3. SKIP
4. SKIP
5. SKIP
6. SKIP
7. SKIP

pots, metal objects etc.) in the archaeological data. It would also be
possible to examine whether, even though the design elements and motifs
varied from region to region, the formal logic remained the same. In
addition, to what extent are the design structures in adjacent regions
logically incompatible? It may be suggested that such questions can be
answered following procedures similar to those outlined above, especially
if an emphasis is placed on examining what designs are *not* found. Both
the work on the Mesakin design grammar and Faris' (1972) similar work
on southeast Nuba personal art were conducted without interview data.
Indeed, it is difficult to see how verbal information could add to the
analyses. In this respect the archaeologist is in the same position as the
student of the art and design of modern societies. In addition, the
analytical procedures suggested, far from reducing creativity to a dull
mechanical computer programme, have the potential to define the *full*
richness, complexity and subtlety of style and design.

On the other hand, the above 'linguistic' description of the design grammar can be severely criticised as being abstract, analytical and unrelated to the production of design and its use in social contexts. It seems extremely unlikely that the formal grammatical rules adequately capture the procedure of design construction by Mesakin artisans. However, the whole design 'language' would be produced 'by accident' if the aim of the painter or engraver was to remain close to the star motif of figure 81: 1. As already suggested, all the designs use elements of the one star pattern but they are never drawn or painted so as to destroy intimations and evocations of that motif. The painted decoration in the house compounds is associated with various protective symbols including skulls and plants. The symbolic effects of the star or cross motif may be enhanced by its 'hidden' presence. The motif may also be 'here but not here' in the main area of female activities in the compound because of the star's frequent association with men (scarred on their bodies). As regards the calabashes, the transfers of consumables between social categories are symbolically protected by the 'hidden' motif, but at the same time the evocations of the widely recognised and historically significant star or cross design draw attention and add significance to the exchanges or transfers. Thus, although the linguistic method of analysis of Mesakin designs may be useful for identifying both the limits of the design and some aspects of the way in which the designs are built up, the grammar itself may be illusory. The apparent rules may result from the artist's intention to produce a certain social effect in a particular cultural context, by 'playing on', hiding and evoking a widely known pattern.

8.8 *Conclusion*

The regional distributions of traits amongst the Moro and Mesakin do not suggest marked material culture boundaries within the Nuba, but they do demonstrate a localisation of traits made up of a complex overlap and interlacing of distributions. The scale of style localisation relates to the degree and scale of cooperation and dependence in community labour. But the boundaries between hill communities and 'tribes' are only slightly marked and the degree of between-group competition is much less than was noted, for example, in Baringo. Membership of tribes was not traditionally important. Rather it is at the scale of the local hill community that mutual inward-looking dependence is supported in cultural traits. This local cohesion and common access to land is also maintained in the social system and in the burial in common cemeteries located near the settlements.

Although 'tribal' boundaries are not clearly marked by most traits, certain styles and customs do show widespread distributions within tribes and boundaries between Moro and Mesakin. These are traits closely tied to the slightly different conceptual schemes of the two groups, including construction of pig pens, the emphasis on house and body decoration and display, the position of the jaw bones in the compounds, and the patterning of refuse. The Mesakin have a greater sense and fear of pollution, partly related, as noted above, to the greater ambiguity in the male–female relationship and to greater interaction with the dominant Arab groups. The Moro have fewer indications of a pollution taboo, perhaps because of the less ambiguous male–female relationship in their society and less contact with the Baggara Arabs, and they cope with what pollution fears they do have by the physical separation of men from pigs and by private precautions such as the placing of jaw bones inside granaries. The Mesakin are more concerned with emphasising boundaries by surrounding them in ritual. They emphasise the decoration and purification of the compounds, of the self, and personal items are more frequently displayed at boundaries around the home, the body and on burial mounds. The Mesakin hut compounds have higher walls, are more closed with carefully modelled entrances and special entrance huts. The separation between male and female, between pure and impure, is projected onto the compound construction, house decoration and art, onto the decoration of calabashes and onto the world of domestic animals leading to the particular bone refuse patterns that have been described. Thus many of the distinct differences between Moro and Mesakin concern different world views rather than being related directly to competition between Nuba groups.

More generally, the Nuba groups studied illustrate one of the categories of society and symbol system identified by Douglas (1970). She suggested two independently varying aspects of society – group and grid. Membership of groups varies in that in some societies individuals are less subordinate to groups. The Nuba have well-developed local groups – the hill communities which are emphasised and supported by local material culture distributions, common cemeteries and mutual labour. Although the tribe is weakly developed in many spheres of activity, it has been shown that the Mesakin form a fairly exclusive social group (p. 153). Within a group, the grid describes the roles and networks of relationships centred on individuals. Within some societies, roles are undefined and ambiguous. To a certain extent this is true of the Nuba, and especially of the Mesakin. The frequent ambiguity of descent rules, and the mixture of matrilineal and patrilineal principles, mean that the complex cross-cutting series of roles and relationships centred on an individual are subject to frequent reinterpretations. In such a context of strong group and weak grid, Douglas suggests that the emphasis is on the purity of the group, and on the insider/outsider dichotomy. Danger is associated with boundaries, there are cleansing rituals, and the body interior is protected at its boundaries from pollution coming from the outside. There is an emphasis on classification, categorisation and logic-chopping exercises. All these aspects of ritual and world view are present in Nuba society, and particularly in Mesakin society where the tribal group is strongest and grid is weakest. From the emphasis on spatial group seclusion to the pollution taboos, to the concern with body, home and granary boundaries, to the ritual surrounding the boundary between life and death and the breaking of items associated with a dead man, to the regular placing of items in particular places in the huts, to the detailed classification and categorisation of form and design, to the logically consistent set of generational rules in the art, Douglas' scheme is supported. The type of amalgamation of different strands of symbolic behaviour identified by Douglas provides the archaeologist with a rich body of ideas to test and experiment with in his own data. The Nuba example demonstrates the potential of such an approach in which the structures in many aspects of material culture patterning can be related to a common scheme, and to a coherent underlying meaning. But, as interpreted here, the concepts of group purity and boundedness are not simply abstract principles. Rather they have meaning in the context of a set of socio-economic relations. These social and economic actions concern the competitive dependency of Nuba minority groups on Arabs, and the ambiguous tensions within Nuba society between patrilineal and matrilineal interests. The concept of group purity is also consonant with and constitutive of the localised cultural marking of intra-community dependencies, and the maintenance of intra-group cooperation in subsistence labour through time.

There is yet another aspect of the emphasis on purity and boundedness which remains to be considered. The Nuba are in a state of flux. Recently there have been important social and economic changes as the young have moved down from the hill villages, and patterns of landholding have altered (Roden 1972). The region is rapidly becoming incorporated into the wider Sudanese and world economies. Police, government and missionaries have increased their influence. Much of the present concern with the purity and boundaries of the hill communities may represent a traditional ideal and traditional rights which are gradually being eroded. The clearly defined Nuba cemeteries represent an ideal of continuity with the ancestors which is fast becoming difficult to maintain in reality. The enclosed and bounded hut compounds hide the increasing break-up and dispersal of families. It has been demonstrated that there is little movement of outsiders into Nuba communities. But Roden (1972) has documented the considerable out migration into new labour markets and into closer contact with Arabs in the plain. The material symbols of boundedness and pollution comprise an ideology of group cohesion and purity, an ideal world of traditional values and rights, which is daily becoming contradicted by other forces. The numerous repetitions of the same structural scheme support an ideology which denies the changing pattern of day-to-day relationships. The competition between patrilineal and matrilineal rights and the concern with Arab influence must both be seen as components in wider changes in Nuba society. The ideology which is partly constituted in material culture is negotiated and manipulated as traditional rights and interests come under threat.

9

Implications for archaeology

Two conclusions can be drawn from the ethnoarchaeological studies presented in this book. The first concerns the active part played by material symbols in social and economic relations between ethnic, age, sex, status, and family groupings. This book emphasises symbols in action in contrast to the passive, reflective nature of material culture which, as was shown in chapter 1 and as will be further discussed in this chapter, appears to be assumed in the interaction hypothesis and in the hypothesis that regional styles of material culture reflect scales of craft production. In all the studies in this book it has been shown that the extent to which cultural similarity relates, for example, to interaction depends on the strategies and intentions of the interacting groups and on how they use, manipulate and negotiate material symbols as part of those strategies. Thus, spear and calabash styles in Baringo disrupt boundaries which are distinct in other aspects of material culture because the spears and calabashes are employed by young men and women in their opposition to the dominant elders. Also in Baringo, particular types of body decoration worn in common by young men and women constitute a means by which the authority of the older men is contradicted (p. 84). Whether stylistic variation in stool and spear types (chapters 3 and 4) and other craft items (chapter 7) do or do not reflect variation in the scale of production depends on 'consumer' preferences and on the symbolism of the objects. The way in which Dorobo groups (chapter 6) do or do not associate economic symbiosis with competition and cultural distinctions depends on their intentions as regards regaining cattle and becoming pastoralist. Status groups in the Lozi kingdom (chapter 7) carefully and actively use material culture to legitimise their authority, while within a Lozi village family tensions are supported and continued in pottery decoration. Thus there are no simple relations between, on the one hand, degrees of interaction or scales of production, and on the other, material culture patterning, because other factors intervene – intentions, strategies, attitudes and ideologies.

But this concern with the active use of symbols in social strategies leaves much unanswered. In particular, why are individual items chosen to be used in this or that strategy? What factors affect the non-utilitarian form of artifacts, which artifacts are decorated and with what styles of design? What decides the overall form of the cultural patterning and how it varies from group to group? If material culture is used as part of ideologies to mask, contradict or exaggerate social relations, what decides the form of these ideologies and transformations? The second conclusion to the ethnoarchaeological studies is that answers to such questions must acknowledge culture as being meaningfully constituted in the sense that each material trait is produced in relation to a set of symbolic schemes, and in relation to general principles of symbolic meaning which are built up into particular arrangements as part of social strategies. The effects of local conceptual schemes were most clearly recognised in the Nuba study (chapter 8). Here all aspects of material culture from burial and settlement to decoration and refuse play a part in forming, and are formed by, the same symbolic scheme. The concepts also frame the social and economic relations and the adaptive strategies of the Nuba tribes and hill communities.

So, while it can be said that material culture is actively involved in the adaptive strategies of groups, it is now clear that the explanation of those strategies and the way in which material culture is involved in them depend on internally generated symbolic schemes.

The two conclusions, but in particular the second, can now be assessed in terms of current work in prehistoric archaeology with the aim of demonstrating some further implications of the ethnoarchaeological work. The enquiry which initiated the ethnoarchaeological approach concerned the nature of material cultures and their interpretation in prehistory. It is possible to reconsider these archaeological entities, 'cultures', in the perspective of the conclusions reached above, and then to move on to a discussion of other spheres of archaeological analysis.

9.1 *Cultures*

If, as has been demonstrated, there can be no simple relationship between information flow and material culture patterning, what factors are to be used in explaining archaeological cultures?

In answering this question, it is helpful to return to figure 1 where two aspects of regional cultural patterning are identified – discontinuity and scale. The ethnoarchaeological work has suggested several types of explanation which are relevant for variation along both these axes.

Discontinuity or boundedness in cultural distributions result from the nature of between-group relations and within-group organisation and structure. In terms of between-group relations, one strategy may be complete assimilation between groups, as in the case of the Kisima Dorobo (chapter 6). Here plateaux of stylistic uniformity occur. But several other examples have shown (chapters 2, 3, 6, 7) that restricted access to resources and competition may be associated with overt expression of distinct material culture identities. Groups may support and justify competitive interaction in areas of economic stress by emphasising overt material culture differences. The competitive relationship may be based on the overt distinctions. However, not all traits may be involved in such differentiation since, typically, interaction continues between competing groups. Boundaries do not restrict the movement of all traits and the between-group interaction and the diffusion of cultural styles may be used to disrupt the ethnic distinctions. But the archaeologist can measure directly, using techniques such as regression analysis and association analysis, if any traits are showing discontinuities and boundaries (kinks) in their distributions. If there are other reasons for inferring conditions of stress, then it may be possible to interpret such boundaries as being related to an enhanced consciousness of ethnic differences with increased competition between ethnic groups. Cohen (1977) has suggested that bone assemblages, population densities and soil degeneration may be used as indicators of economic stress. But while the archaeologist may in some cases be able to identify high degrees of ethnic competition, he cannot identify all ethnic groups since many, though having had a name and perhaps even a language of their own, will not have used an overt ethnic affiliation in material culture as part of competitive economic strategies. These latter ethnic groups are 'hidden', in the archaeological record, somewhere beneath continuous variation in material culture (the various tribes of the Lozi – Tc̣tela, Subiya etc. – provide an example in chapter 7).

But the above explanation of discontinuities in terms of between-group ecological relations is insufficient and overly simplistic because of the importance of the second series of factors affecting overt boundary maintenance – within-group organisation and structure. By 'organisation' here is meant social roles and relationships, and by 'structure' is meant the framework of ideas and concepts. Chapter 5 demonstrated that in the Baringo area social tensions between young and old men play an important role in maintaining distinct and competitive boundaries. Ethnic boundary maintenance is here organised as part of within-group strategies. More generally, it is through the internal organisation of social relations that strategies of economic competition are chosen and it is in terms of the within-group organisation that, ultimately, the between-group relations must be understood and assessed. A similar point was made in the study of the Nuba (chapter 8), but here the organisation concerns the structure of concepts and ideas. The structure of meanings associated with purity and boundedness provides a framework in terms of which the regional distributions and regional boundary maintenance must be assessed.

Regional cultural discontinuities are linked to aspects of society and economy by local concepts, by principles of symbolic meaning (e.g.

pure/impure) and by the way those meanings are used and manipulated in each particular context. So any ecological or behavioural view which expects straightforward relationships between material culture boundaries and competition, interaction or ethnicity is inadequate. Any such relationship in a particular case depends on prior analysis of the internal organisation of social relations and of concepts and symbolism. During the latter part of this chapter and in the chapter which follows, some ways of examining the mediating concepts will be discussed.

The above observations allow a reconsideration of the relationships between cultures and peoples and of the ever present concern in European prehistory with defining cultural entities. Even when cultural boundaries (discontinuities) are closely tied to the internal structures of societies, they also become involved in external relations; they are often maintained as part of between-group interaction. Material culture discontinuities may be foci of social and economic interchange. The internal conceptual and social spheres are involved in the crystallisation or appearance of overt cultural boundaries as one strategy in the social and economic interdependencies between groups. The question as to whether cultures (of the kind shown in the upper half of the graphs in figure 1) represent peoples is by-passed by a concern with the role of overt boundaries in between-group interaction. In fact it seems likely that markedly discontinuous cultural areas often do relate to peoples in some non-material sense, but interpretation in terms of political or language units or of self-conscious tribes is not necessarily relevant to the examination of the role and meaning of the cultural boundaries themselves. To break prehistoric Europe up into blocks of material culture which are discussed in isolation and in terms of origins, assimilation and movements of peoples is to miss the central issue: what form of social and economic strategies led to boundary maintenance? To discuss the economies of cultures in isolation, to list separately the economic traits of each culture group, may well completely distort the picture since the very existence of cultural discontinuities suggests the likelihood of economic interdependencies between cultural entities. The economies of different contemporary and adjacent cultures in prehistoric Europe should be studied in relation to each other as interdependent parts in a total system, rather than in isolation. Internal relations and concepts and between-group social and economic interaction often combine to produce a strategy in which overt cultural distinctions play a major part in economic interdependencies.

Figure 1 depicts an aspect of material culture variation apart from discontinuity that requires explanation. The scale of cultural similarity has been shown in the preceding chapters to be related not only to the friction effect of distance, but also to the degree of economic dependence between groups, to the nature of the artifact types being examined, to social and political organisation, and to the meanings associated with an artifact type. In the Baringo area, widespread economic relationships (such as cattle sharing) and pastoral interdependencies are associated with widespread trait distributions. The Nuba, in a segmented environment, with a mainly arable economy and with an internal conceptual emphasis on categorisation and 'groups', have localised relationships and local styles. However, different scales can exist in the same region. In the Baringo area, calabash styles are highly localised relating to localised learning networks among women and to local disruptions of societal constraints by the women (chapter 4). Most types, however, especially those associated with men, are widely distributed. Different artifacts get caught up in different scales, and yet a dominant scale often emerges. Even if very few types of artifact survived, one would have to be exceptionally unlucky to miss the major difference between the mainly widespread Baringo distributions (covering the square kilometres indicated in table 1) and the mainly localised Nuba distributions (figure 77). Thus the material culture patterning for any one region could often be located on the graphs in figure 1. Scale is also related to socio-political organisation. Widespread styles occurred in the Lozi area (chapter 7) because long-distance reliance on the central authority partly replaced the local ties and dependencies.

It should be mentioned in passing that much of the above discussion of cultures, but especially that concerned with discontinuities, is relevant to the overt expression of age, sex and status groups within societies. In chapter 5, the distinctions in dress between women of different ages could be linked behaviourally to the degree of economic and social tensions prevalent within local areas. But these ecological relationships must be understood in terms of the attitudes and intentions of the women of different ages and in terms of the principles of symbolic meaning within which women act and through which women are viewed. The latter point is made in chapter 8, where all aspects of female attire and of the domestic world associated with women are shown to be infused with conceptions of fertility and impurity. So, as archaeologists, we cannot assume that burial information on age and sex differentiation in items of dress relates directly to social organisation since attitudes and concepts intervene. Similarly, status and ranking, as suggested in chapter 7, may or may not be reflected in overt material symbols depending on the way in which principles of symbolism and meaning are manipulated in the particular context.

Having suggested some implications of the ethnoarchaeology for the definitions and interpretation of archaeological cultures, the initial concerns of the fieldwork, it is now possible to move on to consider some of the broader questions outlined in chapter 1. In that chapter it was shown that the view that cultures reflect areas of interaction is just one example of a wider tendency in archaeology towards behavioural explanations. Many of the archaeologists studying settlement, refuse, burial and exchange, have appeared to assume direct behavioural links between material culture and social organisation. If it is accepted, in line with the results of the ethnoarchaeological studies in this book, that material culture is meaningfully constituted, then the implications for the various areas of archaeological work can be assessed. No complete review of archaeology is intended in what follows. The aim is to highlight some of the limitations inherent in particular aspects and areas of archaeological interpretation.

9.2 *Within-site artifact distribution*

There have been many criticisms and reassessments of the suggestion (Longacre 1970; Deetz 1968; Hill 1970) that the matrilocal residence of female potters is reflected in clustered style distributions on sites (e.g. Allen and Richardson 1971), and, more recently, work by Longacre (1981) has been concerned to provide a surer basis for such hypotheses. The matrilocal residence hypothesis is one example of the more general assumption that material similarities reflect degrees of interaction and patterns of information flow. The Stanislawskis (1978) have pointed to one of the difficulties with the application of this assumption to within-site artifact distributions. They have shown how design learning and copying may cut across family and clan lines. There are numerous cross-cutting flows of information in any society and pottery designs can rarely reflect them all. But the Stanislawskis do not provide alternative hypotheses. When do pottery styles reflect particular types of information flow, and why? In chapter 7 it was shown that similarities in pottery styles in a Lozi village cut across learning networks because those styles are used strategically in family struggles over dominance. It is necessary to obtain further examples of the complex way in which pottery styles may be used within small communities to support, hide, justify or comment on power relations.

But further criticisms of the matrilocal residence hypothesis have come from those concerned with post-depositional theory. Work from Kenya (Gifford 1978) and Australia (Gould 1971) to modern Tucson (Rathje 1974) has emphasised the indirect and complex relationships between refuse and behaviour. Schiffer (1976, 4) has offered the principle that archaeological remains are a distorted reflection of past behavioural systems and he has suggested two links between behaviour and material culture which are relevant here. These links are seen as cultural laws called 'correlates' and cultural formation processes (c-transforms).

'Correlates' relate behavioural variables to variables of material objects within a living system (*ibid.*, 13). Schiffer gives Rathje's (1973) hypothesis about the relationship between social mobility and status symbols as an example of such law-like links. There is no indication in Schiffer's account that the material correlates for the same behaviour (for example, social mobility) may vary according to the different ways symbols are negotiated within different frameworks of meaning and within different ideologies.

Cultural formation laws relate variables of a living society to variables concerned with the deposition or non-deposition of artifacts (Schiffer 1976, 14). These c-transforms predict (*ibid.*, 15) the materials that will or will not be deposited (on sites, in burials etc.) by a socio-cultural system, and Schiffer gives as an example the law that, with increasing site population or size and increasing intensity of occupation, there will be a decreasing correspondence between the use and discard locations of artifacts. Other studies concerned with depositional processes have examined the relationship between the life-span of an artifact and its frequency in refuse (David 1972), and the effects of curation (Binford 1976).

Schiffer (1976) suggests that c-transforms can be of value in interpreting archaeological remains cross-culturally so that any influence from the particular framework of cultural meaning appears to be denied. A more specific attempt to demonstrate that cultural traditions are irrelevant to the behavioural study of the distributions of discarded artifacts is presented by Binford (1978), who asks whether the Nunamiut use of animal resources is the result of 'cultural bias' or of 'objective food preferences' (*ibid.*, 38). He shows that the Nunamiut Eskimos maximise their use of different parts of animal carcasses in terms of their meat, marrow and other products. Differences between the Nunamiut and the !Kung Bushmen (Yellen 1977) in terms of variability in butchering practices (Binford 1978, 87–8) and in whether parts of animals are distributed differentially to individuals with different social roles (*ibid.*, 144) are related behaviourally to factors such as distance from kill-site to camp, and the amount of meat coming into the community. It is suggested that the Nunamiut use of animal resources is expedient and adaptively responsive and that it can be seen to be objectively rational.

The fact that the Nunamiut have a good knowledge of which parts of the animal carcass have most meat, and which bones have most marrow is reasonable in view of their heavy dependence on animal food products. But to show that the Nunamiut act 'sensibly' or even 'predictably' is not to offer a full interpretation of their actions. The Nuba also know a lot about animal anatomy and the meat value of different parts of carcasses. But it would be insufficient to describe the Nuba use of animal resources in maximising and functional terms. The mundane practices of cutting up, eating and discarding animal products are enmeshed in a frame of meaning. Sahlins (1976) has shown how, in Anglo-Saxon society today, the maximising logistics of the use of horse and dog meat, and the eating of offal depend partly on a particular symbolic scheme (see also Douglas 1970). Binford provides no evidence at all of the cultural and symbolic context within which the Nunamiut carry out their food processing activities, and it is impossible to evaluate the integration of 'cultural' and 'objective' food preferences in his example.

If it really were to be shown that the Nunamiut have no symbolism whatsoever associated with animals, eating and refuse, then the objective maximisation of resources must itself be understood in its own cultural context. Binford (*ibid.*, 44) accepts that maximisation depends on the social and cultural context but he explains this relationship only in terms of the adaptive role of maximisation. However, the emphasis on function, utility and maximisation in reference to meat, eating and food residues must be seen itself as an ideology or conceptual framework which has to be interpreted as part of the attitudes and beliefs of groups within societies.

Gifford (1977) and Yellen (1977) are more sensitive to the role of cultural context in the on-site patterning of bone residues and they note that different parts of carcasses are given to different statuses and subgroups within societies in their study areas. Yet they provide no general discussion of the way in which 'rational' behaviour in terms of refuse disposal may vary according to underlying ideological or conceptual differences. In Britain, Gypsies live on their rubbish in a way which is considered intolerable to most non-Gypsies. The external appearance of their encampments seems to us to be dirty, unpleasant and unhygienic. But in an interesting study, Okely (pers. comm.) has shown that Gypsy refuse disposal habits are not a function of the short-term nature of their camps. Rather, Gypsies use refuse as part of a demonstration of hostility towards non-Gypsies and as part of an underlying concept of the world. The insides of the caravans are spotlessly clean and great care is taken to ensure that what passes into the body as food is uncontaminated by contact with dirt, itself associated with non-Gypsies. The internal purity and cleanliness are therefore in opposition to the external hostile world of non-Gypsies who are categorised as dirty. The refuse disposal is a marker of this perception. The perception is itself closely integrated into the Gypsy economic strategy by which they fill an important minority niche within the wider society. Gypsies as travellers and as scrap dealers, and non-Gypsies as stable scrap producers are hostile to each other within a competitive symbiotic relationship. The structure of refuse disposal plays a part in forming this hostile socio-economic relationship, but the refuse disposal cannot be linked directly and behaviourally to the socio-economic strategies. The concepts of internal purity and cleanliness intervene.

The ethnoarchaeological study amongst the Sudan Nuba (chapter 8) noted that many aspects of refuse deposition could only be understood in terms of a particular set of Nuba ideas and values. Any archaeological study of the Nuba bone distributions would have to consider the placing of different parts of the carcass and the bones of different animal species around the settlement according to distinctive rules. The discovery of these rules and symbolic principles in settlement organisation and refuse distributions must be a primary concern if the functioning of society and the behaviour of its members are to be interpreted adequately. The Nuba study described the way in which the principle of purity/impurity lay behind the artifact distributions, and such a principle is often likely to be of fundamental importance in interpretations of refuse deposits in view of the clear indications (Douglas 1966) that attitudes to refuse are deeply enmeshed in conceptual schemes. Ethnoarchaeological studies of discard must discover other symbolic principles in relation to refuse and the different ways those principles can be articulated in social and economic strategies. Refuse distributions do not 'transform' aspects of society according to behavioural predictions but according to principles of symbolic meaning.

9.3 *Settlement patterns*

Concepts and symbolism mediate between refuse distributions and on-site behaviour. Recent hypotheses concerning settlement size and the distribution of buildings on sites have had a behavioural emphasis and have neglected symbolic meanings. Settlements are practical and functional, they are lived in and used from day to day, but our ideas of space are not a ragbag of behavioural responses.

As an example of the necessity of examining the symbolic use of space in prehistoric settlement studies, it is possible to reconsider the mathematical relationships which have been set up between settlement and population size. Constant figures or formulae for the settlement area needed per person have been derived cross-culturally (Naroll 1962) and from a sample of Californian aboriginal populations (Cook and Heizer 1968). More complex regression models have also been constructed. Wiessner (1974) suggests that her regression model, derived from Bushman camps, will vary in different types of society such as hunter-gatherer, settled village or urban. Yet in all these studies the link between area and population is assumed to be direct and relatively non-problematic. If we can just collect enough examples, the behavioural law can be refined with confidence. But, in a very large ethnographic survey, Fletcher (1981) has cast considerable doubt on any idea that settlement size reflects population size. Fletcher has shown that while there is an absolute upper limit to the density of people and the frequency of interaction that can be tolerated by people living together, populations in settlements exist at all densities so that any relationship between area and population is difficult to define. The point at which a settlement is considered over-crowded depends to a large degree on the social and conceptual context within which interaction occurs (Yellen 1977, 118), and on the steps taken to restrict the frequency of interaction by, for example, building boundaries and channelling movement. Casselbury (1974, 119) suggests that size/population formulae depend on human proxemic systems and may be unique for each dwelling type and social context. In certain social and constructed environments people are able to withstand very high densities and it is necessary for archaeologists to probe the relationship between settlement and population size from a different perspective, examining how density variation is dealt with conceptually and socially and how attitudes to such variation are linked to beliefs within the total cultural framework.

That spatial organisation in settlements is not a neutral referent of behaviour and social organisation has also been suggested more generally for within-site and regional settlement studies. Hillier *et al.* (1976, 180) show that spatial patterning may not be a reflection of social organisation, but complementary to it. They quote the example of the strung-out settlements of the Tallensi and note that this dispersed pattern complements a very tightly knit social system which holds the community together despite physical separation. Space is not a reflection of society but is organised in relation to social form, often providing an alternative to it. Within the concepts of a society, settlement space may provide a necessary but separate forum for symbolic expression. This is not to say that the organisation of settlement space is unrelated to other aspects of life, but it is to suggest that it is more than a mere epiphenomenon of other realities.

In the Nuba study the organisation of the compound into male and female halves and the relations of the positioning of spears, showers and eating activities to this division was described (for further ethnographic examples see Bourdieu 1977 and Humphrey 1974). Clarke (1972) has demonstrated the ability to interpret male/female oppositions in the distribution of buildings and artifacts in the Iron Age Glastonbury settlement in England. Isbell (1976), in his archaeological study of houses and ceremonial centres in the South American Andes, also recognised male/female distinctions. Yet these archaeological studies (see also Fritz 1978 for an interesting account of settlement symbolism) lack any models of the way in which such oppositions as male/female might be used and might give meaning to social actions and intentions. In the Nuba example, Douglas' (1966) model of sex pollution was described. It is the concept of sexual impurity which links the male/female oppositions in the Nuba settlement pattern to wider concerns within the society such as relations with outsiders and relations between matrilineal and patrilineal lines. An archaeological study incorporating the same model will be presented in chapter 10. Other divisions of space, such as the separation of Mongolian tents into the back honoured or high-status half, and the front low-status half may also constitute and frame social relations (Humphrey 1974). Such symbolic oppositions can be identified archaeologically in the associations of artifact types and in the types of 'furniture' found in different parts of the houses and settlements (see, in an historical context, the work of Glassie 1975, and the prehistoric example in chapter 10). But the models used to relate material oppositions to other aspects of life must not assume any simple reflection of social organisation in settlement pattern. The models must concern the way that concepts such as purity and impurity, constituting and being constituted by the settlement form, are strategically negotiated, sometimes transforming and disguising the social relations.

The two conclusions which resulted from the ethnoarchaeological studies and which were summarised at the beginning of this chapter (the active role of symbols, and the importance of concepts and symbolic meaning in the relationship between material culture and social organisation) have led to an awareness of some of the limitations of settlement studies in archaeology. In the same vein, recent studies of prehistoric burial practices can be assessed.

9.4 *Burial*

Tainter (1978, 107) has suggested that Binford's (1971) ethnographic survey of mortuary practices confirms 'beyond serious contention the argument (still rated sceptically by some) that variability in mortuary practices must be understood in terms of variability in the form and organisation of social systems, not in terms of normative modes of behaviour'. In contrast, it is claimed here that it is not only right to be sceptical of the social reconstruction of cemetery evidence, but that it is also necessary to develop a new approach, based on different principles from those followed by, for example, Binford (1971), Tainter (1975), Saxe (1970), Goldstein (1976), Shennan (1975) and Chapman (1977).

The social aspects that are revealed in patterning in burial data have been the main concern of recent work. In building up a criticism of this position, current interpretations of patterns at three levels or scales will be considered. Some of the types of interpretation that have recently been offered at each of these three scales will be discussed. Ethnographic examples will then be used to outline the limitations of the social approach at the three scales.

Social interpretations

Scale 1: regional patterning. Studies of regional cemetery distributions may identify relationships with political, administrative or social boundaries. Following Bonney (1966), Ellison and Harris (1972), for example, suggest that Saxon burials often occur on present-day parish boundaries in Wiltshire and around the edges of model catchment areas of sites with names with *-ingas* or *-inga-*. Anthropologically, death is often associated with 'liminal' places – peripheral no-man's lands, betwixt and between, boundaries.

A further important aspect of cemetery regional patterning is the relationship between burial and settlement. In some periods in the past, cemeteries occur within or adjacent to settlements, while in other periods cemeteries may be isolated, well away from any settlements. A social interpretation of such variability might be that cemeteries occur adjacent to settlements when the dead and the ancestors are seen as being directly connected to the contemporary community. In such cases, communities may wish to stress their ties and rights to land through their links with the past. Where society and land rights are not closely linked, it may be easier for cemeteries to be placed well away from settlements on peripheral or unused land.

Scale 2: within-cemetery patterning. A similar interpretive model is relevant for the organisation of graves within cemeteries. In some societies, as for example at the late Iron Age Owslesbury site in Hampshire, a distinct and bounded cemetery occurs (Collis 1968) with enclosing and sub-dividing ditches. In other periods in the past, a distinct disposal area for the dead is not found. In some parts of the European Neolithic or in the British early Iron Age, parts of human skeletons are incorporated in normal domestic refuse within sites, in pits or ditches, or in proper graves amongst or under the houses. So a cemetery may be organised and bounded, or it may be scattered and diffuse.

Social interpretations of this type of variation include the hypothesis developed from Saxe (1970) and further refined by Goldstein (1976). 'To the degree that corporate group rights to the use and/or control of crucial but restricted resources are attained and/or legitimised by means of lineal descent from the dead (i.e. lineal ties to ancestors), such groups will maintain formal disposal areas for the exclusive disposal of their dead, and conversely' (Saxe 1970, 119). Thus the presence of formal, including bounded, cemeteries is consistently associated with corporate groups practising lineal descent. Such a group's communal rights to restricted resources, usually land, are justified by links with the common ancestors who worked the land – that is, with the dead.

Another aspect of within-cemetery patterning is clustering of graves. Degrees of clustering can be identified by various forms of spatial analysis. If clusters occur, and if they do not result from chronological variation, they may be interpreted in terms of families, subgroups, clans, moieties, etc.

Scale 3: within-grave patterning. Analysis at this scale may concern the micro-location of artifacts in the grave, placed around or on the body. In the late Iron Age Dorset burials, there is a tendency for ox and pig bones to be located near the head of the corpse, and for sheep bones to be placed near other parts of the skeletons, mainly of women (Chambers 1978). Alternatively, the distribution of the human bones themselves can be examined, as in studies of body position and orientation. Work on burials in British Neolithic megaliths has shown that there is great ritual organisation in the placing of different parts of the skeleton in different parts of the tomb (Shanks, pers. comm.).

Most work on within-grave patterning, however, has concentrated on questions of age, sex and status differentiation, based mainly on the co-occurrence of artifact types. One of the social hypotheses to which much attention has been paid concerns whether status is ascribed or achieved (e.g. Shennan 1975). It is assumed that the recovery of wealthy child burials indicates that status is ascribed at birth, not achieved during life. Since the achieved status of adults may be expressed in the wealthy graves of their children, the hypothesis necessitates difficult assumptions which are discussed fairly by Shennan.

A further important social hypothesis concerning grave content is derived from Binford (1971). The suggestion was made that there should be a strong relationship between the complexity of the status structure in a social and cultural system and the complexity of differential treatment of persons in mortuary ceremonialism. In an ethnographic sample of forty non-state organised societies, Binford claimed some support for his hypothesis although this claim will have to be criticised below. Despite these criticisms, it remains the case that in certain contexts, as the number of cross-cutting roles which are signalled in life increases, so does the complexity of artifact associations and differentiations increase. But if the society then changes and becomes less complex, then it is also assumed that the amount of organisation in the burial data will decrease.

This brief introduction demonstrates that current interpretations of burial data, at whatever scale, are largely concerned with explanation in terms of social behaviour. Crudely, cemetery organisation equals social organisation. Biassing factors such as lack of chronological precision, partial survival, post-depositional disturbance and so on are acknowledged. But the belief remains that patterns in death reflect patterns in the life of a society. The validity of this view is already suspect as a result of the ethnoarchaeological study of the Nuba in chapter 8. The implications of the Mesakin and other ethnographic burial data can be considered at the three scales defined above.

Scales 1 and 2. At the regional scale, Mesakin cemeteries are located adjacent to and within settlements. A social model suggests that this propinquity of cemetery and settlement concerns common and continuous links with the dead ancestors. The same model was seen to be relevant to the bounded character of cemeteries (scale 2). The Nuba cemeteries do not have ditches nor walls round them, but they do often have paths which mark out the perimeters. So is the social model correct? Do the Mesakin Nuba stress common rights to the land which are justified by descent from dead ancestors?

At first sight, the answer to both these questions would seem to be affirmative. The earlier ethnographic accounts (Nadel 1947) record that most land is passed down in matrilineal lines. The community at any one time depends on the communal labour invested by the ancestors. The bounded cemeteries near the settlements could be taken as stressing the links through time in the common ownership and labour placed in the land. Yet these earlier ethnographic accounts are only partially relevant today. At present, as Roden (1972) has shown, a new social and economic situation has developed. There has been out migration and integration into the national Sudan economy. Despite, or perhaps because of, these changes involving different social relations and different patterns of land ownership, the burial pattern remains unchanged to form a certain stability and to act as a key for cooperation and continuity in labour and settlement. Burial customs present an ideal and are not a full or accurate reflection of what actually happens today in social and economic life. This disjunction between burial pattern and social pattern will become clearer as more of the Nuba data are considered.

A further characteristic of patterning at the within-cemetery scale is the distinct clustering of graves. Each cluster tends to have a major chief's grave and those buried in the cluster are usually related in some way. Each cluster in a Mesakin cemetery correlates with a named community section. So the social model that cemetery clusters may relate to 'family' or clan groupings appears to fit the Nuba data. But again, when looked at in detail the correspondence breaks down. In the first place, the distribution of Mesakin compounds is fairly dispersed, not highly clustered in contrast to the graves in cemeteries. Second, the individuals in a cemetery cluster may have lived in completely different off-shoot communities miles away from the community by which the cemetery is located. Many off-shoot groups still think of themselves as belonging to their area of origin and wish to be buried in the original cemetery.

Third, the females buried in a cemetery group have usually spent their lives in quite other communities. Amongst the Mesakin, virilocal residence means that a wife moves to live with her husband in her husband's community. But there is matrilineal succession which means that the children are tied to and often live with the mother's brother and the mother's family back in her home area. So, many parents and children live separated. But the mother is usually buried back in her own home area where her family and children live, not in her husband's area where she has lived most of her life, nor in the same cemetery cluster as her husband. So who gets buried where is a complex question. Neither the composition nor the nature of the social and settlement pattern in life seems to be reflected in burial. Similarly, the artifacts found in the graves of any one cemetery cluster were once used in a variety of different settlement areas, social groups and community sections.

What the cemetery clusters do express is not the totality of what actually happens in social relations, but one aspect of it which is seen as an ideal – the ideal of matrilineal groups. In practice in daily life the matrilineal line is continually frustrated by male dominance and competing paternal rights. But in death the matrilineal group is assembled 'pure', without the husband's presence. As in the Madagascan example to be considered below, the pattern of death reinforces a societal ideal which is only part of what exists in practice and about which there is concern. Once again there is a distortion and structured disjunction between patterns in death and patterns in the living society.

Scale 3. At the within-grave scale, the hypothesis that complexity of artifact associations in graves relates to or mirrors social complexity in life will be examined. More generally, what goes in the grave, the form of the grave and burial ritual can be considered in terms of their relationships to social organisation.

Chapter 8 showed that there is a clear relationship between death and grain in Nuba burials. The emphasis on fertility suggests a fear that misfortune in death may adversely affect the fertility and continuity of the crops and of the family and society. The frequent breaking on the grave of personal items – the items which 'are' the deceased – also removes the impurity and ill-effects of the dead. The Nuba have a strong sense of purity and impurity. Given this strong sense of purity, death is considered as an impure threat. This general attitude to death results in the great amount of effort and ritual which surrounds the boundary between life and death, and, as was shown in chapter 8, the attitude also produces a particular structure to the death ritual itself – the shape of the grave, the breaking of artifacts and vessels, the number and types of artifact placed in and on top of the grave, and the use of ash. The threat of impurity is related to the social position and role of the deceased. In addition, the items owned by the deceased in life must be disposed of. Through such factors, status, age and sex are reflected in Nuba burial. These aspects of social organisation (but not, as we have seen, many other aspects) are reflected in death ritual, but only because of and through the particular attitudes to death found in the Nuba.

If, in the archaeological record, the Nuba case was followed in time by a society without all this ritual, where death was less feared as impure, where little effort was expended in surrounding death and the dead with ritual, and here age, sex and hierarchical divisions were not expressed in graves, it could not be assumed that the society had become less complex. A change to a less complex or less differentiated burial rite does not necessarily entail a change to a less complex society. If age, sex and status are not differentiated in grave content, this does not mean they were not differentiated in life. Rather, the change to less differentiation in burial may relate to changes in both attitudes to death, themselves structurally related to changes in an overall world view, and aspects of social organisation other than hierarchy or overall complexity.

The Nuba example, at the three scales of analysis, suggests that many aspects of social organisation (as, in this case, residence patterns) are not expressed in burial, whereas some aspects are (in this case, for example, the matrilineal group), but that what is represented depends on attitudes to death structurally related to attitudes in life. Because of the dominant role of these attitudes, the aspects of societal organisation which are represented in burial may be ideals picked out from practical social relations or even in contrast to them, reverting and distorting. These characteristics of burial are clarified in two further examples.

As in the case of the Nuba, the British Gypsies studied by Okely (1979) have a strong sense of group purity which is seen as being threatened at death – a polluting event (*ibid.*, 87). All through life, Gypsy is contrasted with non-Gypsy (Gorgio). Gypsies associate Gorgios with dirt and pollution and it is partly because of this that, in the impurity of death, a Gypsy can become Gorgio in that he dies in a non-Gypsy hospital and is buried in a non-Gypsy church graveyard. The society and attitudes of the living are inverted or disguised in death. Everything is turned inside out at death, and in the Gypsy burial, when the body is in the coffin, it is dressed in new clothing put on inside out.

The Gypsy fear of impurity in death also leads to many other characteristics of the death ritual. Before burial the corpse is kept outside the camp; replicas of things liked by the dead person are given as wreaths; actual personal possessions (clothing, bedding, personal crockery, tools) are broken up and burned on the perimeters of the camp, or buried a distance away or dropped in deep water. All this is to ward off the pollution resting with the dead person's objects. The deceased's animals, horses and dogs are killed or got rid of, and his or her hearse trailer is burned. All members then leave the camp in which death occurred, at least for a while.

The Gypsy example shows again how the study of burial must be primarily concerned with attitudes to death and life, and that as part of these attitudes we must expect distortions, partial expressions and even inversions of what happens in social life. The same point is made most forcefully in the data collected by Bloch (1971; 1975) on Merina burial in Madagascar. In his study area Bloch found collective and repeated burial in ancestral tombs often located in the ancestral heartland well away from where the deceased had lived. In day-to-day life, villages move and fission and there is a complex and widespread network of interpersonal relationships. In the sphere of everyday behaviour, the Merina peasant is part of a practical organisation adapted to the economy and ecology of his region and involving flux. But he identifies through the tomb and in sacred behaviour with a quite different ideal organisation of ancestors and stability. The tombs and death ritual support an ideological and social framework (local stable groups) which does not exist in the practice of the dispersed networks and overlapping, ungrouped, social relations. The tombs are a denial of the fluidity of the Merina society.

The possibility of inversion, disguise or distortion of social reality in burial practices seems adequately documented: Church of England burial in modern society expresses an ideal of equality, humility and non-materialism which is blatantly in contrast with the way we live our lives in practice.

A new approach to burial must not expect simple correlations between social organisation and burial. Rather, it must identify the way in which prevailing attitudes to death can be derived from different conceptions of the living practical world. For example, societies have been illustrated which emphasise group purity in their relations to others and in relation to dirt and uncleanliness, and which often view death in a distinctive way. It can only be through such attitudes that mortuary ceremonialism can be interpreted.

In the review of social and behavioural interpretations of burial data in the first part of this discussion, cross-cultural studies were mentioned which purport to demonstrate that the links between society and burial are real and straightforward. Why is it that the complexity of the situation has been overlooked? How have archaeologists been able to derive simple correlations from ethnographic surveys? In Binford's (1971) cross-cultural survey, forty non-state organised societies were examined. It is not clear how this sample was derived, but in any case Binford was unable to test for correlations between death and societal organisation because of lack of data on the latter variable. The link had to be examined indirectly by correlating death practice with means of subsistence. It is not surprising, then, that any real relations were masked.

But we have also seen that while burial behaviour may distort and invert, it does not totally hide. There will always be some aspect of the societal organisation which can be picked out in the gross cross-cultural reviews as being reflected in burial. In the Saxe (1970) and Goldstein (1976) surveys of ethnographic literature, formal disposal areas for the dead were correlated with corporate lineal groups. The Merina formal tomb burial does, superficially and partially, relate to descent groups in society. Yet a closer examination shows that the everyday social relations are based on a totally different scheme.

There is a need, then, for a careful, detailed and critical examination of ethnographic data on the relationship between social and burial organisation. In contrast to the existing surveys, this new work must attempt not only to catalogue and to set up behavioural correlates, but also to interpret in terms of concepts, symbolic principles and ideologies. Interpretation must be in terms of attitudes to death and the way in which those attitudes are integrated within practical living systems and the associated beliefs. In death people often become what they have not been in life. When, why and how this should be so have yet to be fully understood, but we cannot assume simple and direct links.

9.5 *Exchange*

How does the emphasis on meaning and symbolism affect studies of the distributions of exchanged items in prehistory? In answering this question, two aspects of recent studies of prehistoric exchange systems can be highlighted. The first concerns the very broad scale at which the analyses are usually carried out. Thus, studies of Neolithic obsidian exchange concern distributions covering 800 km from source (Renfrew and Dixon 1976); Neolithic Polish flint and Grand Pressigny flint reach 500 and 700 km (Sherratt 1976); *Spondylus gaederopus* has a distribution in prehistoric Europe over 1000 km wide (Shackleton and Renfrew 1970); and in the later Iron Age, the coin distributions in Britain cover areas 60 to 80 km across (Hodder 1977b; Hogg 1971). The list could be extended but a characteristic of all these studies is that the analyst assumes that he can discuss each distribution as having one, or a few, associated exchanged mechanisms. This assumption is retained despite the fact that most of the distributions mentioned above cross several 'cultural' boundaries and occur in a variety of different contexts. For example, Grand Pressigny flint is found in several different local societies in western Europe (Sherratt 1976).

In *Exchange systems in prehistory* (Earle and Ericson 1977) the articles by, for example, Renfrew, Sidrys and Plog discuss the characteristics of total exchange networks. Despite the very broad scale at which it is accepted that analyses of exchange can properly be conducted, there are clear intimations that exchanged objects might mean different things in different local contexts. For example, *Spondylus gaederopus*, exchanged widely into central Europe during the Neolithic, occurs throughout the Bandkeramik (early Neolithic) culture. Towards the eastern end of the distribution in the Nitra cemetery, these shells occur mainly in the graves of males over 30–40 years of age. Yet in north central France, *Spondylus* shells are found in Bandkeramik graves only with women (Burkill, pers. comm.; Sherratt 1976, 567). These shells played a different role in two local contexts within the same broad cultural area. Their meanings differed in the two contexts.

The ability of material objects to have different meanings in different contexts is a common characteristic of all symbols. As students of exchange mechanisms, we can only disregard this aspect of the objects we study if it can be assumed that the meaning attached to an item is irrelevant to an understanding of the way it is passed on from person to person. The use of the terms reciprocal, redistributive and so on may be thought to be analytically descriptive and to be unconcerned with meaning. Yet it would seem very difficult to abstract the movement of an object between two participants in an exchange act from the meaning involved in that act and in the object itself. The meaning in an exchange act involves the symbolism attached to an object in a local context and the symbolic power held by an object in being transferred from one context to another. But this symbolism is manipulated as part of the social and economic relations and intentions of the participants. There is a need to move away from broad studies of total exchange distributions to more sensitive studies of the meaning of exchange acts in local contexts.

The second aspect of recent exchange studies that is to be discussed here follows on from the the first. The broad-scale studies involved statistical manipulations of total patterns, fall-off curves and the like. The aim was to 'play' with these 'end-result' patterns, using regression analysis, gravity models and simulation studies (e.g. Hodder and Orton 1976) in the hope of inferring exchange processes. My own involvement in these approaches has convinced me of their limited value. Some difficulties in the interpretation of fall-off curves were identified in the analysis of pottery distributions in chapter 3. One reason for the lack of success in archaeological exchange studies has been, again, that the symbolism of the object within a social act has been sacrificed for the sake of analytical tractability. 'Behind' the 'end-result' patterns are strategies and intentions involving the manipulation of material symbols in local contexts. For example, 'shoe-last' axes are found widely in Neolithic contexts in central Europe including the Nitra cemetery mentioned above. At Nitra the axes are found only with older men. As in Sharp's (1952) study of the Yir Yoront in Australia, the association of widely traded axes with older men may suggest that axe symbolism constituted the prestige and central position of older males (seen also in the *Spondylus* shells). In the Yir Yoront case, a monopoly by the older men of the axe exchange and their control over who used the axes provided both a real and a symbolic basis for their social position. Whatever the resulting regional pattern of exchanged objects, the local manipulation of the axes as symbols to reproduce a specific set of social relations provides the 'meaning' behind the distribution. The same point is relevant to the distribution of spears and the manipulation of spear symbolism in the Baringo area (chapter 4).

It can be claimed that many recent archaeological studies *have* examined exchange within a social context. However, many of these studies have been concerned less with a specific cultural and historical context and more with general relationships between exchange systems and types of society. For example, links have been examined between reciprocal and redistributive exchange and degrees of social ranking (for example, Renfrew 1972; Hodder 1978). These cross-cultural law-like links are seen as acceptable because of the functional relationships which are assumed to tie exchange systems to social forms. Thus, in one category of society prestige exchange may function to regulate and facilitate the flow of subsistence goods (Rappaport 1968; Sherratt 1976). Exchange is frequently seen as a 'regulatory mechanism' functioning to maintain the social system (e.g. Pires-Ferreira and Flannery 1976, 289), and the inter-regional exchange of goods may function to smooth out local resource scarcities and variations. Such studies fail to give an adequate account of the symbolic meaning in the exchange act since everything is reduced to function.

Other 'social' studies of prehistoric exchange have, on the other hand, examined how the exchange act and the artifacts and symbols exchanged are manipulated within a set of social strategies. In particular, several studies have linked long-distance movement of prestige goods with the development of hierarchies, the elites being supported by, or being dependent on their trade monopoly (Bender 1978; Frankenstein and Rowlands 1978; Pires-Ferreira and Flannery 1976). Yet because of a lack of emphasis on the internally generated meaning of the exchange symbolism, these studies cannot be concerned with why any particular artifact types are conceived as having 'prestige', or some other value, in a local context. Nor do these studies demonstrate how the choice of a particular object as an elite exchange item might, by its associated symbolism, play a part in 'naturalising' or making acceptable the trade monopoly and so the social order. Any particular object type may, in a local context, have a meaning and power resulting from its place within a structured set of symbols. This meaning could be appropriated by an elite group as part of an ideology of legitimation, but such symbolism can only be examined by structural and contextual studies.

Despite the great variety of existing prehistoric exchange studies, there is still a need to break away from broad regional analyses of fall-offs and 'dots on maps' towards an approach which examines how traded items are involved in internally generated strategies within societies, and which examines how the items are given a local meaning, incorporated via local conceptual schemes into strategies and intents.

9.6 *Style*

As for exchange processes, style is now frequently defined and analysed by prehistorians in functional and behavioural terms (e.g. Conkey 1978; Plog 1978). Style is seen as being explicable in terms of its function in expressing roles and relationships and in integrating individuals within groups (that is, groups with common styles). Wobst (1977, 321) defines style as being concerned with the participation of artifacts in information exchange. Style is that which has social and ideological functions as opposed to utilitarian functions. Given this functional view of style, behavioural models can be applied. For example, Wobst (*ibid.*) suggests that style will vary according to the social and spatial distance between 'emitter' and 'receiver'. He indicates that style is important in sending messages between socially distant individuals. Some doubts concerning Wobst's hypothesis were encountered in chapter 3 where intimate and everyday domestic aspects of material culture such as hearth position 'reflected' ethnic identity as much as did items of dress and decoration. Whereas the latter items could be said to concern information exchange between socially distant communicators, the same can hardly be said for hearth position, nor for many of the other humdrum aspects of daily life which are distinctive of ethnic groups in the Baringo area.

The fact that Baringo 'styles' vary equally in both the public and private domains suggests that a functional view which utilises concepts drawn from information theory may be inadequate. The 'styles' of the Mesakin and Moro Nuba differ. But this difference is difficult to explain simply in terms of lack of information flow or in terms of overt ethnic display at a certain social distance. The groups are not 'closed' to each other, and while the argument concerned with ethnic display may help to explain the content of the differences between Moro and Mesakin (i.e. that they *are* different), it does little to explain the nature of the difference (i.e. why they are different in terms of particular cultural traits). In explaining the Moro and Mesakin differentiation it was necessary to examine the attitudes and concepts of the two groups. In other words it was necessary to interpret the form and structure which lay behind the stylistic differentiation.

Style, then, must concern structure as well as function. The different hearth positions in the Baringo area must relate to as yet unexamined variation in concepts concerning the organisation of items and features within the domestic world, in the same way that the organisation of domestic refuse amongst the Moro and Mesakin could be related to differences in attitudes regarding purity. So, styles may well express and justify ethnic differentiation, but the manner in which they do this can only be understood by examining structures of symbolic meaning. Style is the form and structure which lies behind all social functions and all information flows (Conkey 1980); it is the particular way in which general principles of meaning are assembled and reorganised in a local context as part of the social strategies of individuals and groups.

Sackett (1977) accepts that 'style' is the way something is done, the manner in which artifacts function in a specific time and place. But Sackett discusses this 'other', stylistic, component only in terms of its diagnostic value and in terms of its material, social and ideational functions. There is no indication here of how form and structure might be studied as components of style distinct from function.

The different view put forward by Dunnell (1978) that style can be defined as those traits which have no adaptive nor selective value leaves style as peripheral and inconsequential when, on the contrary, it might be brought in as central to all studies of function. It is necessary to develop ways of studying the principles which structure all aspects of life. Such a methodology has been most frequently applied in archaeology to art and design, and it is in these spheres that the word style is most often used. However, the Nuba study showed that the formal and structural examination of decoration and design is only a special case of a more general emphasis on structure as opposed to function that is necessary in studies of cultural styles.

In the analysis of art and design, several ethnographic studies have encouraged archaeologists to do more than simply assign functional significance to particular motifs. Friedrich's study (1970) of potters and their designs noted that specific motifs diffused easily between potters, whereas the arrangement of design, its composition, was more stable. This type of work (see also Munn 1966; Adams 1973; Vastokas 1978; Korn 1978) has led to a wider archaeological interest in the structure of design and a readier acceptance that style concerns more than function. Work on transformational grammars (Muller 1973), various types of symmetry (Washburn 1978), and other aspects of form (Conkey 1977; Leroi-Gourhan 1965; Marshak 1977) has demonstrated the feasibility of structural classifications and analyses of mute archaeological data. These archaeological studies sometimes use the structural classifications simply as additional or alternative ways for discovering population group composition and interaction spheres (e.g. Washburn 1978). But many archaeological studies (e.g. Conkey 1977; Marshak 1977) have been concerned to tie the design structures to other aspects of life. If it is possible to identify coherent grammatical rules in a set of pottery designs, one is often then entitled to ask 'So what?'. It may be possible to demonstrate similarities in the structures of design in settlement and exchange patterns (Adams 1973) but the 'So what?' question still seems appropriate unless an adequate linking hypothesis can be supplied.

It has already been suggested that studies of design styles must be integrated into studies of the overall 'style' of a community. But how is this to be done? In the Nuba example, various aspects of the design structure (position of the decoration in the compounds, male–female oppositions, and the existence of a limited range of strict design rules) were linked to the overall structure of ideas in Mesakin society through the concepts of purity and boundedness. The constraint and classification in the design generation symbolise the general concern with the boundaries between interacting categories (Nuba as opposed to Arab, patrilineal rights as opposed to matrilineal rights). But the design structure does not 'express' the social concerns and adaptive strategies in any simple or direct way since the expression takes place through the medium of the concept of purity. In addition, it was suggested at the end of chapter 8 that the Nuba material culture patterning may not relate to an actual set of socio-economic relations, but that it may be manipulated to represent an ideal that is fast disappearing.

In the study of Njemps calabashes (chapter 4) it was suggested that the greater use of decoration amongst the Njemps and their use of 'zoned' as opposed to 'floating' designs could also be related to a concern with marking boundaries around food and drink, and to a concern with purity and boundedness. But this interpretation in terms of concepts and ideas is not sufficient on its own. Studies of stylistic variation must examine both structure and function. In the Njemps example, the zoned decoration varied within the tribal area. Explanation of this variation concerned the strategies of individuals in their social and ecological relationships. Hypotheses which adequately link design styles to other aspects of cultural patterning must concern both the structure of concepts and the way those structures are manipulated in personal and group adaptive strategies.

There is a need for the further development of models concerning the full variety of ways in which design arrangement can be articulated in socio-economic action. In answering the 'So what?' questions that are put to students of design grammars, the archaeologist must concern himself with how and why those grammars make 'sense', as in the Nuba example, in the overall style of the society. Any study of design form on its own cannot answer major questions of interpretation. There is an interplay between structure and function in style which neither the 'linguistic' nor the 'behavioural' approaches in archaeology can adequately examine. Styles of design are not explainable simply in terms of a set of grammatical rules, nor are they simply functional tools. Rather the design styles comment on, transform or disrupt the styles in other aspects of life. Design styles do not 'reflect' behaviourally, but they are made to 'transform' structurally.

9.7 *Social stratification*

Various types of archaeological data have been examined, and some of the implications of the ethnoarchaeological studies suggested. Whether archaeologists are concerned with regional distributions of artifacts or settlements, with burials or with pottery decoration, they have frequently assumed behavioural links between material culture and society. But the ethnoarchaeological studies indicated that material culture does not reflect, it transforms the relationships in other non-material spheres, and it does so within a particular framework of beliefs, concepts and attitudes. The term transformation as used here differs from the use in Schiffer (1976) where 'transforms' are seen as predictable behavioural reflections, rather than as structural rearrangements within particular conceptual frameworks. The importance of the transformational aspect of material culture can be clarified by considering an area of archaeological interest which cuts across the categories of data so far examined. Social stratification has been studied in archaeology by examining regional and within-site settlement patterns, burials, exchange distributions, and styles of elite artifacts. How does the hypothesis that culture is meaningfully constituted affect our studies of ranking in prehistoric societies?

In answering this question it is necessary to define system and structure in studies of prehistoric societies. Most archaeological work on hierarchisation has been concerned with *social systems* (Brumfiel 1976; Carneiro 1970; Cherry 1978; Crumley 1976; Earle 1977; Flannery 1972; Gall and Saxe 1977; Johnson 1973; Renfrew 1975; Wright 1977; Yoffee 1979). By social system I mean the pattern of relationships and roles, the communication and use of power, relations of dependence and authority, the movement of resources and trade. It is in discussions of social systems that archaeologists talk descriptively of degrees of complexity and of adaptation and homeostasis. Functional relationships are set up between trade, hierarchy, subsistence and so on – between the different subsystems of the total social system. This functional and utilitarian view of society has been the main concern of recent work.

By *social structure*, on the other hand, I mean the rules and concepts which order and give meaning to the social system. The framework of rules is built up from general principles which exist in all societies but which are manipulated and negotiated in particular ways specific to each context. These structural and symbolic principles by which interaction is organised include, for example, the rules of ideologies of domination and the symbolic principles of purity, hygiene, godliness etc. All these various dimensions of meaning are organised and continually reorganised in relation to each other. The structures are continually being renegotiated and manipulated as part of the changing strategies and relations between groups with different powers.

In examining ranking in the social system we can describe burial and settlement patterns, and look at relationships with trade, subsistence and so on (Flannery 1972; Peebles and Kus 1977; Renfrew 1975; Wright 1977). But the real difficulty with this work is: how can we ever go beyond a descriptive exercise of typologising societies into chiefdoms, stratified societies or states, or into degrees of complexity, with associated categories of exchange (reciprocal, redistributive, prestige), and with associated typologies of evolutionary development (however multilinear; Sanders and Webster 1978). Ranking itself, at the level of its description and functional relationships, seems reduced to its barest essentials. To identify, typologise (at whatever scale of detail) and then to set up functional relationships means that if ranking 'works' (i.e. it functions to do something like coping with exchange or a very dry environment or just to keep itself going), then the 'working' is seen as a sufficient explanation. An awareness of the circularity of these functional arguments is shown in the work of Flannery (1972), Flannery and Marcus (1976), Renfrew (1972) and Friedman and Rowlands (1977).

To concentrate on social structure in the sense defined here is, however, to say that there is more to explaining ranking. What archaeologists descriptively call ranking or asymmetry involves domination, power and authority. And in all societies this domination is daily and in each action negotiated and renegotiated between power groups within a dynamic and changing framework of meaning. Domination is accepted within a symbolic or conceptual framework which gives meaning to socio-economic interactions. These conceptual frameworks through which ranking is viewed and accepted are ideologies of legitimation. Through the ideologies, the exercise of power is negotiated and understood. The various principles of meaning (e.g. pure/impure) and the structures built up from them are manipulated ideologically to represent, misrepresent, disrupt or deny social reality.

Domination might become accepted ideologically in a number of different ways. Three of the many ways in which principles of meaning and ideologies might be used in social contexts can be outlined (Giddens 1979). First, an ideology can be used to *deny* the conflict within society. It is normally in the interests of dominant groups if the existence of contradictions is denied or their real locus is obscured. Amongst the Lozi (chapter 7), restriction of Mbunda rights was obscured by the encouragement to adopt Lozi material symbols. Secondly, an ideology can represent the sectional interests of one group as the *universal interests* of the total society. So the ideas of the ruling class become the ruling ideas. In Baringo societies, the dominance of the older men is presented as being necessary to ensure the safety of all under the ideology associated with distinct, competitive and overt ethnic boundaries. Thirdly, *naturalisation* occurs in an ideology when the arbitrary existing system of relations appear immutable and fixed, as if they are natural laws. The Lozi elite naturalised its rights and divine powers by the repetition of cultural differences in all aspects of life, from mundane stools and fences to the regalia of high office.

Some archaeologists might allow that meaning, symbolism and ideology *are* important in social stratification while denying any need to concern themselves with what are thought to be 'intangibles'. The participants in Hill (1977), and Thomas (1974, 75) assert that systems can be studied without reference to structures of meaning or to people's thoughts and feelings. But it is possible to see the dangers of such a viewpoint by considering the three types of ideology outlined above in reference to the one class of material culture which is used most frequently by archaeologists to infer ranking; that is, burial. Depending on the ideology, material symbols in burial could be used and could relate to ranking in different ways. If there was an ideology of denial, we might find that burial pattern denied the social differentiation. Something of this type happens in modern Britain (Parker Pearson, pers. comm.). The material culture associated with burial ritual can be used as part of an ideology which makes domination acceptable by denying it. The same pattern might occur in burial when sectional interests are presented as universal – the second type of ideology.

But with the third type, naturalisation, we might find that burial differentiation accurately reflects social differentiation. Indeed *all* aspects of material under such an ideology might reinforce social differentiation and make it appear natural by endlessly repeating the same organisation in all spheres, down to the trivia of cooking pots, stools and hair combs.

So, how material culture relates to society depends on the ideological structures and symbolic codes. The archaeologist cannot disregard meaning and symbolism in analysing ranking because behind the social system is a structure and society.

Various archaeological studies of ranking influenced by structural-Marxist theories (Friedman and Rowlands 1977; Frankenstein and Rowlands 1978; Bender 1978) do see material items such as prestige goods as maintaining relations of dominance and dependence. But there is, in the archaeological applications and discussions, almost no account of legitimation or of the symbolism of material culture as part of ideologies. The emphasis is on material correlates and on the reflective nature of material culture. It is difficult for archaeologists to understand the way the system of ranking and exchange is allowed to develop because the ideology under which the domination and monopoly of prestige goods are accepted and negotiated is little examined. Other, functional, studies of the role of 'cognised models' in ranked societies have emphasised the importance of belief and cognition in regulating social relations (Flannery 1972; Flannery and Marcus 1976). But again the role of material culture in transforming those relations under different ideologies is little discussed.

9.8 *Conclusion*

By the end of chapter 7, the studies in Baringo, the Leroghi plateau and western Zambia had indicated that any hypothesis that material culture passively reflected other aspects of life was inadequate. Objects as symbols were seen to be actively used in social strategies. But as a result of the work in chapter 8, this view could itself be questioned because the use of symbols, and the social strategies themselves, are couched within conceptual schemes. These schemes utilise general principles of meaning (pure/impure etc.) to build a framework which lies behind, or 'structures' all aspects of action and all the uses of material symbols. Material culture patterning is thus a structural transformation of other aspects of life. By 'structural transformation' is meant that the link between material culture and social relations lies in the conceptual schemes. Thus refuse and burial patterns relate to social organisation via such concepts as purity and pollution. But by 'structural transformation' is also meant that the concepts can be manipulated ideologically to represent, mis-represent or disrupt social realities. Structural transformations are thus different from Schiffer's (1976) behavioural transforms in that the latter involve direct and predictable functional links between social and 'environmental' conditions and artifact patterning; 'if A then B'. There is little place for the mediation of symbolic principles in the behavioural viewpoint.

The relevance of the idea that material culture transforms structurally rather than reflects behaviourally has been demonstrated in this chapter by considering briefly a variety of different areas of archaeological analysis. In all the areas examined, the dominant concern in recent work has been with the behavioural links between society and material culture. Yet the links between society are much more complex than has been allowed because principles of symbolic meaning intervene. The archaeologist is unable to interpret information on settlement, burial, refuse, pottery decoration and so on without considering the role of the structure of beliefs and concepts in social action. An acceptance of the notion that culture is meaningfully constituted leads to an awareness of limitations in existing approaches and will lead to different types of archaeological analyses and interpretations.

10
Conclusions and prospects

> Environments to which societies are adjusted are worlds of ideas,
> collective representations that differ not only in extent and content,
> but also in structure.
>
> (Childe 1949, 22)

In the preceding chapter it was suggested that there are few areas in
prehistoric archaeology in which there has been sufficient emphasis on
symbolism and conceptual schemes. Such an emphasis is of importance
in reconstructing the past since material culture transforms, rather
than reflects, social organisation according to the strategies of groups,
their beliefs, concepts and ideologies. In this final chapter I wish to
consider briefly some broader aspects of a less behaviourally and less
ecologically oriented archaeology.

10.1 'Wholeness'

It is suggested that interpretation of the past might make use of a concept
of structure as demonstrated in the Nuba study (chapter 8) and defined
more clearly in chapter 9. Each aspect of the material culture data,
whether burial, settlement pattern, wall design or refuse distribution, can
be interpreted in terms of common underlying schemes. These structures
of meaning permeate all aspects of archaeological evidence. Each
material item has significance in terms of its place in the whole. This is
not to say that the patterns in the different types of data are always direct
mirror images of each other. Rather, the identifiable patterns are
transformations, often contrasting, disrupting or commenting on basic
dichotomies and tensions within the social system and within the
distribution of power. Yet the emphasis on 'wholeness' remains. The
structures behind the patterning in one type of data must be interpreted
by reference to other structures in other categories of information.

An emphasis on wholeness is also the hallmark of the application of
systems theory in processual archaeology. But it is possible to identify
differences in the concept of wholeness or totality as used by systems
theorists and as described here. All applications of systems theory in
archaeology have begun with a definition of a subsystem, or with a list
of all subsystems (e.g. Clarke 1968; Renfrew 1972). The aim of the
analysis is then to examine the interrelationships between the different
subsystems, and to explain one in terms of its connections to others.

Indeed, it is the very essence of systems theory that the behaviour of one subsystem can be understood and predicted from its functional links to others. As one part of the system changes, the others regulate and adapt to regain homeostasis (Plog 1975, 208; Binford 1972, 20; Flannery 1972, 409; Hill 1971, 407). One subsystem which has recently been seen as important is the 'ideational' (Drennan 1976; Fritz 1978; Flannery and Marcus 1976). Flannery (1972, 409) accepts that the human population's 'cognised model' of the way the world is put together is not merely epiphenomenal but plays an essential part in controlling and regulating societies. Everything ideational is put in a separate subsystem and then the functional links between this and the other subsystems are examined in terms of regulation and management.

The concept of wholeness in archaeological systems theory thus concerns the functional relationships between separate subsystems. In assessing this viewpoint it should first be recognised that the subsystems are of the analyst's own making. He decides on separating out, for example, everything ideational, and then examines the links between categories which have been arbitrarily defined (Sahlins 1976). Second, the structure of the whole derives from the functional links between the parts, and there is no real concept of wholeness itself except as a by-product of the relationships between parts. Few archaeologists have claimed that there are absolute one-to-one behavioural links between environments and human societies. So if one asks 'Why does the system have the form it does?', 'What structures the whole?', the functional view inherent in systems theory can only provide partial answers.

On the other hand, it may be easier to answer such questions satisfactorily if archaeologists consider the symbolic principles which link the parts together. These principles permeate the functional relationships, and they form the whole. The whole does not come from the parts but from the underlying structures. It is not adequate to separate everything ideational into a separate subsystem. Rather, idea and belief are present, and are reproduced, in all action, however economic or mundane. Structures of meaning are present in all the daily trivia of life and in the major adaptive decisions of human groups. Material culture patterning is formed as part of these meaningful actions and it helps to constitute changing frameworks of action and belief. The concept of wholeness from this structural point of view is more absolute and more far-reaching than in systems theory as used by archaeologists.

In practical terms the need for systems theorists to locate separate subsystems has been associated with a concern for identifying variability (e.g. Binford 1978, 3). In its annual adaptive cycle, a community is seen as going through different tasks at different positions on the landscape. In different environmental and strategic contexts, different assemblages will be left as a result of variation in adaptive behaviour. So the search of the archaeologist is for adaptively linked variation in cultural assemblages. This approach pays little attention to schemes common to the varying assemblages. Binford (*ibid.*, 3) accepts that adaptive responses 'draw upon a repertoire of cultural background', but this cultural component is considered peripheral and unimportant. Under this behavioural view, there is little emphasis on methodologies for examining how variability can be studied and interpreted as transformations following underlying rules. That which articulates and gives meaning to the variability is given less attention than the variability itself and its functional relationships.

On the other hand, the traditional 'normative' emphasis (see chapter 1 and Binford 1978) concerned with cultural norms and mental templates has contrasting limitations. Here the examination is of the cultural codes held in common by members of society regardless of the setting in which they find themselves. This approach is less able to cope with variability and with expedient adaptive responses.

It is necessary then to bridge the gap between the emphasis on variability and the emphasis on static, shared norms and templates. There is a need to move away both from studying variability without examining the structures which bind that variability together, and from studying cultural codes which do not allow for adaptive intelligence. In the ethnoarchaeological studies in this book I have tried to examine symbols in action, and I have shown how structures of meaning relate to practice – how symbol sets are negotiated and manipulated in social action. Cultural patterning is not produced by a set of static fixed norms but is both the framework within which action and adaptation have meaning, and it is also reproduced in those actions and in the adaptive responses that are made. There is no dichotomy between an interest in culture and meaning and a concern with adaptive variability. Indeed, interpretation of the past must integrate both research aims. The examination of variability on its own is insufficient.

Processual, behavioural and systems theory archaeology have accompanied a massive fragmentation and compartmentalisation of archaeological research. The discussion above suggests one of the reasons why this should be so. The emphasis in recent archaeology has been on defining subsystems and their law-like behavioural links with an 'environment'. The initial need to define subsystems in analytical research has provided a framework for the specialisation of methods, theories and generalisations relevant to each subsystem. There are those who work on settlement studies or spatial analysis, while others write books or conduct cross-cultural research on burial, exchange, subsistence economies, art and so on. Despite attempts to break down these barriers (e.g. Flannery 1976), each subsystem realm is developing its own vocabulary which is fast becoming incomprehensible to specialists in other fields. Much of the literature, teaching and research in archaeology is divided along these lines. There is a need for integration, which would be the logical result of a symbolic and 'contextual' archaeology.

10.2 *The particular historical context*

The type of prehistory that is implied by a concern with the meaningful constitution of material culture patterning is likely to be more particularistic and less concerned with cross-cultural behavioural laws. Material culture patterning cannot be derived directly from the 'environmental' conditions of behaviour. But this is not to say that some form of generalisation will not be used in interpreting the past. If the Nuba data and some of the ethnoarchaeological information are considered as if prehistoric and archaeological, it can be seen that, in giving 'meaning' to the finds and in placing them in a structured 'whole', two broad types of generalisation might be used.

1. Symbolic or structural principles occur widely although they are used and emphasised in different ways in each society. In the Nuba case, the structural oppositions clean/dirty, male/female and life/death would be seen to be marked. These symbolic principles are found in most societies, and knowledge of them aids the analysis in the particular case. The identification and analysis of symmetry in the Nuba art and decoration might make reference to general studies of types of symmetry (e.g. Washburn 1978). We might also include generalisations concerning the relationships between structural principles. For example, in the Nuba case, Douglas' model for the link between pure/impure and an emphasis on categorisation is applicable.

2. As well as generalisations concerning structures and symbolic principles themselves, there are also models and analogies concerning the way man gives meaning to his actions. Such generalisations give indications about the way beliefs and concepts can be integrated into social and ecological strategies, and about the way the structures of the first type of generalisation are used in day-to-day life. In chapter 8, Douglas' model for the relationship between the principle pure/impure and sex dichotomies was described, while it has also been suggested in the accounts of the Njemps, Nuba and British Gypsies that dependent subgroups within larger dominant societies often have a strong sense of purity and boundedness, and place an emphasis on classification and categorisation.

Despite the use of these two types of generalisation, the interpretation of each set of material culture data is unique. The general principles are rearranged into unique patterns in each 'whole'. The particular nature of each set of cultural data occurs for two reasons.

i. The general symbolic principles of the first type are assembled in particular ways. In the archaeological study of the Nuba, it would first be necessary to identify the particular use of general structural oppositions such as clean/dirty, life/death, male/female and the degree of emphasis on classification and categorisation. In comparing the Moro and Mesakin areas it would be noted that decoration surrounds zones with more refuse, suggesting the marking of boundaries between clean and unclean, while the decoration around the flour in the grinding huts and in the toilet areas might also be identified. Many of the rituals marking the life/death boundary could be recovered archaeologically, and if the grave fills were sieved some idea of the association of grain with death might be found. Within the compounds, the division into two halves, male and female, could be identified in the distribution of male and female artifacts and in the overall arrangement of the different types of buildings. An emphasis on symbolic categorisation and separation would be recovered from the distributions of cattle and pig bones, and body and skull bones, while in the art of the Nuba a series of simple but distinct rules would be found.

It would also be necessary to examine the relationships between these different symbolic oppositions. It would be found that cattle/pig could be associated with male/female because of the association of male items with cattle remains in cattle camps and in burials, and because of the association of female items with pigs. So male/female = cattle/pig rather than pig/cattle. This is a particular relationship. In the art, general principles (rotational symmetry etc.) are assembled by the idea of a particular cross or star design. The particular way the elements are arranged into a whole is aided by general hypotheses concerning the relationships between types of symbolic principle. The Nuba dichotomy clean/dirty could be linked to the emphasis on categorisation and boundedness by positing Douglas' model concerned with purity. By suggesting an additional dichotomy such as pure/impure, it may be easier to tie different components into the 'whole'. But the arrangement pure/impure = cattle/pig = male/female = clean/dirty = life/death is particular and specific to the Nuba context.

ii. Really inseparable from (i), except in the stages of analysis, is the articulation of the symbolism and beliefs in social and ecological action. In the archaeological study of the Nuba, reference could be made to models and analogies in the second type of generalisation. Economic evidence and the regional distributions of cultural material would indicate the overt separation of a distinct Nuba group with economic and resource interchange with their more widely spread neighbours (the Arabs). The minority, dependent but symbolically separate position of the hill communities in relation to the Arabs is consistent with the overall concern with the marking of conceptual boundaries and with the principle of purity. Although in this case the Nuba fit one of the models in (2), we cannot predict that the same integration of structure and practice will occur in all similar social and ecological environments, nor that material culture will always be involved in the same way. Other groups in similar situations may manipulate concepts and material symbols differently. As the Nuba communities undergo radical changes, with out migration, closer contacts with Arabs, and the break-up of family groupings, interest groups have chosen to emphasise certain traditional values and certain concepts have come to the fore. The ideological manipulation of symbolism to justify, disrupt, mask or comment on aspects of social reality was examined especially in the studies in Baringo and Zambia. In each particular context, beliefs and material symbols are negotiated and manipulated in different ways as part of individual and group strategies.

Because of the transformations in (i) and (ii), we cannot *predict* what material culture patterning will result in any human and physical environment, but we can *interpret* the past by using our contemporary knowledge of symbolism and ideologies (1 and 2). There can never be any direct predictive relationships between material culture and social behaviour because in each particular context general symbolic principles, and general tendencies for the integration of belief and action are rearranged in particular ways as part of the strategies and intents of individuals and groups. The 'whole' is particular, dependent on context.

An archaeology in which an emphasis is placed on the particular way that general symbolic and structural principles are assembled into coherent sets and integrated into social and ecological strategies can be called a 'contextual' archaeology. The advantage of the term 'context' is that it can be used to refer both to the framework of concepts and to the articulation of that framework in social and ecological adaptation. As in the Nuba example, a cultural item or a social or ecological action can be interpreted in terms of its place within a structured set or whole. But the notion of context must be extended to include historical context. The framework within which actions and strategies are given meaning is built up over time and at each new development this framework is itself altered and transformed from within. The structures at phase B cannot be understood without reference to the structures in phase A. In the Nuba study, the ideology which accompanies the present changes and flux derives from a traditional framework with a long history. In the example of the Merina of Madagascar given in chapter 9, the ideal of stable descent groups which contrasts with the day-to-day links and social relations derives from an older structure of beliefs. Equally, reference to the history of a particular cultural trait is fundamentally important in the interpretation of its position and use within a new phase. Amongst the Dorobo (chapter 6), the Maasai quality of the cultural items is critical, while spear and weapon types may be borrowed from successful groups within the Baringo area (chapter 4) precisely because the types have a history of association with highly esteemed warrior groups.

10.3 *Applying the contextual approach in archaeology*

It has been suggested as a result of the ethnoarchaeological studies that material culture is meaningfully constituted. Material culture patterning transforms structurally rather than reflects behaviourally social relations. Interpretation must integrate the different categories of evidence from the different subsystems into the 'whole'. It has also been suggested that each particular historical context must be studied as a unique combination of general principles of meaning and symbolism, negotiated and manipulated in specific ways. I have already indicated briefly how these points might be followed up in the practice of archaeology by imagining what the Nuba would look like if dug up. This is, of course, a slight of hand. It is now necessary briefly to describe a truly archaeological analysis which illustrates the points made so far in this chapter. The case study cannot be exhaustively described here. It is introduced simply as an illustration, to demonstrate the feasibility and potential of the approach and to provide some flavour of its nature.

Late Neolithic Orkney

The archaeological study concerns the late Neolithic on the Islands of Orkney in northern Britain (figure 84). In Orkney, settlements have been excavated at Skara Brae (Childe 1931; D. V. Clarke 1976), Rinyo (Childe and Grant 1939; 1947) and at the Knap of Howar, Papa Westray (Traill and Kirkness 1937; Ritchie 1973; 1975). Excavations of communal burial tombs have provided general information on ritual and form (Henshall 1963), while the recent excavations at Quanterness (Renfrew 1979) provide an important account of the detail and dating of an Orkney tomb. The 'henges' of Stenness (Ritchie 1976) and Brogar represent a third type of site on Orkney connected with 'ritual' but not demonstrably primarily concerned with burial. The settlements, burials and ritual sites all occur within a relatively small area, the Orkney Islands, and a relatively short period of time, the second half of the third millenium bc. It is possible, then, to compare the information excavated from the different types of site.

Within the terms of the 'processual' approach in archaeology such comparison of information from different types of site would, as has been shown, be of interest. Indeed, in the site report of Quanterness, it is stated (Renfrew 1979, 160) that the comparison of Quanterness and Skara Brae should allow the special factors governing the selection of the fauna used in funerary practices to be assessed. Yet such a comparison is never carried out in the report, and there is no comparison of the information from the different types of site. As was indicated above, this lack of integration is paradoxically symptomatic of much of recent archaeology. The systems approach involves the separation of spheres, subsystems, and then the analysis of the links between them. But the initial separation

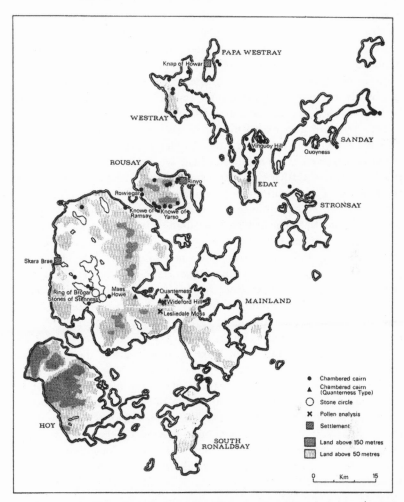

84. The distribution of Neolithic sites on Orkney. *Source*: Renfrew 1979.

hinders the further integration. All that can be achieved is a demonstration of the possible functional links between subsystems, and there is no method for examining the structure which runs through the whole. A systems framework has not provided methods or theories which would focus attention on the comparison of faunal material from a burial (such as Quanterness) and a settlement (Skara Brae). These two types of site are in separate subsystems and the functional links are obscure. It is perhaps partly for this reason that a comparison between the different types of site is never carried out in the Quanterness report.

On the other hand, the focus of interest in the contextual approach is precisely on the comparison of information from different spheres within the same cultural frame and on the identification of common structural schemes. So what similarities and differences do occur between the settlement, burial and ritual sites? In general, there are many similarities in the artifacts found. On the Orkney mainland, Grooved Ware is found at all three types of site, as are particular artifacts such as a highly distinctive decorated three-spiked macehead which occurs at both Skara Brae and in the Quoyness chambered cairn.

Yet there are also major differences in the artifacts found in the different types of site. Although the mainland Orkney pottery is all of the same Grooved Ware tradition, there are distinctions. At the Skara Brae and Rinyo settlements, decoration is more elaborate and more common than at Quanterness tomb and Stenness henge (although such differences could be due to variation in recovery methods, with more attention paid to decorated pottery in the earlier excavations of the settlements). Applied decoration is common at the settlements but rare at Quanterness and absent from the small sample at Stenness. Some particular decorative motifs occur at Quanterness but not at Skara Brae (Renfrew 1979, 79). While many of these pottery differences could be due to chronological variation which is too slight to be identified by radiocarbon dating, the distinctions are supported in other spheres. For example, beads, extremely common at Skara Brae where they often occur in large concentrations in 'stores', are extremely rare in the burial and ritual sites.

The faunal assemblages also vary between the different site types, although the discussion here is hampered by only approximate recording of the faunal material and by the fact that some of the recent excavations have yet to result in fully published bone reports. Yet there are certainly differences in the percentages of animal bones (cattle, sheep, pig) present in the different types of site. There are also differences in the ages of the animals. The bones which occur in both the Skara Brae and Knap of Howar settlements indicate large proportions of very young cattle with sheep being of all ages, while this situation is reversed at the Quanterness tomb. Here there are very many young sheep but relatively few young cattle. Different parts of the animal carcasses are also predominant in the different types of site. Childe's Skara Brae report gives indications of the presence of all parts of the animal carcass including skull, jaw, ribs and vertebrae. Although the account of the Skara Brae animal bones is inadequate for purposes of detailed comparison with the tombs and henge, the latter sites are distinctive in showing lack of particular parts of the animal carcass. At Quanterness the sheep bones include many limbs and feet, but few skull fragments. At Stenness both cattle and sheep are represented by very few ribs, vertebrae, scapulae and skulls. The magnitude of these variations is considered in both bone reports to be too great to be due to differential survival and some cultural selection is assumed.

So the artifactual evidence, including animal bones, from Orkney suggests major differences between the settlement, burial and ritual sites, and in particular between the settlements and the other two types of site. Although slight chronological variation may account for some of these differences, the substantial series of radiocarbon dates from Orkney demonstrate contemporaneity in the late third millenium bc. It would also be possible to argue that the coastal settlement sites, partly dependent on fish (Clarke 1976) and shells, are different from other, as yet unexamined, inland sites whose assemblages may prove to be more similar to the inland henges and tombs. This would seem to be a difficult hypothesis to support in view of the short distances from interior to coast, and in view of the artifactual evidence of the social and economic integration of the different sites (similar pottery styles and other artifact types) but it must remain a competing hypothesis to be examined by future fieldwork.

In any case there is other evidence of the special conceptual importance of the boundary between life and death, settlement and tomb, in Orkney. This evidence resides in the long sequence of complex ritual that can be associated with death as a result of the detailed analyses by Chesterman (in Renfrew 1979) of the human bones from Quanterness. Analysis of the bleached condition of the bones, their fragmentation and placing in the tomb, suggested excarnation of the bodies outside the communal tombs, selection of certain parts of the body, and the placing of these parts in the tombs. There is a large preponderance of feet over hand bones. In the tomb the bones were burnt in a central fire. All this, and the very existence of these large burial structures suggest the special importance attached to the life/death boundary in the particular context of late Neolithic Orkney.

While such evidence of the special distinctiveness of the boundaries between life (settlement) and death (burial) and ritual (henge) is unlikely to be of any surprise to archaeologists, it is important for my purposes to document the importance of the boundaries before moving on to a further characteristic of the Orkney data. This further aspect is that what is reconstituted on each side of the boundaries has many structural equivalencies.

Structural similaries across conceptual boundaries. The overall plans of the Skara Brae and Rinyo settlements are markedly *cellular* with huts leading off long corridors and, within the huts, small 'cupboards' leading off the central area (figure 85). The entrances to both the hut 'cells' and the cupboard 'cells' are small and low.

In the centres of the Skara Brae huts there is always a hearth surrounded by stones placed on edge. Adjacent to the hearth are frequently found artifacts such as flint and stone tools, bone adzes and piercing tools. Although the hearth is usually seen as central, many of

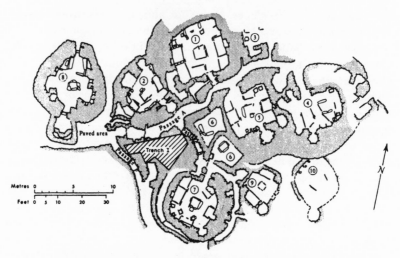

85. Plan of the Skara Brae settlement on Orkney. *Source:* Clarke
1976. Reproduced by permission of the Controller, HMSO.

the huts have the entrance door slightly to the right of the hearth on
entering (e.g. huts 2, 4, 5 in figure 85).

Despite the slightly off-centre position of the hearth and door, the huts
demonstrate a clear left/right symmetry (as seen by a person standing
in the hut entrance). The overall plan shows similar features, in
particular the 'beds', in the left and right of the approximate central axis
from the door to the hearth to the 'dresser' at the back of the hut. Yet
closer examination shows that this apparent symmetry hides repeated
differences, left from right. The right hand bed is always larger (1·5 to
2 m long) than the left hand bed (1·1 to 1·7 m). Childe records (1931,
15) that receptacles (for example of whalebone) containing traces of paint
always occur under the left bed, while beads are also distinctively on the
left side (*ibid.*). It would be tempting to relate this right/left difference
to male/female. However, such an interpretation is not part of my
argument and other interpretations are possible – for example, an
adult/child distinction or some difference in function which is not
involved in sex, age or status differentiation.

While the left and right halves of the huts show both symmetry and
opposition, there is also a cross-cutting distinction between the interior
of the huts, behind the hearths, and the front of the huts between the
hearths and the entrances. The back half of the hut contains a major
'dresser' set in the back wall, and frequently contains 'limpet boxes' set
in the floor. The precise interpretation of the functions of these features
is unclear although some type of storage is usually supposed (Clarke
1976). At the Rinyo settlement (Childe and Grant 1939) a large pot was
found in a recess in the wall facing the door in hut D. Near the hearth
and the front of the hut are the main activity areas at Skara Brae (as

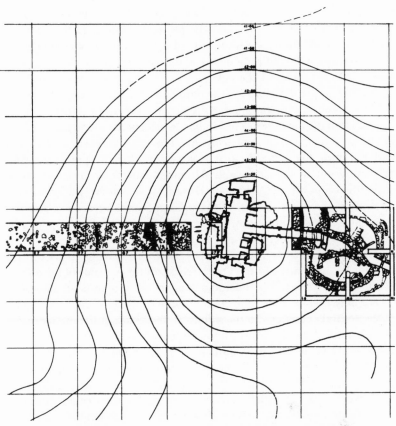

86. Plan of the Quanterness tomb on Orkney. *Source*: Renfrew
1979.

seen in the distributions of tools) and the right hand near corner is
interpreted by Childe, especially in hut 7, as a kitchen or dining area.

A final characteristic of the arrangement of information in the huts to
be mentioned here is the positioning of some engraved decoration around
the walls within the settlement and huts.

The main structural components of the Skara Brae settlement, ap-
parently duplicated in the less extensively excavated Rinyo site, are the
cellular arrangement with cells linked by small, low and often long
entrances, the hearth approximately on the central axis of the hut with
the entrance slightly to the right, the left/right symmetry and opposition,
and the decoration of the inside of the settlement boundary. Many of
these structural characteristics also occur in the chambered tombs. Most
obviously, the overall plan of the tombs is cellular, with six chambers
leading off the central chamber at Quanterness (figure 86) and Quoyness,
and with three side chambers at Maes Howe. At Quanterness, as at Skara
Brae, the entrances are low, narrow and long.

This parallel between the cellular structure of the settlements and chambered tombs is so obvious that it has rarely been remarked or thought to be of importance. But the particular similarity between the settlements and burials on Orkney mainland is given special significance by a contrast with the settlements and tombs on the more northerly islands. On Rousay and the northern isles a few chambered tombs do occur, but the great majority of the tombs are 'stalled cairns'. The tombs here are made up of single galleries divided at intervals by stones partially inserted into the long sides. The 'stalled' aspect is also found at the Knap of Howar settlement on Papa Westray. The two huts excavated (Traill and Kirkness 1937) are divided into two or three sections by stones projecting out of the side walls. Although aspects of the Skara Brae structure occur at the Knap of Howar, such as the positioning of cupboards mainly at the end of the hut opposite the entrance, and the location of beds to the sides, the linear partitioning into segments is clearly different and comparable to the stalled cairns.

A further distinctive aspect of the Orkney settlements is the central location of the hearth. In the Quanterness tomb, evidence of burning is confined to the central chamber and does not occur in the side chambers. There may also be some indication of more burning in the central part of the central chamber. To the sides, left and right, of the main central chamber are higher concentrations of human bones and higher densities are also found in the side chambers. Pottery, animal bones and other artifacts are more common in the central area of the main chamber. The overall arrangement of burning and artifacts at the centre, with lower artifact densities and higher human bone densities at the edges is parallel to the central hearth and artifacts in the huts with the beds, dressers and storage facilities around the sides.

The offset entrances in the huts are paralleled in the placing of the side chambers in many of the tombs. For example, at Quoyness the entrances are offset to the right as they are in the huts.

The plans of all the tombs show a left/right symmetry as has already been identified in the concentrations of human bones at Quanterness. The decoration around the sides of the chambers in the tombs is similar to the huts both in its rectilinear zig-zag content and in its placing often round entrances to side chambers (in the huts the decoration often occurs around entrances to different types of side cubicle).

The settlements and tombs thus demonstrate many structural parallels which must be examined against the extensive ritual surrounding the life/death boundary. Some of the same structures can be identified in the henge at Stenness (figure 87). At the centre of the stone circle is a rectangular setting of stones on edge and there is evidence of burning, particularly in the form of burnt sheep bones, within this feature. The shape, position, construction and contents of this feature are parallel to the hearths in the huts.

The axis from the henge entrance to the central square of stones divides

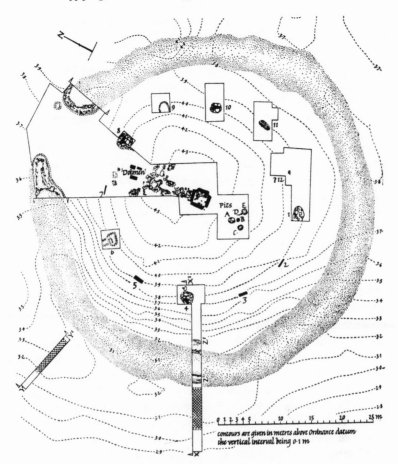

87. Site plan of the Stones of Stenness, Orkney, showing the ring of stones (numbers 1 to 12), the outer bank and inner ditch, and the central setting of stones. *Source*: Ritchie 1976.

the henge into two symmetrical halves, but the bones from the ditches surrounding the two halves indicate an opposition within the symmetry. While sheep bones are found in the ditch to the left of the entrance, no sheep bones are found to the right.

Behind the central stone setting at Stenness are pits, one of which contains a concentation of pure barley while another contains the lower part of a pot. These pits behind the central stone setting are analogous to the storage tanks and facilities behind the hearths in the huts. There is an additional structural parallel between the Maes Howe tomb and the Stenness henge: both have banks *outside* the ditches.

The structural similarities between the settlements, tombs and 'ritual' henges have been described. The parallels concern the cellular arrangement with complex entrances (not found in the henges – see below), the hearth position as part of a centre/periphery pattern, a left/right symmetry and opposition, and a front/back division. The existence of these structural equivalencies on each side of marked boundaries (e.g. between settlement (life) and tomb (death)) suggests that the activities carried out in each context reconstituted and reinforced particular dimensions of order. In ritual and in death the structure is first broken down at the boundaries and then reconstituted on the other side, reinforcing and naturalising the day-to-day order of life in the settlements.

Yet in discussing the henge at Stenness one major aspect of the structure was not examined. Neither the Ring of Brogar nor the Stones of Stenness are in any sense cellular in plan. The henges have centres and encircling rings; they have no cubicles nor cells nor long narrow entrances. Everything is organised around one centre, and in this the plan of the henge denies or leaves out the multi-centred form which is so distinctive of both the burial and settlement plans.

Henges and change. In one respect the Orkney henges reverse the settlement and burial structures. To examine this difference in structure it is necessary to begin to examine changes through time. Renfrew (1979) has suggested that the earlier Neolithic on Orkney is characterised by an egalitarian society. This conclusion is derived from the form and distribution of burials, settlements and artifacts in Orkney which show no indication of ranking. But in the later part of the Neolithic (late second millenium bc) a few monuments of larger scale were constructed such as Maes Howe and the henges themselves. The major monuments occur in close proximity in the central part of mainland Orkney and for the first time suggest some form of centralised organisation. It should be emphasised that the settlements and many of the tombs continue in use during both periods.

The suggested change from local and equivalent communities to some degree of centralisation is supported by evidence from other parts of Britain. The change in burial may indicate a real change in Orkney social organisation. But carbon 14 for the Orkney sequence is of particular interest in that the dates place the Stenness henge earlier than the Maes Howe tomb. A bridge between the decentralised and the centralised phases of the Orkney Neolithic occurs in the 'ritual' of the henges.

The denial in the ritual sites of an aspect of the structure found in the other classes of site marks a contrast. This ritual contrast in structure is similar to what Turner (1969) has termed 'antistructure'. Turner suggests that it is often in the sacred or 'holy' undermining of structure that the structural order is in fact revitalised. The reconstitution of structure out of contrast is often associated with a feeling of community he calls 'communitas'. The central location of the henges in the Orkney Islands suggests a general community focus in ritual even prior to the development of an elite and it indicates that significance may reasonably be given to the lack of cellular structure in the henges. The later association of the especially large tomb of Maes Howe with these central henges is taken here as indicating that the 'communitas' and subversion in ritual were manipulated so that they became associated with the emerging status group. The elite could develop out of the pre-existing system only through the ritual reversal of structure, from cellular to centred, within an otherwise familiar setting in which the settlement and burial activities were repeated and supported. The one part of the structure which was changed concerned the new centred arrangement, the lack of equivalent cells. A henge expressed in one unit the images in numerous individual components in settlements and burials. It provided a ritual symbol of unity which could in turn be used to support an elite. In addition, the reconstitution of the settlement structure in a ritual setting associated with a dominant group may indicate that knowledge about ritual and the symbolic significance of daily activities was controlled by high status individuals and contributed to their legitimation.

Returning to the earlier Neolithic in Orkney, related arguments may be used to account for the similarity between burial and settlement forms. Although Renfrew has described society at this earlier stage as egalitarian, senior males or lineage heads would have been socially dominant (Bloch 1975) within local groups and the burial ritual may have legitimated their authority through ties with the ancestors (Friedman and Rowlands 1977). The burial form, as an image of the settlement form, would relate the ancestors, the past and the ritual to the daily activities within the settlements. The links made in this way between seniors, ancestors, burial and settlement would act to legitimate the dominance of seniors and their central focus in daily activities within settlements and in the social relations there symbolised. The increased dominance of the social group buried at Maes Howe was also based on the manipulation of a familiar organisation of space within the tomb and on symbolic references in the burial ritual to the mundane activities of the individuals inhabiting settlements such as Skara Brae.

Review of the Orkney study. Since the archaeological analysis of the Orkney material was introduced here as an illustration, it may be helpful to examine the procedure of analysis in order to refer back to the more general conclusions at the beginning of this chapter.

a. 'Wholeness'. In the initial stage of the Orkney analysis a set of structural relationships was identified and then 'tested' across different spheres (settlement, burial and ritual) and in different regions (mainland and northern Orkney). It was not assumed that the structure in each sphere should reflect that in others, but rather transformations and contrasts were identified. This stage of analysis, demonstrating and identifying pattern, took up the major part of the account.

In the second stage an idea was taken from Turner that structure and antistructure reinforce each other, that structure exists in reference to antistructure in ritual. This hypothesis expresses a principle concerning the way in which man constructs meaning. It is not a behavioural law since it does not say 'if there are certain conditions, then there will be an interplay between structure and antistructure'. Rather, it suggests that structure and antistructure are logically linked.

b. The particular context. The hypothesis was then made that the structural transformations could have been manipulated as part of social action (the development of an elite), so influencing the particular way in which hierarchisation occurred. It was suggested (again from Turner) that the organisation of ritual may provide 'communitas', and the further hypothesis was then made that this sense of community in an earlier phase could be appropriated by an emerging elite to form a new system in the following phase. Here a general functional model has been used, but understanding of the particular way in which hierarchisation had developed by the end of the period is contributed to by the structural analysis. The structure in the later phase is transformed out of the structure in the earlier phase, manipulated as part of the strategies of groups within societies.

10.4 *Summary and some further prospects*

The ethnoarchaeological studies in Kenya and Zambia led to a realisation that symbols are actively involved in social strategies. Because of the active involvement, the symbols may be used to mask, exaggerate or contradict certain types of information flow and social relationships. The Sudan example showed that the form of these transformations depends on general conceptual principles. An archaeology which accepts and develops these points would probably be relatively particularistic in the sense that the conceptual framework within which man acted and constructed meaning would be seen as being unique to one spatial and historical context. The conceptual framework itself would be seen as having been built up strategically from general and widely found principles. The various principles are combined to provide a structure which runs through the whole of the material culture patterning, through all the types of archaeological evidence. The different subsystems and the behavioural variability from site to site are interpreted in terms of the principles and concepts which play a part in all social and ecological actions.

But it is insufficient merely to describe what might be done in archaeology in reaction to the ethnoarchaeological studies. And so in this final chapter I have provided a brief archaeological illustration. The particular interpretations provided, like most explanations, will ultimately be proved to be wrong. But the very possibility of proof and disproof is important in demonstrating the feasibility of following up the general implications of the ethnoarchaeological work. The archaeological example in this chapter suggests that studies and interpretations of the past may be able to incorporate symbolic principles and the framework within which man gives meaning to his actions.

As the quote at the beginning of this chapter indicates, the conclusions reached in this book are hardly new. Many of the suggestions made here in relation to prehistory are accepted within historical archaeology (Deetz 1967; Ferguson 1977; Glassie 1975; Leone 1977; Schmidt 1978). Yet I think the conclusions have been worth describing in view of the functional, behavioural and ecological emphases in many recent prehistoric studies. Recent approaches in many fields of archaeological research were described and contrasted with the ideas resulting from the ethnoarchaeology in chapter 9.

The prospects for the further development of a non-behavioural, contextual archaeology, depend to a large extent on the further expansion of ethnoarchaeological investigations. We need to know much more about the role of material culture patterning in reproducing conceptual frameworks, and about the ideological manipulation of material items in social and ecological strategies. On a broader front there is a need for archaeologists to integrate theories and ideas from a wide range of studies concerned with structure, meaning and social action. The prospect is for a debate in archaeology concerning structuralism (Piaget 1971; Levi-Strauss 1963) and its various critiques (Bourdieu 1977; Pettit 1975; Sperber 1974), post-structuralism (Ardener 1978; Harstrup 1978), structural-Marxism (Godelier 1977; Friedman and Rowlands 1977) and contemporary social theory (Giddens 1979; Marsh, Rosser and Harré 1978). What is meant by concepts such as ideology, legitimation, power, symbol and social structure must be argued within the archaeological literature and the concepts must be incorporated into interpretations of the past. The ethnoarchaeological studies presented in this book have resulted in the asking of many more questions than have been answered. But they have at least suggested the urgency of developing a broader archaeology, more fully integrated into the social sciences.

BIBLIOGRAPHY

Adams, M. J. (1973). Structural aspects of a village art. *American Anthropologist*, **75**, 265–79.

Ardener, E. (1978). Some outstanding problems in the analysis of events. In E. Schwimmer (ed.), *The yearbook of symbolic anthropology*, **1**. Hurst, London.

Arnold, D. E. (1978). Ceramic variability, environment and culture history among the Pokom in the Valley of Guatemala. In I. Hodder (ed.), *Spatial organisation of culture*. Duckworth, London.

Allen, W. and Richardson, J. (1971). The reconstruction of kinship from archaeological data: the concepts, the methods and the feasibility. *American Antiquity*, **36**, 41–53.

Bakker, J. A. (1979). *The TRB West Group*. University of Amsterdam, Amsterdam.

Bender, B. (1978). Gatherer-hunter to farmer. *World Archaeology*, **10**, 204–22.

Bergmann, J. (1968). Ethnosoziologische Untersuchungen an Grab- und Hortfundgruppen der älteren Bronzezeit in Nordwestdeutschland. *Germania*, **46**, 224–40.

Binford, L. R. (1965). Archaeological systematics and the study of cultural process. *American Antiquity*, **31**, 203–10.

(1971). Mortuary practices: their study and their potential. In J. A. Brown (ed.), *Approaches to the social dimensions of mortuary practices*. Society for American Archaeology Memoir, **25**, Washington D.C.

(1972). *An archaeological perspective*. Academic Press, New York.

(1973). Interassemblage variability – the Mousterian and the 'functional' argument. In C. Renfrew (ed.), *The explanation of culture change*. Duckworth, London.

(1976). Forty-seven trips. In E. S. Hall (ed.), *Contributions to anthropology: the interior peoples of northern Alaska*. Ottawa National Museum of Man, Ottawa.

(1978). *Nunamiut ethnoarchaeology*. Academic Press, New York.

Blackburn, R. H. (1973). Okiek ceramics and evidence for central Kenya prehistory. *Azania*, **8**, 56–70.

(1974). The Okiek and their history. *Azania*, **9**, 139–57.

Bloch, M. (1971). *Placing the dead*. Seminar Press, London.

(1975). Property and the end of affinity. In M. Bloch (ed.), *Marxist analyses in social anthropology*. ASA, London.

Bonney, D. J. (1966). Pagan Saxon burials and boundaries in Wiltshire. *Wiltshire Archaeological Magazine*, **61**, 33–50.

Bourdieu, P. (1977). *Outline of a theory of practice*. Cambridge University Press, Cambridge.

Brumfiel, E. (1976). Regional growth in the eastern valley of Mexico: a test of the 'population pressure' hypothesis. In K. V. Flannery (ed.), *The early Mesoamerican village*. Academic Press, New York.

Burkitt, M. C. (1921). *Prehistory: a study of early cultures in Europe and the Mediterranean basin*. Cambridge University Press, Cambridge.

(1923). *Our forerunners*. William and Norgate, London.

Carneiro, R. (1970). A theory of the origin of the state. *Science*, **169**, 733–8.

Casselbury, S. E. (1974). Further refinements of formulae for determining population from floor area. *World Archaeology*, **6**, 117–22.

Chambers, S. A. (1978). An analysis of Iron Age inhumation burials in the Dorset area and an assessment of their value as indicators of social organisation. Dissertation, Leeds University Extra-Mural Department.

Chapman, R. W. (1977). Burial practices: an area of mutual interest. In M. Spriggs (ed.), *Archaeology and anthropology*. British Archaeological Report Supplementary Series 19. BAR Publications, Oxford.

Cherry, J. (1978). Generalisation and the archaeology of the state. In D. Green, C. Haselgrove and M. Spriggs (eds.), *Social organisation and settlement*, British Archaeological Report International Series **47**. BAR Publications, Oxford.

Childe, V. G. (1931). *Skara Brae. A Pictish village in Orkney*. Kegan Paul, London.

(1948). *What happened in history*. Penguin, Harmondsworth.

(1949). *Social worlds of knowledge*. Oxford University Press, Oxford.

(1950). Social evolution in the light of archaeology. *Mankind*, **4**, 175–83.

(1951). *Social evolution*. Schuman, New York.

(1956). *Piecing together the past*. Routledge and Kegan Paul, London.

(1958). Valediction. *Bulletin of the Institute of Archaeology*, **1**, 1–8.

(1962). *The prehistory of European society*. Penguin, Harmondsworth.

Childe, V. G. and Grant, W. G. (1939). A Stone-Age settlement at the Braes of Rinyo, Rousay, Orkney. *Proceedings of the Society of Antiquaries of Scotland*, **73**, 6–31.

(1947). A Stone-Age settlement at the Braes of Rinyo, Rousay, Orkney. *Proceedings of the Society of Antiquaries of Scotland*, **81**, 16–42.

Clark, G. (1968). *Archaeology and society*. Methuen, London.

Clarke, D. L. (1968). *Analytical archaeology*. Methuen, London.

(1972). A provisional model of an Iron Age society and its settlement system. In D. L. Clarke (ed.), *Models in archaeology*. Methuen, London.

Clarke, D. V. (1976). *The Neolithic village at Skara Brae, Orkney: 1972–73 Excavations: an interim report*. HMSO, Edinburgh.

Cohen, A. (1974). *Two-dimensional man*. Routledge and Kegan Paul, London.

Cohen, M. N. (1977). *The food crisis in prehistory*. Yale University Press, New Haven.

Coles, J. (1963–4). Scottish middle Bronze Age metal-work. *Proceedings of the Scottish Antiquarian Society*, **97**, 82–156.

Collis, J. (1968). Excavations at Owslebury, Hants: an interim report. *Antiquarian Journal*, **49**, 18–31.

Conkey, M. (1977). Context, structure and efficacy in Palaeolithic art and design. Paper presented at the Burg Wartenstein Symposium, **74**.

(1978). Style and information in cultural evolution: toward a predictive model for the Palaeolithic. In C. Redman *et al.* (eds.), *Social archaeology: beyond dating and subsistence*. Academic Press, New York.

(1980). Some thoughts on boundedness in art and society. Paper presented at the Structuralism and Symbolism in Archaeology Conference, University of Cambridge.

Cook, S. F. and Heizer, R. F. (1968). Relationships among houses, settlement areas, and population in aboriginal California. In K. C. Chang (ed.), *Settlement archaeology*. National Press, Palo Alto.

Cordell, L. S. and Plog, F. T. (1979). Escaping the confines of normative thought: a reevaluation of Puebloan prehistory. *American Antiquity*, **44**, 405–29.

Crawford, O. G. S. (1912). The distribution of Early Bronze Age settlements in Britain. *Geographical Journal*, **40**, 184–203.

(1921). *Man and his past*. Oxford University Press, London.

Crumley, C. (1976). Toward a locational definition of state systems of settlement. *American Anthropologist*, **78**, 59–73.

Cunliffe, B. (1974). *Iron Age communities in Britain*. Routledge and Kegan Paul, London.

Dalton, G. (1981). Anthropological models in archaeological perspective. In I. Hodder, G. Isaac and N. Hammond (eds.), *Pattern of the Past*. Cambridge University Press, Cambridge.

Daniel, G. (1962). *The idea of prehistory*. Penguin, Harmondsworth.

David, N. (1971). The Fulani compound and the archaeologist. *World Archaeology*, **3**, 111–31.

(1972). On the life span of pottery, type frequencies and archaeological inference. *American Antiquity*, **37**, 141–2.

Deetz, J. (1967). *Invitation to archaeology*. Natural History Press, New York.

(1968). The inference of residence and descent rules from archaeological data. In S. R. Binford and L. R. Binford (eds.), *New Perspectives in archaeology*. Aldine, Chicago.

Douglas, M. (1966). *Purity and danger*. Routledge and Kegan Paul, London.

(1970). *Natural symbols*. Barrie and Rockliff, London.

Drennan, R. D. (1976). Religion and social evolution in Formative Mesoamerica. In K. V. Flannery (ed.), *The early Mesoamerican village*. Academic Press, New York.

Dundas, K. R. (1908). Notes on the origin and history of the Kikuyu and Dorobo tribes. *Man*, **8**, 136–9.

(1910). Notes on the tribes inhabiting the Baringo district, East African Protectorate. *Journal of the Royal Anthropological Institute*, **40**, 49–72.

Dunnell, R. C. (1978). Style and function: a fundamental dichotomy. *American Antiquity*, **43**, 192–202.

Earle, T. (1977). A reappraisal of redistribution: complex Hawaian chiefdoms. In T. Earle and J. Ericson (eds.), *Exchange systems in prehistory*. Academic Press, New York.

Earle, T. and Ericson, J. (eds.) (1977). *Exchange systems in prehistory*. Academic Press, New York.

Ellison, A. and Harris, J. (1972). Settlement and land use in the prehistory and early history of southern England: a study based on locational models. In D. Clarke (ed.), *Models in archaeology*. Methuen, London.

Ericson, J. (1977). Egalitarian exchange systems in California: preliminary view. In T. K. Earle and J. Ericson (eds.), *Exchange systems in prehistory*. Academic Press, New York.

Faris, J. (1968). Some aspects of clanship and descent amongst the Nuba of South-Eastern Kordofan. *Sudan Notes and Records*, **49**, 45–57.

(1972). *Nuba personal art*. Duckworth, London.

Ferguson, L. (ed.) (1977). *Historical archaeology and the importance of material things*. Society for Historical Archaeology, Special Series Publication **2**.

Flannery, K. V. (1972). The cultural evolution of civilisations. *Annual Review of Ecology and Systematics*, **3**, 399–426.

(ed.) (1976). *The early Mesoamerican village*. Academic Press, New York.

Flannery, K. V. and Marcus, J. (1976). Formative Oaxaca and the Zapotek cosmos. *American Scientist*, **64**, 374–83.

Fletcher, R. (1981). People and space: a case study on material behaviour. In I. Hodder, G. Isaac and N. Hammond (eds.), *Pattern of the Past*. Cambridge University Press, Cambridge.

Frankenstein, S. and Rowlands, M. (1978). The internal structure and regional context of Early Iron Age Society in south-western Germany. *Bulletin of the Institute of Archaeology*, **15**, 73–112.

Fried, M. (1968). On the concept of 'tribe'. In *Essays on the Problem of tribe*, 3–22. American Ethnological Society, New York.

Friedman, J. and Rowlands, M. (eds.) (1977). *The evolution of social systems*. Duckworth, London.

Friedrich, M. H. (1970). Design structure and social interaction: archaeological implications of an ethnographic analysis. *American Antiquity*, **35**, 332–43.

Fritz, J. M. (1978). Paleopsychology today; ideational systems and human adaptation in prehistory. In C. Redman *et al.* (eds.), *Social Archaeology: beyond dating and subsistence*. Academic Press, New York.

Frobenius, L. (1898). *Der Ursprung der Kultur*. Forschungsinstitut für Kulturmorphologie, Berlin.

Gall, P. L. and Saxe, A. (1977). The ecological evolution of culture: the state as predator in succession theory. In T. Earle and J. Ericson (eds.), *Exchange systems in prehistory*. Academic Press, New York.

Giddens, A. (1979). *Central problems in social theory*. Macmillan Press, London.

Gifford, D. P. (1977). Observations of modern human settlements as an aid to archaeological interpretation. PhD thesis, University of California, Berkeley.

(1978). Ethnoarchaeological observations of natural processes affecting cultural materials. In R. A. Gould (ed.), *Explorations in ethnoarchaeology*. University of New Mexico Press, Albuquerque.

Gladwin, W. and Gladwin, H. S. (1934). *A method for the designation of cultures and their variation*. Globe Medallion Papers **15**, Globe Arizona.

Glassie, H. (1975). *Folk housing in Middle Virginia: a structural analysis of historical artifacts*. University of Tennessee Press, Knoxville.

Gluckman, M. (1941). *Economy of the central Barotse plain*. Rhodes-Livingstone Paper **7**, Rhodes-Livingstone Museum, Lusaka.

(1949). The role of the sexes in *wiko* circumcision ceremonies. In M. Fortes (ed.), *Social structure*. Oxford University Press, Oxford.

Godelier, M. (1977). *Perspectives in Marxist anthropology*. Cambridge University Press, Cambridge.

Goldstein, L. (1976). Spatial structure and social organisation: regional manifestations of Mississippian society. PhD dissertation, Northwestern University.

Goody, J. (1962). *Death, property and the ancestors*. Stanford University Press, Stanford.

Gould, R. (1971). The archaeologist as ethnographer: a case study from the Western Desert of Australia. *World Archaeology*, **3**, 143–77.

Harstrup, K. (1978). The post-structuralist position of social anthropology. In E. Schwimmer (ed.), *The yearbook of symbolic anthropology*, **1**. Hurst, London.

Hennings, R. O. (1951). *African morning*. Chatto and Windus, London.

Henshall, A. S. (1963). *The chambered tombs of Scotland*. Edinburgh University Press, Edinburgh.

Higgs, E. S. (1968). Archaeology – where now? *Mankind,* **6,** 617–20.
   (ed.) (1972). *Papers in economic prehistory.* Cambridge University Press, Cambridge.
   (ed.) (1975). *Palaeoeconomy.* Cambridge University Press, Cambridge.
Hill, J. N. (1970). *Broken K Peublo: prehistoric social organisation in the American southwest.* Anthropological Papers of the University of Arizona **18,** Tucson, Arizona.
   (1971). Report on a seminar on the explanation of prehistoric organisational change. *Current Anthropology,* **12,** 406–8.
   (ed.) (1977). *The explanation of prehistoric change.* University of New Mexico Press, Albuquerque.
Hillier, B., Leaman, A., Stansall, P. and Bedford, M. (1976). Space syntax. *Environment and Planning B,* **3,** 147–85.
Hivernel, F. (1978). An ethnoarchaeological study of environmental use in the Kenya Highlands. PhD thesis, University of London.
Hobley, C. W. (1906). Notes on the Dorobo people and other tribes. *Man,* **6,** 119–20.
Hodder, I. R. (1974). Regression analysis of some trade and marketing patterns. *World Archaeology,* **6,** 172–89.
   (1977a). The distribution of material culture items in the Baringo district, W. Kenya. *Man,* **12,** 239–69.
   (1977b). Some new directions in the spatial analysis of archaeological data. In D. L. Clarke (ed.) *Spatial Archaeology.* Academic Press, London.
   (ed.) (1978). *The spatial organisation of culture.* Duckworth, London.
   (1981). An ethnographic study amongst the Lozi, W. Zambia. In I. Hodder, G. Isaac and N. Hammond (eds.), *Pattern of the past.* Cambridge University Press, Cambridge.
Hodder, I. R. and Orton, C. (1976). *Spatial analysis in archaeology.* Cambridge University Press, Cambridge.
Hogg, A. H. A. (1971). Some applications of surface fieldwork. In M. Jesson and D. Hill (eds.), *The Iron Age and its hillforts.* Southampton University, Southampton.
Holmes, W. H. (1914). Areas of American culture characterisation tentatively outlined as an aid in the study of the antiquities. *American Anthropologist,* **16,** 413–46.
Humphrey, C. (1974). Inside a Mongolian tent. *New Society,* **31,** 273–5.
Huntingford, G. W. B. (1951). The social institutions of the Dorobo. *Anthropos,* **46,** 1–48.
   (1953). *The southern Nilo-hamites.* Ethnographic Survey of Africa, International African Institute, London.
Isbell, W. H. (1976). Cosmological order expressed in prehistoric ceremonial centres. Paper given in Andean Symbolism Symposium. Part 1: Space, time and mythology. International Congress of Americanists, Paris.
Johnson, G. (1973). *Local exchange and early state development in Iran.* University of Michigan Museum of Anthropology, Anthropological Paper **51,** Ann Arbor.
Johnston, H. (1902). *The Uganda Protectorate.* Hutchinson, London.
Kenya Land Commission 1934. Evidence, Part II. Nairobi.
Kidder, A. V. (1924). *An introduction to the study of southwestern archaeology, with a preliminary account of the excavations at Pecos.* Papers of the Southwestern Expedition, Phillips Academy. New Haven, **1,** New Haven.
Kleindienst, M. and Watson, P. J. (1956). Action archaeology: the archaeological inventory of a living community. *Anthropology Tomorrow,* **5,** 75–8.

Klejn, L. S. (1977). A panorama of theoretical archaeology. *Current Anthropology*, **18**, 1–42.

Knöll, H. (1959). *Die nordwestdeutsche Tiefstichkeramik und ihre Stellung im nord- und mitteleuropäischen Neolithikum.* Provincialinstitut, Münster Westfalen.

Korn, S. M. (1978). The formal analysis of visual systems as exemplified by a study of Abelam (Papua New Guinea) paintings. In M. Greenhalgh and V. Megaw (eds.), *Art in society.* Duckworth, London.

Kossinna, G. (1911). *Die Herkunft der Germanen.* Kurt Kabitsch, Leipzig.

(1926). *Ursprung und Verbreitung der Germanen in vorund frügeschichtlicher Zeit.* Germanen-Verlag, Berlin.

Leone, M. P. (1977). The new Mormon temple in Washington D.C. In L. Ferguson (ed.), *Historical archaeology and the importance of material things.* Society for Historical Archaeology, Special series Publication **2**.

Leroi-Gourhan, A. (1965). *Préhistoire de l'art occidental.* Mazenod, Paris.

Levi-Strauss, C. (1963). *Structural anthropology.* Basic Books, New York.

Longacre, W. (1970). *Archaeology as anthropology.* Anthropological Papers of the University of Arizona, 17, Tucson, Arizona.

(1981). Kalinga pottery: an ethnoarchaeological study. In I. Hodder, G. Isaac and N. Hammond (eds.), *Pattern of the past.* Cambridge University Press, Cambridge.

Lüning, J. (1972). Zum Kulturbegriff im Neolithikum. *Prähistorische Zeitschrift*, **47**, 145–73.

Macalister, R. A. S. (1921). *A textbook of European archaeology.* Cambridge University Press, Cambridge.

Maher, C. (1937). *Soil erosion and land utilisation in the Kamasia, Njemps and East Suk reserve.* Kenya National Archives, Nairobi.

Mainga, M. (1973). *Bulozi under the Luyana kings: political evolution and state formation in pre-colonial Zambia.* Longman, London.

Marsh, P., Rosser, E. and Harré, R. (1978). *The rules of disorder.* Routledge, London.

Marshak, A. (1977). The meander as a system: the analysis and recognition of iconographic units in upper Palaeolithic compositions. In P. J. Ucko (ed.) *Form in indigenous art.* Duckworth, London.

Martin, P. S., Lloyd, C. and Spoehr, A. (1938). Archaeological works in the Ackman-Lowry area, south-western Colorado, 1937. *Field Museum of Natural History Anthropological Series*, **23**, 217–304.

Meillassoux, C. (1972). From reproduction to production. *Economy and Society*, **1**, 93–105.

Middleton, J. (1965). Kenya: changes in African life, 1912–1945. In V. Harlow, E. M. Chilver and A. Smith (eds.), *History of East Africa.* Clarendon Press, Oxford.

Muller, J. (1973). Structural studies of art styles. Paper presented at IXth International Congress of Anthropological and Ethnological Research. Chicago.

Mungeam, C. H. (1966). *British rule in Kenya 1895–1912.* Clarendon Press, Oxford.

Munn, N. D. (1966). Visual categories: an approach to the study of representational systems. *American Anthropologist*, **68**, 936–50.

Nadel, S. F. (1947). *The Nuba.* Oxford University Press, Oxford.

Naroll, R. (1962). Floor area and settlement population. *American Antiquity*, **27**, 587–8.

Okely, J. (1979). An anthropological contribution to the history and archaeology of an ethnic group. In B. C. Burnham and J. Kingsbury (eds.), *Space, hierarchy and society.* British Archaeological Report International Series **59**, 81–92. BAR Publications, Oxford.

Peebles, C. and Kus, S. (1977). Some archaeological correlates of ranked societies. *American Antiquity*, **42**, 421–48.

Pettit, P. (1975). *The concept of structuralism: a critical analysis*. Gill and MacMillan, Dublin.

Phillips, P. (1975). *Early farmers in west Mediterranean Europe*. Hutchinson, London.

Piaget, J. (1971). *Structuralism*. Routledge and Kegan Paul, London.

Pires-Ferreira, J. W. and Flannery, K. V. (1976). Ethnographic models for Formative exchange. In K. V. Flannery (ed.), *The early Mesoamerican village*. Academic Press, New York.

Plog, F. T. (1975). Systems theory in archaeological research. *Annual Review of Anthropology*, **4**, 207–24.

Plog, S. (1976). Measurement of prehistoric interaction between communities. In K. V. Flannery (ed.), *The early Mesoamerican village*. Academic Press, New York.

(1978). Social interaction and stylistic similarity. In M. B. Schiffer (ed.), *Advances in archaeological theory and method*, *1*. Academic Press, New York.

Rathje, W. L. (1973). Models for mobile Maya: a variety of constraints. In C. Renfrew (ed.), *The explanation of culture change*. Duckworth, London.

(1974). The Garbage Project: a new way of looking at the problems of archaeology. *Archaeology*, **27**, 236–41.

Ratzel, L. (1896). *Anthropogeography – the application of geography to history*. J. Engelhorn, Stuttgart.

Rappaport, R. A. (1968). *Pigs for the ancestors*. Yale University Press, New Haven.

Renfrew, C. (1972). *The emergence of civilisation*. Methuen, London (1973). Monuments, mobilisation and social organisation in neolithic Wessex. In C. Renfrew (ed.), *The explanation of culture change*. Duckworth, London.

(ed.) (1974). *British prehistory: a new outline*. Duckworth, London.

(1975). Trade as action at a distance. In J. Sabloff and C. C. Lamberg-Karlovsky (eds.), *Ancient civilisation and trade*. University of New Mexico Press, Albuquerque.

(1977a). Alternative models for exchange and spatial distribution. In T. K. Earle and J. E. Ericson (eds.), *Exchange systems in prehistory*. Academic Press, New York.

(1977b). Space, time and polity. In J. Friedman and M. Rowlands (eds.), *The evolution of social systems*. Duckworth, London.

(1979). *Investigations in Orkney*. Society of Antiquaries, London.

Renfrew, C. and Dixon, J. (1976). Obsidian in western Asia: a review. In G. Sieveking, I. Longworth and K. Wilson (eds.), *Problems in economic and social archaeology*. Duckworth, London.

Ritchie, A. (1973). Knap of Howar, Papa Westray. *Discovery and Excavation in Scotland*. 1973, 68–9.

(1975). Knap of Howar, Papa Westray. *Discovery and Excavation in Scotland*. 1975, 35–7.

Ritchie, J. N. G. (1976). The stones of Stenness, Orkney. *Proceedings of the Society of Antiquaries of Scotland*, **107**, 1–60.

Roden, D. (1972). Down-migration in the Moro hills of S. Kordofan. *Sudan Notes and Records*, **53**, 79–99.

Rouse, I. (1939). *Prehistory of Haiti, a study in method*. Yale University, New Haven.

Rowlands, M. J. (1971). The archaeological interpretation of prehistoric metalworking. *World Archaeology*, **3**, 210–24.

(1976). *The organisation of middle Bronze Age metalworking in southern Britain*. British Archaeological Report 31. BAR Publications, Oxford.

Sackett, J. R. (1977). The meaning of style in archaeology: a general model. *American Antiquity*, **42**, 369–80.

Sahlins, M. (1968). *Tribesmen*. Englewood Cliffs, New Jersey.

(1976). *Culture and practical reason*. University of Chicago Press, Chicago.

Sanders, W. and Webster, O. (1978). Unilinealism, multilinealism and the evolution of complex societies. In C. Redman *et al.* (eds.), *Social archaeology: beyond dating and subsistence*. Academic Press, New York.

Saxe, A. A. (1970). Social dimensions of mortuary practices. PhD Thesis, University of Michigan.

Schiffer, M. B. (1976). *Behavioural archaeology*. Academic Press, New York.

Schmidt, P. R. (1978). *Historical archaeology. A structural approach in an African culture*. Greenwood Press, Westport, Connecticut.

Seligman, C. G. and Seligman, B. Z. (1932). *Pagan tribes of the Nilotic Sudan*. London.

Shackleton, N. and Renfrew, C. (1970). Neolithic trade routes re-aligned by oxygen isotope analysis. *Nature*, **228**, 1062–5.

Sharp, L. (1952). Steel axes for stone-age Australians. *Human organisation*, **11**, 17–22.

Shennan, S. E. (1975). The social organisation at Branc. *Antiquity*, **49**, 279–88.

Shennan, S. J. (1978). Archaeological 'cultures': an empirical investigation. In I. Hodder (ed.), *The spatial organisation of culture*. Duckworth, London.

Sherratt, A. (1972). Socio-economic and demographic models for the Neolithic and Bronze Ages of Europe. In D. L. Clarke (ed.), *Models in archaeology*. Methuen, London.

(1976). Resources, technology and trade in early European metallurgy. In G. Sieveking, I. Longworth and K. Wilson (eds.), *Problems in economic and social archaeology*. Duckworth, London.

(1981). Aspects of the secondary products revolution: plough and pastoralism in prehistoric Europe. In I. Hodder, G. Isaac and N. Hammond (eds.), *Pattern of the past*. Cambridge University Press, Cambridge.

Sidrys, R. (1977). Mass-distance measures for the Maya obsidian trade. In T. K. Earle and J. E. Ericson (eds.), *Exchange systems in prehistory*. Academic Press, New York.

Spencer, P. (1965). *The Samburu*. Routledge and Kegan Paul, London.

(1973). *Nomads in alliance*. Oxford University Press, Oxford.

Sperber, D. (1974). *Rethinking symbolism*. Cambridge University Press, Cambridge.

Stanislawski, M. B. and Stanislawski, B. B. (1978). Hopi and Hopi–Tewa ceramic tradition networks. In I. Hodder (ed.), *Spatial organisation of culture*. Duckworth, London.

Stevenson, R. C. (1957). A survey of the phonetics and grammatical structure of the Nuba Mountain languages. *Afrika and Ubersee*, **41**, 27–35.

(1962 and 1964). Linguistic research in the Nuba Mts. *Sudan Notes and Records*, **43** and **45**, 118 and 79.

Steward, J. H. (1955). *Theory of culture change*. Urbana, Illinois.

Struever, S. and Houart, G. L. (1972). An analysis of the Hopewell Interaction Sphere. In E. N. Wilmsen (ed.), *Social exchange and interaction*. University of Michigan Museum of Anthropology, Anthropological Paper, **46**, Ann Arbor.

Sutton, J. E. G. (1973). *The archaeology of the western highlands of Kenya*. British Institute in East Africa, Nairobi.

Tainter, J. A. (1975). Social inference and mortuary practices: an experiment in numerical classification. *World Archaeology*, **7**, 1–15.

(1978). Mortuary practices and the study of prehistoric social systems. In

M. B. Schiffer (ed.), *Advances in archaeological method and theory, 1*. Academic Press, New York.

Thomas, D. H. (1974). *Predicting the past*. Holt, Rinehart and Winston, New York.

Traill, W. and Kirkness, W. (1937). Howar, a prehistoric structure on Papa Westray, Orkney. *Proceedings of the Society of Antiquaries of Scotland*, **71**, 309–21.

Turner, V. W. (1952). *The Lozi peoples of north-western Rhodesia*. Ethnographic survey of Africa, International African Institute, London.

(1969). *The ritual process*. Routledge and Keegan Paul, London.

Vastokas, J. M. (1978). Cognitive aspects of North Coast art. In M. Greenlagh and V. Magaw (eds.), *Art in society*. Duckworth, London.

Washburn, D. K. (1978). A symmetry classification of Pueblo ceramic designs. In P. Grebinger (ed.), *Discovering past behaviour*. Academic Press, New York.

Wedel, W. R. (1941). *Environment and native subsistence economies in the Central Great Plains*. Smithsonian Miscellaneous Collections 100, Washington D.C.

(1953). Some aspects of human ecology in Central Plains. *American Anthropologist*, **55**, 499–514.

White, C. A. (1949). *The science of culture: a study of man and civilisation*. Grove Press, New York.

Whitehouse, R. (1969). The neolithic pottery sequence in southern Italy. *Proceedings of the Prehistoric Society*, **35**, 267–310.

Wiessner, P. (1974). A functional estimator of population from floor area. *American Antiquity*, **39**, 343–9.

Willey, G. R. (1946). Horizon styles and pottery traditions in Peruvian archaeology. *American Antiquity*, **11**, 49–56.

Willey, G. R. and Phillips, P. (1958). *Method and theory in American archaeology*.

Willey, G. R. and Sabloff, J. A. (1974). *A history of American archaeology*. Thames and Hudson, London.

Wobst, H. M. (1977). *Stylistic behaviour and information exchange*. University of Michigan Museum of Anthropology, Anthropological Paper **61**, 317–42.

Wright, H. T. (1977). Toward an explanation of the origin of the state. In J. N. Hill (ed.), *The explanation of prehistoric change*. University of New Mexico Press, Albuquerque.

Yellen, J. (1977). *Archaeological approaches to the present*. Academic Press, New York.

Yellen, J. and Harpending, H. (1977). Hunter-gatherer populations and archaeological inferences. *World Archaeology*, **4**, 244–53.

Yoffee, N. (1979). The decline and rise of Mesopotamian civilisation. *American Antiquity*, **44**, 5–35.

INDEX

adaptation, 5, 6, 7, 10, 11, 85, 125, 208, 213, 214, 217
  ecological, 4, 85, 217
adaptive strategies, 10, 11, 35, 73, 124-6, 186, 206, 207, 213
age-sets, 16, 18, 67, 75, 77, 78, 83, 88, 90, 102, 104, 125
agriculture, 16, 34, 84, 87, 90, 98, 101, 103, 105, 129, 151, 154, 189
  hoe, 129
  irrigation, 16, 17, 34
  shifting, 129
Anderri, 132, 165
animal carcasses, 158, 161, 191, 192, 220
Arabal, 14, 29, 32, 60
Arabs, *see under* Baggara
artifact associations, 1, 194, 197, 199
artifact distributions, 6, 10, 58, 63, 64, 68, 118, 119, 190, 193, 207, 226, *see also* calabashes, pottery, spears, stools
artifact production, 9, 58-63, 75, 118, 119, 185
  of pottery, 37-48, 92, 93, 142-5
  of spears, 60-3
  of stools, 48-53, 93, 95
artifact styles, 9, 119, 122, 123, 124, 207
  distribution, 75, 122, 150
ash, 156, 168, 199
assemblage, 6, 59, 97
  bone, 158, 187, 220
  cultural, 25, 213, 214
  faunal, 220, 221
association analysis, 187
association patterns, 6
  non-random, 6, 7, 41, 43
  random, 6, 7
axes, 114
  adzes, 114, 166, (bone) 221
  iron, 101
  Middle Bronze Age palstaves, 59
  'shoe-last', 203

Baggara, 129, 142, 143, 146, 154, 155,
162, 163, 168, 182-4, 206, 216, 217
Bandkeramik culture, 202
Bantu, 105
  language, 105
Baringo, 13-18, 24-6, 31, 34-6, 41, 43, 44, 46-8, 56-8, 60, 62, 67, 68, 71, 73-7, 83-5, 90, 96, 99, 104, 111, 117, 125, 126, 162, 181, 185, 187-9, 203, 205, 209, 210, 217
  lake, 13, 14, 16, 37, 72
Barotseland, 105, 117
basketwork, 18, 52, 114, 115, 117, 118, 134
  distribution, 134
  kerebé (bowl), 32, 34
  tokei (drinking cup), 22, 31
beads, 79, 80, 92, 96, 101, 166, 220
beans, 129, 136, 147, 154, 158, 166
beer, 30, 129, 147, 156
behavioural explanation, 4, 5, 10, 11, 188, 189, 193, 201, 204, 207, 211, 214, 229
behavioural laws, 215, 228
Binford, L. R., 5, 9, 10, 52, 191, 192, 195, 197, 201, 213, 214
body scars, 141, 146, 149, 150, 161, 166, 171, 174, 181, 182, 185
  distribution, 151
bones, animal, 155-9, 161, 181, 182, 196, 216, 220, 221, 224
bones, human, 221, 224
  refuse, 157, 159, 161, 182, 192
boundaries, 73, 74, 125, 126, 151, 156, 162, 182, 183, 185, 187, 188, 193, 195, 216
  social, 8, 68
Brogar, henge, 218, 226
burial patterns, 208, 210, 212, 226
  practices, 9, 134, 152, 153, 155, 156, 163, 165-70, 186, 189, 195, 196, 198-201, 207, 209, 211, 216, 219
  sites, 220, 221, 227, *see also* cemeteries
  tombs, 218, 220, 221, 223-7

c-transforms, 190, 191, 207, 210

calabash, 37, 52, 58, 68–70, 72, 73, 75, 95, 126, 134, 140, 142, 147–50, 161, 165–7, 171, 172, 181, 185, 189, 206
decoration, 68–70, 72, 73, 75, 126, 147–50, 171, 172, 174, 182, 206, 207
distribution, 68, 69, 134, 150, 151

cattle, 14–16, 23, 25, 26, 28, 29, 31, 32, 34, 50, 60, 65, 67, 76, 84, 87, 88, 90, 92, 98, 99, 101, 102, 104, 105, 109, 114–17, 120, 129, 154, 156, 158, 159, 161, 162, 165, 167, 168, 170, 185, 188, 216
bones, 155–9, 216, 220
meat, 157, 165
milk, 158, 159

cattle friends (partners), 23, 24, 29, 31, 34, 90

cemeteries, 134, 153, 155, 163, 165–8, 170, 181–3, 195–8
distribution, 195, 196

Chebloch, 41, 44, 45

chickens, 156

chief, 16, 17, 27, 90, 99, 106, 109, 133, 134, 167, 198

Childe, V. G., 3–6, 10, 59, 218, 220, 222, 223

Chokwe, 111, 116, *see also* Mbunda

circumcision, 25, 31, 77, 88, 92, 99, 101, 102, 105, 116, 117
dress, 18, 116

Clark, G., 4, 5, 10

Clarke, D., 3, 4, 6, 8, 10, 194, 212

clay, 37, 40, 92, 114, 142, 146

clean–dirty opposition, 215, 216

compounds, 16–18, 27–9, 31, 40, 43, 44, 46–8, 51, 54, 60, 62, 66, 82, 90, 92, 95, 97–9, 129, 131, 133–6, 138, 139, 142, 143, 145, 147, 151, 153, 155–61, 166, 169, 170, 181–3, 194, 198, 206
plan, 25, 134–9

contextual archaeology, 217, 219, 229

cooking pots, 37, 43, 45, 46, 92, 142, 144, 146, 210
metal, 18

'correlates', 10, 11, 190, *see also* cultural laws

Crawford, O. G. S., 3, 6

cultural laws, 190, 191

cultures, archaeological, 1–7, 9–11, 59, 125, 186, 188, 189

curation, 10, 191

dancing, 66, 80, 129, 154

design, 72, 73, 144–7, 170–81, 183, 205–7, 215, 216
distribution, 144, 145, 150, 151
see also style

Dorobo, 87, 88, 90–103, 126, 185, 217

Elmolo, 100, 101, 103, 104
Kisima, 98, 100, 101, 103, 104, 186
Leroghi, 98, 103
Lonkewan, 98–101, 103, 104
Maasai, 98, 99, 103
potter, 92
Tindiret, North, 101, 103, 104
Tugen, 99

dress, 17, 18, 21, 22, 24–7, 29, 32, 34, 54, 69, 77, 78, 81, 83, 84, 101, 102, 205
ceremonial, 31, 102
female, 69, 97, 189

drinking, 70

Durotriges, 7

ear decoration, 18, 22, 27, 40, 43, 77, 79, 80, 84, 85, 92, 96–8, 151
female, 31, 79, 80, 84, 92, 96, 101
flap, 32, 34, 78–80, 85, 92, 97
male, 77, 84, 102
ring, 92, 97, 101, 102, 151

eating, 70, 134, 150, 156–61, 191, 192, 194
taboos, 157

ecological relationships, 126, 127, 187, 189, 207

ecological strategies, 215, 217, 229

ecology, 2, 4, 5, 7, 11, 85, 188, 229
cultural, 2

Eldumē area, 72

Elkeyo–Marakwet, 44

Elmolo, *see* Dorobo

ethnoarchaeology, 1, 7–9, 11, 13, 125, 126, 185, 186, 189, 190, 192, 193, 195, 197, 207, 214, 215, 218, 228, 229

ethnography, 1, 11, 12, 14, 17, 105, 195, 197, 198, 201, 206
of metalworking, 59

exchange, 10, 13, 17, 28, 48, 65, 98, 100, 101, 108, 119, 134, 148, 189, 202–4, 206–8, 210
down-the-line, 10
'friends', 24, 90
networks, 202
prestige, 10, 203, 204, 208
reciprocal, 10, 26, 108, 202, 203, 208
redistributive, 10, 202, 203, 208
secondary, 48, 62

fall-off curves, 10, 41, 43, 47, 48, 203, 204

farms, 129
'far', 129, 169, 170
'hillside', 129, 133
'house', 129, 132, 133, 169, 170

feasting, 129, 156

feasts, cattle, 165
funeral, 165, 167, 168, 170

fertility, 156, 157, 168–70, 189, 199

fishing, 28, 29, 66, 100, 105, 221
functionalism, 2, 5, 7, 10, 11, 125, 192
  anthropological, 2
  explanation, 204–6, 210, 229
  relationships, 85, 203, 208, 213, 214
funerals, 165, 167, 168, 170, *see also* burial
  practices, feasts

goats, 14, 23, 25, 26, 28, 34, 45, 50, 60,
  61, 63, 88, 90, 98, 100, 101, 129, 136,
  154, 156, 158, 159, 161
  bones, 155
grain, 90, 101, 129, 137, 139, 146, 156,
  157, 160, 161, 168, 170, 199, 216
granary, 16, 134–9, 141, 142, 155–61,
  166, 168, 170, 182, 183
graves, 163, 165–8, 170, 182, 196–9, 202
  fill, 216, *see also* tombs
grinding hut, 134–8, 162, 216
Grooved Ware, 220
Gypsies, 162, 192, 200, 215

hearths, 37, 57, 58, 84, 221–5
  position, 54–6, 126, 204, 205, 221–5
henges, 218–21, 223–7
hierarchy, 105, 208, 228
  political, 105
  social, 105
hoards, 62, 63
hoes, 114, 129
homeostasis, 208, 213
honey, 29, 93, 95, 98, 100, 101, 114
  collecting, 60, 87, 90, 93
honey pots, 50, 97, 100
  sendere, 95
house decoration, 134, 137, 138, 140–2,
  152, 154, 156, 161, 162, 171, 174,
  181, 182, 223, 224
hunter–gatherers, 8, 87, 98, 101, 102, 103,
  193
hunting, 66, 90, 93, 98, 100, 102, 103
huts, 16–18, 54, 56, 96, 105, 134, 135,
  154, 155, 171, 182, 221–5
  construction, 25, 141, 142
  plan, 41

Ila, 109, 111, *see also* Ila–Tonga; Lozi
Ila–Tonga, 109, 111, 114–16, *see also* Lozi
industry, 59
  organisation, 59, 60, 63
  tradition, 59
  see also artifact production
information flow, 1, 13, 35, 58, 68, 85, 117,
  125, 186, 190, 205, 228
information theory, 3, 4, 8, 205
inheritance patterns, 169, 170
interaction, 1, 7–9, 13, 23, 35, 52, 58–60,
  63–5, 68, 74, 75, 84, 85, 115–17, 119,
  121, 124, 152, 182, 185, 187–90, 193,
  209

social, 5, 8, 9, 11, 13, 35, 58, 125
  spheres, 5, 206
interpretive model, 1, 86, 196
iron, 108, 115–17, 120
  axes, 101
  implements, 114
  mining, 115
  production centres, 115
Iron Age, 7, 194, 196
  coin distribution, 202
  Dorset burials, 196
  Glastonbury village, 194
  Owslebury, 196

Kalenjin, 14, 16, 28, 44, 46, 66, 87, *see
  also* Pokot, Tugen
  language, 16, 87
  Nandi, 101, 104
Kampi-ya-Samaki, 37, 40, 54
Karau, 41
  potter, 43–5
Kerbej, 145, 163
  cemetery, 165
  potter, 146
Kikuyu, 48, 87
kinship, 16
Kisima, 90, 92, 93, 95, 97, 98, 100
  Dorobo, 101, 103, 104
  potter, 92, 93
Kisumu, 46, 48
  pottery, 47
kitchen, 105
Knap of Howar, 218, 220, 224
knives, 101, 117, 118, 134, 154, 166, 169
  distribution, 134
Kokwa Island, 37, 44
  potter, 40, 41, 43, 92
  pottery, 41, 43, 45, 47
Kwandi, 109, 111, 114, *see also* Lozi
Kwangwa, 109, 114, 117, *see also* Lozi

Laikipia escarpment, 90, 97, 98
laws, 10, 203
  behavioural, 193, 215, 228
  cultural, 190, 191
Lealui, 105, 106
leather, 96
  bag, 92
  ear straps, 79, 92
  skin dress, 92
  skins, 101, 108
Lebu, 130, 132, 142, 143
  cemetery, 165
Leroghi plateau, 62, 84, 87, 90, 97–9,
  103, 104, 210
  Dorobo, 103
Lerupē (stoolmaker), 50, 51, 53, 54
Lesaia (stoolmaker), 50, 54
Letrugga (stoolmaker), 48, 50, 51, 54

life–death opposition, 183, 200, 215, 216, 221, 224, 226
Limulunga, 105, 106
Lokridi (stoolmaker), 51, 54
Longacre–Deetz–Hill hypothesis, 8, 122, 190
Lonkewan, 90, 92, 93, 97–102, *see also* Dorobo
Lozi, 105–9, 111, 114–22, 124, 125, 185, 187, 189, 190, 209
  language (Kololo), 105, 109
Luchazi, 111
Lunda, 109, 111, 114, 116, *see also* Mbunda
Luvale, 109, 111, 116, *see also* Mbunda

Maasai, 13, 15, 66, 68, 87, 90, 92, 97–104, 126, 217
  language, 16, 87, 88, 101
Madagascar, 199, 200, 201, 217
Maes Howe, 223, 225–7
maize, 28–30, 45, 114, 129
male–female opposition, 83, 139, 140, 146, 149, 159–63, 169, 172, 182, 194, 206, 215, 216, 222
  in compound, 139, 159–62, 182, 194
Marigat, 17, 46–8
  pots, 41, 47
markets, 16, 37, 40, 44, 46, 48, 54, 80, 93, 95, 101, 108
marriage, 16, 18, 23, 24, 27–9, 31, 34, 67, 69, 76, 80, 87, 88, 90–2, 96, 98, 99, 101, 102, 111, 116, 129, 133, 134, 148, 149, 150, 152, 153, 155–7
  exogamy, 16, 88, 132, 133
  matrilocal, 122
  polygamy, 16, 75, 83, 102–4
material culture, 1, 3, 4, 6, 7, 9, 11, 13, 17, 18, 22, 24–9, 31, 32, 34–6, 55–9, 63, 73, 75–7, 83, 85–7, 96–9, 100–5, 111, 116, 117, 119, 121, 124–6, 130, 140, 151, 152, 154, 182, 184–90, 195, 204, 207, 209–12, 215–8
material culture boundaries, 1, 6, 30–2, 35, 37, 73, 76, 77, 84–6, 104, 125, 153, 181, 185, 188, 202
material culture distribution, 2, 6–8, 13, 116, 186, 216
material culture patterning, 1, 10, 11, 17, 27, 35, 58, 60, 65, 68, 73, 77, 83, 85, 86, 97, 99, 100, 103, 104, 116, 117, 122, 124–6, 152, 183, 185, 186, 189, 206, 207, 210, 213–15, 217, 218, 228, 229
material culture similarity, 6–9, 11, 26, 35, 58, 85, 114, 115, 124, 185, 188, 190
matrilineal descent, 105, 133, 152, 153, 160, 169, 170, 182–4, 194, 198, 199, 206

matrilocal residence theory, 8, 122, 190
Mbowe, 109, *see also* Lozi
Mbunda, 105, 109, 111, 115–17, 120, 124, 209
  language, 105
megalith, 197
Merina burial, 200, 201
Mesakin Qisar, 130, 133, 134, 136, 140, 142, 143, 145, 146, 151, 154, 157, 159, 160, 165, 166, 170, *see also* Nuba
Mesakin Tiwal, 130, 133, 134, 136, 140, 143, 145, 150, 154, 161, 166
  hills, 152
  see also Nuba
metal items, 9, 60, 63, 117, 154, 180
  containers, 46
  metal styles, 59
milk, 23, 68, 114, 157–9
milk jug, 25, 27, 96
  ilkilip (containers), 95, 97, 102
millet, 32, 34, 45, 129
model, 3, 160, 194, 195, 207, 215, 216
  behavioural, 204
  distance, 8
  functional, 228
  geographical, 8
  gravity, 203
  predictive, 73, 85
  social, 197, 198
moran, 25, 66–8, 76–8, 80, 84, 88, 90, 96, 98, 99, 101, 102, 104, 126
Moro, 130, 131, 133, 134, 136, 137, 142–5, 147, 150–3, 155–7, 159, 161–3, 165, 166, 168, 169, 170, 181, 182, 205, 215, *see also* Nuba
  language, 130
Mukutan, 14, 25, 28, 29, 32, 37, 43–5, 51, 54, 82, 83
  stoolmaker, 50, 51, 53
Muoyo, 105, 106

Nalolo, 105, 106
necklace, 78, 80, 82, 92, 96, 97, 101, 102
negative reciprocity, 26, 27, 35, 37, 55, 56, 74
Nitra, 202, 203
Neolithic, 3, 8, 196, 197, 202, 203, 218–21, 226, 227
  axes, 203
  flints, 202
  megaliths, 197
  obsidian, 202
  in Orkneys, 218, 226, 227
  settlements, 218–21
Njemps, 13–18, 22, 25–32, 34, 37, 40, 41, 44, 46, 50, 51, 53–5, 62, 64–6, 69–73, 75, 77–80, 82–4, 93, 96, 98, 100, 104, 162, 206, 207, 215
  language, 23, 24
Nkoya, 109, 114, 116, 122, *see also* Lozi

nomads, 29, 88, 154, *see also* Baggara
normative approach, 5, 7, 8, 214
norms, 7, 11, 214
nose decoration, 151
ring, 151
Nua, 145
cemetery, 165
potter, 146
Nuba, 70, 72, 127, 129, 130, 136, 139–42,
152, 154, 155, 159, 160, 161, 163,
168–72, 174, 178, 181–4, 186, 187,
189–94, 197–200, 206, 207, 212,
215–18
language, 130
Mesakin Nuba, 129, 131, 133, 138,
140–2, 144, 147, 150, 152–7, 161–3,
166, 169, 170, 172, 173, 177, 178,
180–3, 197, 198, 205, 215
mountains, 127, 130, 160
Nuer, 67
Nunamiut Eskimoes, 191, 192
Nyengo, 109, *see also* Lozi

obsidian, 202
Ongata Leroi, 98
Ongata Nairobi, 98
Orkney, islands of, 218, 220–7
Brogar, 218, 226
Knap of Howar, 218, 220, 224
Maes Howe, 223, 225–7
Neolithic settlements, 218–21
Quanterness, 218–21, 223, 224
Quoyness, 220, 223, 224
Rinyo, 218, 220–3
Skara Brae, 218–24, 227
Stenness, 218, 220, 224–6

pastoralists, 13, 16, 25, 28, 87, 92, 101,
103, 104, 185
pigs, 129, 154, 156–62, 168, 169, 182, 216
bones, 196, 216, 220
jaws, 154–6, 168
meat, 157–9
pens, 134, 136, 154, 157, 159, 162
skull, 155–9, 168
Pokot, 14, 16–18, 25–9, 34, 35, 43–6, 50,
54, 64, 66, 69, 72, 98–100
language, 23, 24
pollution, 126, 157, 159–62, 169, 170,
172, 182, 183, 194, 200, 210
population, composition, 206
size, 10, 187, 191, 193, 194
figures, 15, 16, 105
pottery, 5, 8, 9, 18, 37, 40, 41, 43–8, 54,
56, 58, 69, 84, 93, 96–8, 100, 101,
108, 114, 117, 119, 120, 122–4, 134,
137, 140, 142–4, 146, 147, 154,
165–7, 180, 190, 206, 224
Beaker, 6

decoration, 41, 92, 122, 144–6, 185,
206, 207, 211, 220, 221
distribution, 37–45, 47, 48, 108, 134,
143–5, 147, 151, 203
Grooved Ware, 220
Principal Components Analysis, 66
processual archaeology, 5, 7, 11, 212, 214,
218
purity, 70–2, 126, 154, 157, 159–63,
168–70, 172, 182, 183, 187, 189,
192–5, 199–201, 205, 206, 208, 210,
215, 216

Quanterness, 218–21, 223, 224
Quoyness, 220, 223, 224

race, 3
random walk procedures, 41, 47
ranking, 121, 189, 203, 207–10, 226
refuse, 9, 147, 156, 161, 162, 182, 186,
189–93, 196, 205, 210–12, 216
bone, 157, 159, 161
dispersal, 134, 191, 192
regression analysis, 187, 193, 203
Renfrew, C., 4–7, 10, 47, 202, 203, 208,
212, 218, 220, 221, 226, 227
Rinyo, 218, 220–3
ritual, 218, 224, 226, 227
sites, 218, 220, 221, 225, 226

Salabani, 40
Samburu, 16, 64, 75, 83, 84, 87, 88, 90,
91, 93, 95–104
self-decoration, 18, 26, 27, 82, 96, 101,
134, 151, 156, 182
settlements, pattern, 10, 16–18, 129–33,
194, 195, 198, 206–8, 212, 226
size, 9, 10, 193, 194
space, 194
sesame, 129, 136, 154, 165–8
Shanjo, 109, *see also* Lozi
sheep, 14, 28, 48, 50, 88, 90, 100, 162
bones, 196, 220, 224, 225
shield, 18, 22, 31, 41, 66, 166, 167
'shower', 139, 142, 161, 194
sili, 136, 137, 142, 168
simulation, 203
Skara Brae, 218–24, 227
slaves, 109
sleeping hut, 134–9
smiths, 59, 60–4, 66, 116, 120
Arabal, 60–5
Marakwet, 60
Pokot, 60
Samburu, 60, 62–5, 96
workshops, 59
social organisation, 9, 10, 13, 16, 73, 85,
99, 103, 104, 188–90, 194, 195, 197,
199–201, 210, 212, 226

social strategies, 58, 73, 75, 85, 86, 124, 185, 186, 188, 193, 204, 210, 215, 217, 228, 229
sorghum, 129, 136, 137, 147, 154, 156, 158, 165–8
spatial autocorrelation tests, 52, 53, 62, 66, 118
spatial patterning, 1, 8, 48, 52, 59, 68, 73, 119, 194
spatulae, 119
spears, 18, 52, 58, 60–9, 73, 75, 77, 96, 100, 114, 126, 134, 139, 154, 166, 167, 169, 185, 194, 217
    distribution, 134, 203
Spondylus gaederopus, 202, 203
spoons, 115, 119, 134
    calabash, 150, 152
    decoration, 150
    distribution, 134
staff, 67, 101
status, 9, 13, 119–21, 125, 185, 189, 197, 199, 227
    achieved, 197
    ascribed, 197
Stenness, 218, 220, 224–6
stick fighting, 148, 152, 154
stool, 18, 37, 48, 50–4, 56, 58, 84, 93, 95, 96, 98, 100, 121, 185, 209, 210
stoolmaker, 48, 51, 53, 54
    Kisima, 93, 95
storage huts, 105, 129, 137–9
storage pots, 137, 142, 146, 167, 168
structuralism, 229
structural-Marxist theories, 210, 229
style, 204–7, 215, *see also* design
Subiya, 109, 122, 185, *see also* Ila–Tonga; Lozi
sword, 50
symbiotic relationship, 34, 100–3, 109, 114, 115, 154, 155, 185, 192
symbols (material), 11, 12, 36, 56, 57, 73, 75, 83, 85, 86, 97, 103–5, 121, 124–6, 185, 189, 195, 203, 204, 209, 210, 214, 216, 217, 228
systems theory, 4, 5, 212–4, 218, 219
    cultural systems, 5, 188, 197
    exchange systems, 10
    ideational subsystem, 213
    past behavioural system, 190
    social systems, 9, 195, 197, 203, 207, 210

subsystem, 5, 6, 208, 212–4, 218, 219, 228

Tilumbu, 150, 152, 154
Tindiret, North, 101, 103, 104, *see also* Dorobo
Tiwal, North, 150
tobacco, 101, 129
Toka, 109, 111, *see also* Ila–Tonga; Lozi
Tonga, 109, 111, *see also* Ila–Tonga; Lozi
Tosari, 142, 151
    cemetery, 167
Tot, 44, 60
    pots, 45
    smiths, 60, 63
Totela, 109, 114, 187, *see also* Ila–Tonga; Lozi
transformations, 206, 207, 210–12, 214, 217, 227, 228
    cultural, 10
tribal borders, 18, 22–5, 27–9, 31, 32, 34, 55, 57, 58, 64–6, 69, 71, 73, 75, 84, 86, 145, 181
Trichterbecher culture, 2
Tugen, 14–18, 22, 25–8, 30–2, 34, 41, 43, 44, 46, 50, 54, 55, 64–7, 69, 71–3, 77–80, 82, 84, 95, 99, 104
    Hills, 14
    language, 23, 24
Turkana, 24, 25, 28, 34, 35, 51, 99
    lake (Rudolf), 100
Tuwia, 166
'type', 3, 5, 66, 92, 97
    metal types, 59
typology, 59, 63, 172, 173, 208

virilocal residence, 16, 80, 122, 152, 198

warriors, 24, 66–8, 217, *see also* moran
water pots, 37, 43, 45, 46, 137, 142, 144, 146, 166–8
weapons, 18, 66, 217, *see also* shields, spears, swords
wooden containers, 18, 52, 114
    tubē (eating bowls), 22, 31
workshops, 63, 129, 145, 146

Zambezi, river, 105, 109
Zambia, 63, 105, 111, 210, 217, 228

1337237R0

Printed in Great Britain by
Amazon.co.uk, Ltd.,
Marston Gate.